INDRIDI
INDRIDASON

INDRIDI INDRIDASON

The Icelandic Physical Medium

by

ERLENDUR HARALDSSON
and
LOFTUR R. GISSURARSON

www.whitecrowbooks.com

CONTENTS

FOREWORD XI

INTRODUCTION...................................... XIII

CHAPTER 1: WHO WAS INDRIDI INDRIDASON? 1

CHAPTER 2: IMPORTANT EVENTS IN HIS LIFE 7

CHAPTER 3: THE BEGINNING - TABLE-TILTING, AUTOMATIC
    WRITING AND TRANCE SPEECH 15

CHAPTER 4: LEVITATIONS, DIRECT VOICE AND
    LIGHT PHENOMENA............................... 19

CHAPTER 5: THE FIRE IN COPENHAGEN 29

CHAPTER 6: ANY NORMAL EXPLANATION? 35

CHAPTER 7: SWEDENBORG AND THE FIRE IN STOCKHOLM ... 39

CHAPTER 8: THE SEARCH FOR EMIL JENSEN 43

CHAPTER 9: DISAPPEARANCE OF INDRIDI'S ARM 47

CHAPTER 10: HEALING, OLFACTORY (ODOR)
    PHENOMENA AND SURGICAL-LIKE OPERATIONS......... 53

CHAPTER 11: PROOF OF IDENTITY 67

CHAPTER 12: MATERIALIZATIONS AND APPORTS 71

CHAPTER 13: VIOLENT DISTURBANCES AND
    THE PHOTOGRAPHY EXPERIMENT 81

CHAPTER 14: DESTRUCTIVE ASSAULTS 89

CHAPTER 15: RETURN TO ORDINARY SÉANCES 95

CHAPTER 16: JON BECOMES PEACEFUL 101

CHAPTER 17: CONTROLS AND COMMUNICATORS 105

CHAPTER 18: DIRECT VOICE PHENOMENA -
    SPEAKING AND SINGING 109

CHAPTER 19: THE FRENCH SINGER AND
    "MUSICA TRASCENDENTALE" 113

CHAPTER 20: THE NORWEGIAN DOCTOR AND THE COMPOSER
    EDVARD GRIEG 125

CHAPTER 21: ANALYSIS OF INDRIDI'S PHENOMENA 133

CHAPTER 22: D.D. HOME, THE WORLD'S
    MOST FAMOUS PHYSICAL MEDIUM 137

CHAPTER 23: BASIC DIFFERENCES
    BETWEEN THE MEDIUMSHIP OF INDRIDI INDRIDASON
    AND DANIEL DUNGLAS HOME 145

CHAPTER 24: RUDI SCHNEIDER AND
    EINER NIELSEN 149

CHAPTER 25: CONTEMPORARY CRITICISM 155

CHAPTER 26: DR. GUDMUNDUR HANNESSON'S
    INVESTIGATIONS 163

CHAPTER 27: HANNESSON IMPOSES STRICTER CONTROLS .. 169

CHAPTER 28: TIGHTLY CONTROLLED SÉANCE
    AT HANNESSON'S HOME 175

CHAPTER 29: HANNESSON'S LAST
    TWO SITTINGS WITH INDRIDI 181

CHAPTER 30: HANNESSON'S CONCLUSIONS 195

CHAPTER 31: LATE OBSERVATIONS OF
    LEVITATIONS AND DIRECT VOICE PHENOMENA 205

CONTENTS

CHAPTER 32: THE LIFE BEYOND 215

CHAPTER 33: UNTIMELY DEATH 219

CHAPTER 34: CONCLUDING REMARKS -
   THE EVIDENCE FOR SURVIVAL 225

REFERENCES 229

APPENDIX A 237

APPENDIX B 241

APPENDIX C 247

APPENDIX D 253

ACKNOWLEDGEMENTS 261

THE WRITING OF THIS BOOK 263

INDEX 265

Indridi Indridason, the great physical medium.

FOREWORD

I have been interested in the miraculous for as long as I can remember. As a child I read countless books on conjuring, and performed tricks for long-suffering friends and family, and soon learnt that even the smartest of people can often be fooled by the simplest of tricks.

Fascinated by these experiences I enrolled for a psychology degree at University College London, and then for a doctorate at Edinburgh University's Koestler Parapsychology Unit. At the Unit I met Loftur Gissurarson - a jovial, convivial, pipe-smoking Icelandic parapsychologist who, at the time, was carrying out experiments into the possible existence of psychokinesis. Through Loftur I eventually met Professor Erlendur Haraldsson - an equally jovial, equally convivial, but non-pipe-smoking Icelandic parapsychologist who had travelled the world investigating the paranormal.

A few years later Erlendur kindly invited me to accompany him to India and help to investigate several gurus claiming paranormal powers. This lead to two joint papers: "Investigating Macro-PK in India: Swami Premananda" and "Reactions to and assessment of a videotape on Sathya Sai Baba" (*Journal of the Society for Psychical Research*, 1995, no. 839, pp. 193-202 and 203-213).

In this book Erlendur and Loftur present a clear and concise description of several investigations into the Icelandic physical medium Indridi Indridason. Much of this work was carried out by the Experimental Society in Reykjavik, just after the turn of the last century. Members of the Society regularly staged séances with Indridason and carefully recorded the results of their work in a series of "Minute Books." It was commonly believed that these books had been lost over time. However, several years ago two of the books came to light, and provided researchers with detailed descriptions of 56 of the Indridason's séances. Erlendur and Loftur have combined this material with other contemporary reports, letters, newspaper articles, and scientific papers, to produce their own detailed assessment of Indridason's alleged abilities.

During his séances, Indridason appeared to produce an impressive range of paranormal phenomena, including the movement of objects, levitations, weird knocking sounds, strange odours, and the direct channelling of "spirit" voices. Many of those attending the séances had no normal explanations for these phenomena, and Erlendur and Loftur draw parallels between Indridason and perhaps the best known of Victorian physical mediums - Daniel Dunglas Home.

There is little doubt that the testimony describing Indridason's alleged phenomena sounds impressive. However, those skeptical of the paranormal will be quick to point out that such testimony can often be unreliable. In contrast, proponents of the paranormal will point to the large amount of evidence in favour of Indridason's abilities, and ask whether *all* of this could really have been due to a mixture of gullibility, misreporting, suggestion and cheating?

Erlendur and Loftur are to be commended on collecting together a huge amount of fascinating material, and presenting it in a way that is as accessible as it is entertaining. Their wonderful work allows readers to travel back in time over a hundred years, and join a group of dedicated investigators as they attempt to answer perhaps the most fundamental question possible - is there really life after death?

Whatever your current belief about the paranormal, or the conclusion that you arrive at, you are about to embark on the most fascinating of journeys.

Richard Wiseman,
Professor of the Public
Understanding of Psychology
University of Hertfordshire

INTRODUCTION

In an article published in 1924 in the *Journal of the American Society for Psychical Research* Gudmundur Hannesson (1866-1946), a professor of medicine at the University of Iceland, presented an account of physical phenomena observed around an Icelandic medium. Having placed luminous tape on objects in order to see them in darkness, he wrote:

> It was a shock to me to see the zither start. The movement was entirely different from what I had anticipated, and most resembled the play of children throwing a ray of the sun about a room with a mirror. The phosphorescent spot shifted from one corner of the room to another with lightning speed, but in between remained almost stationary; now floating with varied speed in different directions, sometimes in straight lines, sometimes curved lines, sometimes spiral lines; now flashing again in all directions in lines several yards long, as far as one could judge in the dark. This was repeated several times over a period of a few minutes. Finally the zither fell on the table again, and the phosphorescent spot was seen in the same place as before (Hannesson, 1924, p. 262).

The medium in question, who had died by the time this and other reports appeared outside Iceland, and the topic of the present work, was Indridi Indridason (1883-1912), who was known to produce most of the classic phenomena of mediumship, with emphasis on physical ones. Although current students of the old mediumship literature know about his case he is not as well known as other mediums.

When I think about physical mediums from the old days of Spiritualism and psychical research I tend to remember, among several others, figures such as Eva C., Florence Cook, Kathleen Goligher, D.D. Home, Franek Kluski, Eusapia Palladino, and Rudi Schneider. These, and so many other mediums, introduced past generations, and some younger ones as well, to the possible reality of events such as movement of objects without contact, apports, luminous and auditory manifestations, and materializations.

Indridi Indridason deserves to be included in this list of important mediums, even if he is less known. Knowledge about him and his phenomena has already increased thanks to the work of psychologists Erlendur Haraldsson and Loftur R. Gissurarson, both of whom have a track record of previous investigations into psychic phenomena. They have several previous publications about Indridason (for example, Gissurarson & Haraldsson, 1989), works which are enlarged in the present book, *Indridi Indridason: The Icelandic Physical Medium*.

The current study is an excellent work about the life and career of Indridason, bringing together information from many difficult to obtain sources, some of which have never been translated from the Icelandic. This includes works authored by the above mentioned Gudmundur Hannesson, and by others, such as writer and editor Einar Hjorleifsson Kvaran, and professor of theology Haraldur Nielsson.

Several chapters are dedicated to physical phenomena, among them "Levitations, and Direct Voice and Light Phenomena," "Healing, Olfactory Phenomena and Surgical-like Operations," "Materializations and Apports," and "Direct Voice Phenomena – Speaking and Singing." The accounts of materializations presented are fascinating, many of which were luminous. Interestingly, a case of something described as a figure between a horse and a calf was once seen outside the séance room in the presence of the medium, bringing up the topic of animal materializations. The authors, in my estimation, are right in saying that animal materializations are rare, although they mention instances with mediums Franek Kluski and Jan Guzyk. This is also remindful of an incident with medium Eusapia Palladino in which "the bizarre form of a large head of a goat" was reportedly seen in a séance (Morselli, 1908, vol. 1, p. 301).

Similar to other mediums mainly known for their physical phenomena, such as D.D. Home, Indridason also produced mental phenomena, among them trance, and trance speaking. Mental phenomena are the topic of chapters such as "Proofs of Identity," and "Communicators and Controls." In the chapter about "The Fire in Copenhagen" the authors report an incident in a 1905 séance in which a spirit communicator named Jensen stated that he had been in Copenhagen, where there had been a fire in a factory, which eventually was extinguished in about an hour's time. Investigation revealed that there had indeed been a fire that had been put under control in an hour. The authors point out that Copenhagen was more than 1,300 miles from Reykjavik, where the séance was held, and that at the time there were no means of communication between the cities. Interestingly in other séances Jensen was said to have materialized.

The authors devote a chapter to a few incidents in which one of the medium's arms was dematerialized. In one instance, they summarize, "five men searched many times for the missing arm by feeling Indridi's upper body all over. They did this repeatedly, and matches were lit many times during the search, but no one found the arm." For those who, like myself, are not only interested in specific physical phenomena, but also in the history of explanations offered to account for physical mediumship, an incident like this is a connection with a conceptual tradition of biophysical forces in physical mediumship that preceded Indridason's mediumship. This was the idea that the vital forces of mediums (and sometimes of sitters as well) were used in the production of materializations and other phenomena. That is, the medium's matter was believed to be transformed and exteriorized to produce physical phenomena. Observations such as these, remindful of those reported with medium Elizabeth d'Espérance (Aksakof, 1898), illustrate the importance of some mediums, as well as specific phenomena, to inspire and inform theoretical speculations, a topic I have discussed in the case of Eusapia Palladino (Alvarado, 1993).

Another connection with these ideas of forces, as Haraldsson and Gissurarson point out in their book, is that in unpublished séance notes about Indridason's séances "there is much talk about the power or energy that is needed for the communications; the need to gather and collect energy, mending lack of energy, that the energy has been stolen by some undesirable entities, that the controls need to prepare energy for the next séance, that the energy is strong or weak, and so on." Such issues have also been mentioned in relation to other mediums.

In addition to connecting physical phenomena to ideas about the medium's psychic force, the authors discuss the spontaneous manifestations that happened around the medium which suggest a connection between poltergeist activity and physical mediumship. These manifestations, including the medium being pulled and dragged by an unknown force, have been cited before in influential works such as George Owen's *Can We Explain the Poltergeist?* (1964).

Also fascinating are accounts of levitations of the medium, a phenomenon also occasionally observed with others, and in other contexts such as around mystics and saints. Like other manifestations these took place mainly in darkness. In an early observation a sitter said that the medium's feet were on a table and when a match was lighted the medium was seen with no other support from the floor. When the light was extinguished Indridason fell to the floor taking the table with him.

Regarding comparison with other mediums, readers should pay particular attention to various chapters in the present book, among them "Basic Differences between Indridi and Home." Also of interest is a table in Appendix C showing the phenomena produced by both mediums which includes over 100 separate manifestations. While both mediums produced similar effects, according to the authors' comparisons each presented some the other did not produce. For example, Indridason, but not Home, was said to have been transported through matter, and to demonstrate two voices singing at the same time, and flashes of light on a wall. Comparisons are also made to the phenomena of mediums Rudi Schneider and Einer Nielsen.

Haraldsson and Gissurarson have done all of us an excellent service in their study of Indridason's phenomena. Not only have they compiled a good dossier of the medium's life and phenomena, but they have showed the variety of physical and mental manifestations obtained, and presented an evaluation of them. In their view the reports they studied "offer strong support for the conclusion that the phenomena were indeed genuine." Their conclusion is bolstered by things such as lack of evidence for fraud, the contemporary recording of facts, and the conviction of some skeptics. They also point out the conditions used in conducting the séance, particularly those imposed by Hannesson. This included, among others, locking doors and windows, isolating the medium and various objects that could be affected from the rest of the hall, examining the hall and the medium, and putting phosphorescent tape on objects.

I not only recommend this book to students of mediumship, but I hope that such clear and straight forward accounts as Haraldsson's and Gissurarson's are emulated to rescue from the pages of yesterday so many other mediums of the past.

Carlos S. Alvarado, PhD
Research Fellow
Parapsychology Foundation
New York, NY

CHAPTER 1

WHO WAS INDRIDI INDRIDASON?

The mediumship of Indridi Indridason[1] (1883-1912) was investigated and tested extensively by members of the Experimental Society in Reykjavik, the capital of Iceland. Remarkable psychokinetic and mediumistic phenomena are described in detail in contemporary reports, from the beginning of Indridi's mediumship in 1905 to its end in June 1909.

These phenomena, some of which occurred in full light, comprised movements and levitations of various objects, of furniture and of the medium himself, knocks on walls and clicking sounds in the air, olfactory (odor) and light phenomena, materializations of human forms, "invisible" playing of musical instruments, apports, independent voices sometimes singing loudly with great force, dematerializations, direct writing as well as automatic writing by the medium, and trance speech.

We probably have information about most of the kinds of phenomena that occurred with Indridi, and the sequence of their appearance,

---

[1]   Icelanders use a patronymic system of names and few have family names. They refer to each other by given name, like Indridi. The second name, Indridason, refers to the fact that his father's name was Indridi. His sister's name would be Indridadottir, the daughter of Indridi.

1

as there exist a substantial number of fairly extensive reports covering his five years of mediumship. The strength and variety of the observed phenomena seem to resemble those associated with the famous Daniel Dunglas Home (1833-1886).

There are no reports to be found of any medium in Iceland before Indridi. Spiritualism was practically unknown in Iceland up to his time, and the persons who experimented with Indridi were facing the phenomena of physical mediumship for the first time.

The Experimental Society was the first society in Iceland devoted to psychical research. Inspired by reading the posthumously published *Human Personality and its Survival of Bodily Death* by the classicist Frederic W.H. Myers (1843-1901), Einar Hjorleifsson Kvaran, himself a prominent writer and editor, established an experimentation circle in October 1904 to investigate the claims of mediumship (Kvaran, 1906, p. 8). This circle became a formal society in the autumn of 1905 (Kvaran, 1934). Einar was president of the Experimental Society for the whole of its existence, and it can be said that he deserves the honor of having established psychical research in Iceland (Nielsson, 1922b, p. 450).

The leading members of the Society were keenly interested in research, and investigated Indridi from the very beginning of his mediumship in 1905 until he became disabled in 1909. He died in 1912. Indridi is probably unique among great mediums in the way that his mediumship was discovered and developed by research-minded scholars and academics. Haraldur Nielsson, Professor of Theology at the University of Iceland, reports (1924a, p. 233) that sittings were usually held once or twice a week from the middle of September to the end of June. It is stated in the two surviving minute books of the Experimental Society that they were sometimes held more often, up to several times a week.

Indridi was paid a fixed modest yearly salary from the Experimental Society and given free lodging, and in return he gave no séances without the Society's permission. Shortly after his death the Society was dissolved, but in 1918 it was resurrected as the Icelandic Society for Psychical Research.

The Experimental Society was in fact founded primarily to investigate the extraordinary phenomena that took place in Indridi's presence (Thordarson, 1942, pp. 1-2). The Society was not Spiritualistic in the ordinary sense of the word, although many of those who frequently took part in the experiments seem gradually to have accepted the Spiritualistic explanation (Nielsson, 1922b, p. 452).

Among the founders of the Experimental Society were Professor Haraldur Nielsson and Einar H. Kvaran, Bjorn Jonsson (1846-1912; later Prime Minister of Iceland), and several other prominent persons in Reykjavik. In 1907 the Society had become so impressed with Indridi that a small house was built to be better able to study him. The building was on one floor, had a flat roof and shuttered windows. There were two rooms for meetings as well as the two rooms in which Indridi lived. The house was referred to as the "experimental house" (see Figure 1 on page 191).

The minute books of the Experimental Society are an important source about Indridi´s mediumship. They were written immediately after each séance or the following day, mostly by Haraldur Nielsson, sometimes by Einar H. Kvaran or Bjorn Jonsson, both of whom were newspaper editors. The minute books were lost for over 50 years when two of them were discovered in the archives of Dagny Auduns (1908-1991). She was the widow of Rev. Jon Auduns (1905-1981), Dean at Reykjavik Cathedral and a prominent Spiritualist, who had studied theology under Professor Haraldur Nielsson.

The first minute book, comprising 46 pages, describes 13 séances held between 4 December 1905 and 6 January 1906. Many of the descriptions are quite detailed and are a few pages long; one is incomplete, containing only a prayer that was said at the beginning of the séance.[2]

The second minute book (159 pages) provides records of 43 séances between 9 September 1907 and 3 February 1908. We have thus minute books for nine months but it is likely that there should be records for another 25 to 30 months.

In addition to the two existing books there are about a hundred loose pages of additional notes, drafts and comments. The total material amounts to around 300 handwritten pages. It is deposited in the Manuscript Section of the National Library in Reykjavik. The original text of the minute books was published in Iceland in 2015 as *Raddad Myrkur* (in English: "Voices through Darkness"), edited by Karlotta J. Blondal.

Apart from the minute books, we have accounts by four persons who observed Indridi extensively and wrote lengthy reports of their investigations of the startling phenomena that occurred in his presence:

1. Gudmundur Hannesson (1866-1946), Professor of Medicine at the University of Iceland.

---

[2] Though a prayer was said at the beginning of every séance, it was not always the same prayer.

2. Einar Hjorleifsson Kvaran (1859-1938), editor and prominent writer.

3. Rev. Haraldur Nielsson (1868-1928), Professor at the University of Iceland. He played an active role in the first two international conferences on psychical research, which were forerunners to the conventions of the Parapsychological Association.

4. Brynjolfur Thorlaksson (1867-1950), organist at Reykjavik Cathedral. He used to play a harmonium[3] at Indridi's séances and became his personal friend.

Many of the reports about Indridi are available only in Icelandic, but some of the key papers were written in, or have been translated into other languages (see especially Hannesson, 1924b; Kvaran, 1910; Nielsson, 1919b, 1922a, 1924a, and 1925). In addition, Haraldur Nielsson read papers on Indridi's phenomena at the First and Second International Congresses for Psychical Research in Copenhagen in 1921 (Nielsson, 1922b) and in Warsaw in 1923 (Nielsson, 1924b). Short reports can also be found in psychical research journals reviewing these two international conferences (for example Nielsson, 1923).

The most detailed reports on Indridi's mediumship, such as those of Gudmundur Hannesson and Haraldur Nielsson, are based on extensive contemporary note-taking. Gudmundur wrote his notes during the séances, but expanded them afterwards, either immediately after each séance or the next morning (Hannesson, 1908-1909; 1924a). Haraldur used the same method, and both trained themselves to write in the dark during séances (Nielsson, 1924a, p. 235). When appropriate, they obtained written testimony from persons observing or connected with the phenomena and included it in the minute books.

Brynjolfur Thorlaksson's memoirs are the basis of the book about Indridi written by Thorbergur Thordarson (1888-1974). It was published in 1942 as *Indridi Midill* (*Indridi, the Medium*). Thorbergur conducted independent interviews with many people who had been present at the séances. He also referred to the articles by Kvaran (1906; 1910), Nielsson (1930) and Hannesson (1910-1911), but more importantly he used two séance minute books that he had access to in 1942. The séance minutes were mostly written by Haraldur and Einar, and in the second book the minutes were authenticated for each séance by two or more sitters.

---

[3] The harmonium is a type of reed organ that generates sound with bellows.

One investigator surpassed the others in the rigorous controls that he imposed in his investigation and in the quality and detail of his reports. This was Dr. Gudmundur Hannesson, who was to become the most prominent scientist in Iceland for his time and was widely respected at home and abroad. During his lifetime, he held many public offices, including: President of the University of Iceland (twice); a founder of the Icelandic Scientific Society; honorary member of both the Icelandic and Danish Societies of Physicians; Director General of Public Health; and Member of Parliament for some years.

In 1908, Gudmundur Hannesson requested permission from the Experimental Society to make an independent investigation of Indridi. He seems to have been known for his skepticism and disbelief in the phenomena. His thorough investigation lasted the whole of the 1908-1909 winter and is described in the latter part of this book. Gudmundur Hannesson was for Indridi what the British chemist and physicist Sir William Crookes (1832-1919) was for D.D. Home.

CHAPTER 2

IMPORTANT EVENTS
IN HIS LIFE

Indridi Indridason was born on 12 October 1883 as the oldest of three sons of the farmer at Hvoll in the rural area of Saurbaer in Dalasysla district at Breidafjordur in the northwestern part of Iceland. Indridi came to Reykjavik about age 21 to become a printer's apprentice. Haraldur Nielsson (1922a, p. 10) wrote that Indridi had never heard of mediumistic phenomena before he came to Reykjavik. His extraordinary psychic gifts were discovered at the beginning of 1905 (Nielsson, 1922b, p. 451), when by chance he happened to be invited to join a sitting of a newly-formed circle, the first of its kind in the country, at the home of a relative. They were attempting to produce table-tilting when Indridi was invited to join. Einar Kvaran (1934) describes the incident as follows:

> ... Then Indridi arrived. He was a printer's apprentice in Isafold. He was related to Indridi Einarsson [1851-1939], economist and prominent playwright, and lived at his home.
>
> Indridi Einarsson was interested in the experiments but his wife much more so. Once whilst she was sitting at a table Indridi approached. She asked him to participate in an experiment.

Indridi had hardly taken his seat, when the table reacted violently and trembled. Indridi became frightened and was going to run out of the house. From that time the experiments with Indridi started.

He came to my home and we sat down at a table. The table trembled, shook, and moved violently around the room and nearly broke. Once it was overturned.

—Authors' translation from Icelandic.

Haraldur Nielsson (1919b, p. 344) writes that Indridi blushed and became almost frightened when he discovered what influence his presence seemed to have on the table at this sitting. The table apparently[1] made strong movements as soon as he touched it. This was the beginning of an ongoing series of macro-psychokinetic effects that occurred more or less undiminished for nearly five years. Shortly after this incident new phenomena appeared. On inquiry, the members learned that Indridi had formerly had some "remarkable visions," but no details are given concerning the nature of those experiences (Nielsson, 1919b, p. 344).

As the son of a farmer, Indridi received minimal education (taught only to read and write), and knew no foreign language except for a few words of Danish he may have picked up after he moved to Reykjavik.

Haraldur writes that the young country boy had never seen a juggler, and conjuring tricks were at the time quite unknown in Iceland (Nielsson, 1922b, p. 451). During his mediumistic career Indridi was probably the biggest celebrity in Iceland, and he became a highly controversial figure. To some he was an object of scorn and derision, to others a source of the most extraordinary psychokinetic powers and/or a man who connected the living with the dead. Indridi himself always interpreted the phenomena that occurred around him as relating to spirits (Kvaran, 1959, pp. 68-70), which he was able to see.

Indridi was the first medium in Iceland. He was primarily a physical medium and probably the only physical medium we have ever had. According to existing reports, the vigour as well as the variety of

---

[1]   Hereafter, use of words such as apparent, alleged, and purported to denote uncertainty about the reality of Indridi's abilities and the authenticity of the phenomena observed in his presence will be used sparingly. In their examination of Indridi's mediumship, the authors demonstrate that the phenomena, though not proven, were observed repeatedly by a large number of credible witnesses.

his phenomena developed steadily from 1905 until they were at their height in the year 1909, when he held his last sitting (Nielsson, 1924a, p. 235). Indridi's powers never decreased and he only stopped because of illness. Most of Indridi's phenomena occurred whilst he was in trance at séances but violent phenomena also occurred when he was in a waking state. In addition, many phenomena took place outside the formal sittings that were held first in the homes of Einar Kvaran and Haraldur Nielsson, and later in the experimental house.

In the summer of 1909, Indridi went to visit his parents in the country (Nielsson, 1922a, p. 30). During this trip he and his fiancée, Jona Gudnadottir (1892-1909), caught typhoid fever from which she died. In 1911 Indridi married Ingveldur Brandsdottir; the couple had one child who died quite young (Nielsson, 1912). Indridi never regained his health after contracting typhoid, and no further sittings took place. Later it was found that he had also contracted tuberculosis, which resulted in his untimely death in the sanatorium at Vifilsstadir on 31 August 1912. He was only 28 years of age.

In concluding this overview of Indridi's life history, it is relevant to introduce here a great-uncle who would figure prominently in Indridi's mediumship, as his main control personality. The brother of Indridi's paternal grandfather, Konrad Gislason (1808-1891), received a higher education than other family members though not by the usual means. Konrad started as a farm hand for Hallgrimur Scheving (1781-1861) who was rector of the Bessastada gymnasium.[2] The rector was so impressed by the young man that he let him assist him with his scholarly work and soon helped him through the gymnasium. After that, Konrad went to Copenhagen to study at the University of Copenhagen and never returned to Iceland. Konrad Gislason became Professor of Icelandic and Nordic Studies and a prominent scholar. Though Indridi did not meet Konrad Gislason, he would have almost certainly heard about him as a child.

Brief Review of Indridi Indridason's Phenomena

The phenomena observed around Indridi began early in 1905 with strong table movements, automatic writing and trance speech in which the

---

[2] Gymnasium is approximately the equivalent of "high school"; Bessastada was the only gymnasium in Iceland that qualified students to enter university.

first controls and direct communicators appeared. The séances were held in darkness with a glimmer of light from a stove or a small red light. After the summer break in 1905, movements and levitations of objects continued. For example, a table would levitate without anyone touching it, and on another occasion the sitters were unable to push a levitated table down with their hands. Knocks and bangs on walls, the floor and in mid-air were common. There were levitations of the medium. The sitters were often touched by invisible hands while the medium was held some distance from them. At this time the first light phenomena appeared, such as flashing lights, or light spots in the air or on the walls of the séance room. For none of these was there any normal light source.

Indridi is primarily known for *physical phenomena*. Here follows a brief list of observations reported at his séances and some that occurred outside formal séances. These phenomena will be described in detail in later chapters.

Raps, cracking sounds in the air, knocks responding to the sitters' demands, some of them loud and heavy, and knocks heard on the body of the medium.

Gusts of wind, cold or hot, were common, strong enough to blow paper, sometimes far away from the medium, and sometimes as if someone was blowing air from their mouth.

Olfactory (odor) phenomena sometimes occurred; a sudden fragrant smell in the presence of the medium, sometimes other smells, such as seaweed. The odor would sometimes cling to a sitter after being touched by the medium.

Movements and levitations were frequent, of objects, small and large, light and heavy, and over short or long distances within a room or hall and sometimes quite high. Some of these objects moved as if thrown forcefully, at other times their trajectories were irregular. Sometimes objects were found to tremble. Curtains were pulled back and forth on request by the sitters.

Levitations of the medium. Many instances of levitation are reported, often with the medium holding onto another person. During violent poltergeist phenomena, the medium was dragged along the floor and thrown up into the air so that his protectors had difficulty pushing him down (Nielsson, 1924b; Thordarson, 1942).

Playing of musical instruments as if by invisible hands, and sometimes while they were levitating and moving around in mid-air. Winding of a music box by itself.

Fixation of objects or the medium. Sitters could not move objects or stop them moving or push them down when they were above the ground. The sitters could not move the medium or his limbs.

Light phenomena. Fire-flashes or fire-balls, small and large fire-flashes on the walls. Luminous clouds as large as several feet across, sometimes described as a "pillar of light" (Thordarson, 1942, p. 99) within which a human form appeared.

Materializations. The shadow or shape of materialized fingers were seen, or a hand or a foot, or a full human figure. Sitters touched materialized fingers, limbs or trunks that were felt as solid. Once a monster-like animal (mixture of a horse and a calf) was observed outside a séance.

Dematerialization of the medium's arm. The medium's shoulder and trunk was inspected through touch by several sitters, yet the arm was not detected.

Sense of being touched, pulled and punched by invisible hands, also of being kissed.

Sounds heard around the medium, laughter, footsteps, buzzing sounds, clatter of hoof-beats and the rustling noise of clothes as if someone was moving.

Direct voice phenomena. Whispers were heard, voices spoke, also through trumpets moving in the air. Voices were heard singing, including a male and female voice at the same time. A choir was heard in the distance.

Direct writing. Writing appeared on paper without human touch.

Two or more phenomena occurred simultaneously, which was deemed impossible for one person to do, such as a musical instrument moving fast in mid-air while being played, or two widely different voices singing at the same time.

Automatic writing, in which Indridi's handwriting would change significantly.

Mental phenomena were also reported; that is, information was communicated that was not available to any of the sitters by normal means. A fire burning in Copenhagen was described at a time when there was no telephone or radio contact with Iceland.

Controls and individual spirit communicators revealed knowledge that the medium could not have known about them.

A Séance in the Experimental House

At this point it would be useful to describe a typical séance in the ex-perimental house during the winter of 1908-1909. The larger hall in the house (see Figure 1 on page 191) could seat 100 people. The benches were in rows as in a church, with the main door at the rear of the hall. There was an empty space at the front of the hall, and in the middle of the wall was a lectern mounted on the pulpit. In front of the first bench stood a small harmonium, and in the empty space close to the lectern were two chairs and a table. Trumpets and a music box were placed on the table. At the beginning of each séance Indridi would sit on one of the chairs, and the person who was to watch him sat on the other. Let us quote Gudmundur Hannesson (1924b, p. 243):

> People seat themselves on the benches and the room is soon filled. Then comes the medium, a young, handsome fellow. He sits down on one of the chairs in front of the lectern, and beside him on the other chair sits a man who is to watch him when the light is put out and report if he finds that he resorts to imposture. The President [of the Experimental Society] scans the hall to see if everybody is present and that everything is in order. Then the door is locked and the lamp is put out, but a candle is lit for the man who is to play the harmonium, care being taken that the light does not fall on the medium. All conversation

12

ceases. A hymn is played on the harmonium and several among the audience sing to it.

There is now semi-darkness in the hall; nevertheless we see the medium plainly. He is sitting motionless on the chair with his hands clasped on his chest, as people saying their prayers are represented in pictures [probably, as if in prayer]. After a little while, he may be seen to make some starts, as if involuntary jerks. All of a sudden his head and his hands fall down and his body seems to become limp. He sits in a stooping position on the chair with his head drooping. The President makes a sign to the musician. The candle is put out and when the tune has been played through, the music ceases. The medium has fallen into a trance and is unconscious. The hall is now pitch-dark and silent as the grave.

When Indridi was in a trance, several of his spirit control personalities spoke through him and greeted the sitters, after which the physical phenomena seemed to start. The musical box was heard playing a tune in the air, and voices were heard speaking through trumpets in different parts of the hall. One person, called "the watchman," was chosen to sit close to the medium, usually holding one or both of his hands and even his feet, so that he could report if the medium were to try to produce phenomena by imposture or fraud. Later he was also responsible for ensuring that nothing dangerous happened to the medium. This person was frequently Professor Haraldur Nielsson. As the phenomena occurred, the watchman would often call out Indridi's position and explain how he was holding him.

Indridi's séances differed in some ways from séances held in other countries during this period, perhaps because none of those present had ever attended a mediumistic sitting abroad:

1. *The large number of sitters that witnessed the phenomena.* To the best of our knowledge, in other countries the number of sitters rarely exceeded ten persons. Haraldur Nielsson, (1924a, pp. 234-235) says that even though 60-70 sitters were present, independent spirit voices were heard, the levitation phenomena occurred and so did all the other telekinetic phenomena. Gudmundur (Hannesson, 1910-1911, p. 208) writes that the larger experimental hall, seating about 100, was full of sitters at ordinary séances.

2. *The sitters were seated on rows of parallel benches with the medium in an empty space in front of them.* None of the available sources explain why this arrangement was used instead of sitting in a circle. Between October 1904 and autumn 1905, before the Society was formally founded, the sitters sat wherever they pleased in the room (Kvaran, 1934). Before moving to the experimental house, which was purpose-built for Indridi's experiments, members seem to have been seated in a circle with Indridi in the middle.

Other séances were held for the so-called "inner circle," which consisted of a small group of specially chosen people. These séances, generally held in the smaller hall at the experimental house, were to develop and "experiment" with some of the phenomena, such as the materializations and the light phenomena (Thordarson, 1942, p. 4).

Indridi's séances usually took place in darkness. Members of the Society seem to have tried a red light a few times, but it was abandoned because it caused the phenomena to diminish (Nielsson, 1922b, p. 452). However, many violent phenomena were reported to have taken place in full light outside of the sittings. These occurred during what seemed to be poltergeist outbreaks during the winter of 1907-1908 (Nielsson, 1925; 1930).

Furthermore, some table-tilting séances, at which, in addition to table movements, knocks on the table were reported, seem to have been held in normal light (Hannesson, 1908-1909, p. 7). Various other phenomena were also reported to have occurred spontaneously now and then in full light (Thordarson, 1942). We have described the light conditions in the accounts of Indridi's phenomena whenever our sources have mentioned them.

In 1905-1906 the sittings took place at the home of Haraldur Nielsson until the tenants on the floor below complained about the noise. Or they were held at the home of Einar Kvaran. At first the sitters were few, but soon their numbers grew as news of the more startling phenomena spread.

We have concentrated on the development of Indridi's physical phenomena but we have not tried to give a comprehensive account of everything that took place. The first part of this book, before the description of Gudmundur Hannesson's investigation, may not provide evidence comparable, for example, to what is found in the classic investigations of Daniel Dunglas Home and Eusapia Palladino. However, in the latter part, we describe séances in which rigorous control methods were imposed by Dr. Gudmundur Hannesson.

CHAPTER 3

THE BEGINNING – TABLE-TILTING, AUTOMATIC WRITING AND TRANCE SPEECH

I n October 1904, Einar Kvaran started to hold irregular sittings with a small group of friends and family members, where they attempted to produce table-tilting and automatic writing (Kvaran, 1906, pp. 8-11). Some automatic writing was produced, but its content made little sense. At this time, Indridi had not yet been discovered.

As has already been mentioned, Indridi joined the group after his first session with strong table movements. Very soon thereafter, in 1905, this group became the Experimental Society. The Society's members spent some months experimenting with and developing Indridi's automatic writing, table movements, mediumistic trance, and trance speaking.

Indridi immediately produced automatic writing when he tried it (Kvaran, 1906, p. 11). It was difficult to read the writing at first, but it became easier to read as time passed. Finally, he wrote with much more speed than he could normally manage when he wrote in a conscious manner—he had only written a few letters in his whole life, according to Einar Kvaran (*ibid.*, p. 16). It was about then that Indridi's first spirit control appeared, probably through the writing. The control claimed to be a woman and constantly begged Indridi to "seek God" and "good manners" (*ibid.*, p. 18). At this time, members of the Society claimed some "proofs of identity" for deceased communicators manifesting through Indridi's automatic writing (Nielsson, 1919b, p. 344; Kvaran, 1906, pp. 12-16).

Indridi fell into trance for the first time at a sitting at Einar Kvaran's home on the Saturday evening before Easter 1905. Until that time, mediumistic communications had been received only through automatic writing (Kvaran, 1906, pp. 16-18). The trance started when Indridi, whilst writing automatically, made some jokes about the entity that he believed was causing him to write. This seemed to create some upset and the writing protested, "You should not make fun of me," and then declared, "Indridi shall now fall into trance." Indridi did not agree at first but again the writing insisted, "He shall." He then agreed and the light was turned off, though we are not told why. A table with a pillow was put in front of his seat, and a small table, on which were placed paper and a pencil, was positioned by his right side. He put his head on the pillow, and after a few minutes he lost consciousness and started to write on the paper. Einar Kvaran (*ibid.*, p. 18) reports on this first occasion:

> He [the medium] wrote a few sentences with harsh jerks, and sighed heavily and screamed from time to time. He spoke with someone he obviously thought of as being with him, asked him not to treat him badly, and expressed disagreement with what he thought was being said to him. Then, after about an hour, he was woken up, apparently by the same force that had put him to sleep. He was woken at our request, as we had never seen this state before and we were uneasy.

—AUTHORS' TRANSLATION FROM ICELANDIC.

Experiments with Indridi were continued until the summer of 1905. But, in the spring of 1905, Indridi became scared whilst in trance and said he saw shadowy beings; he cursed them, trembled and shivered with terror (Kvaran, 1906, p. 19). Eventually a personality claiming to be Indridi's deceased paternal grandfather Indridi Gislason (1822-1898)[1] replaced the woman control and became his second main spir-

---

[1] This second control (Indridi Gislason from Hvoli in Dolum) is not to be confused with the third control, who claimed to be Indridi's paternal grandfather's brother Konrad Gislason.

it control. This control was the first to speak through Indridi's lips (ibid., p. 19).

Little further was accomplished with this personality and he soon disappeared and other controls took over. Members of the Society tested Indridi's trance state many times without prior warning, by poking needles in several delicate spots in his body (in his hands, on the back of his neck, in the corner of his eyes and elsewhere) but he showed no reaction at all (Nielsson, 1919 a,p. 3). They opened Indridi's eyes to test his pupils' reaction to light, but there was no response (Kvaran, 1906, p. 17).

In the trance state, Indridi often spoke in the first person as though he was one of the trance personalities. Also at this time he started to speak with great astonishment about his own body, and he would frequently do so later on, as if he experienced himself out of the body and was viewing it from some external angle. Haraldur Nielsson (1919a, p. 3) writes how Indridi in a trance state often described this split perception (the split between observer and the observed):

> "Oh, see me and me. . . You are there below with the body. The body is not me. I am up here. There are two Indridis. Oh, is it not strange to see the nerve [cord], which lies between me and me! The lips of the body move and they say what I say. The nerve becomes thinner, the further away I am from my body."
>
> —AUTHORS' TRANSLATION FROM ICELANDIC.

Haraldur adds that nobody at that time had heard of this "cord" except Einar Kvaran, who had read about it but had mentioned it neither to Indridi nor to anyone else. Indridi, during these experiments, was the first man in Iceland known to fall into mediumistic trance, so Haraldur doubted if he could have heard of it from others. Later, when Indridi's left arm dematerialized, we notice again a similar split perception in his trance speaking.

The Experimental Society claimed to have trained Indridi as a medium. Some phenomena first occurred spontaneously, for example when the levitations of Indridi began (Kvaran, 1906, pp. 20-22). Other phenomena, such as apports and materializations, were only obtained after experimentation (Thordarson, 1942, pp. 97-98). We do not have any account of how the Society's members actually trained Indridi, but in the end they succeeded in producing all or most of the mediumistic phenomena they attempted. The steps towards new phenomena that the investigators wanted to produce were often discussed at length with the controls or even initiated by them.

Indridi seems to have had the potential to develop most of the phenomena known to be produced by physical mediums. Several mediums, such as the Austrian Rudi Schneider (1908-1957) and the Italian Eusapia Palladino (1854-1918), suffered a decline in their ability to produce phenomena, but this did not happen with respect to most of Indridi's phenomena. The reason may be that Schneider and Palladino were mediums for long periods whereas Indridi practiced mediumship for only five years and died young.

The following chapters deal chronologically with Indridi's phenomena in order to describe the sequences in his development as a medium. Readers who are primarily interested in the evidential value of the reports on Indridi's phenomena might want to turn next to the chapter on Dr. Gudmundur Hannesson's investigations during the winter of 1908-1909. In the next few chapters, various observations of phenomena are described. These are highly interesting accounts of extraordinary phenomena but do not usually provide such detailed descriptions of controls and conditions as are reported in Gudmundur Hannesson's careful investigations.

CHAPTER 4

LEVITATIONS, DIRECT VOICE AND LIGHT PHENOMENA

In the spring of 1905, the number of sitters became so great that the circle members decided to establish the Experimental Society on a formal basis. The members started to experiment with levitations of the medium, light phenomena and healing, and they attempted to get "proofs of identity" from alleged deceased communicators. Other phenomena reported during this period included levitations and movements of objects, knocks on walls and the floor, clicking sounds in the air, dematerializations of Indridi's left arm and fragrant olfactory phenomena.

Levitation of Objects

Indridi was at the home of two friends in Reykjavik on Sunday evening, 12 November 1905 (Kvaran, 1906, pp. 20-21). Haraldur Nielsson (1922b, p. 452) reports that this incident took place in twilight and that three or four men were sitting around a table. Indridi's friends suggested that he should try to "lift" the table and, after a short while, the table suddenly levitated very high and "bumped" into the faces of those who stood by it (Kvaran, 1906, p. 20), probably in the sense of "lifted to their faces."

Three men tried to hold the table down by force, but still it was raised from the floor and lifted up to the level of their faces. Additionally, the table lifted itself up to Indridi's and the sitters' hands while they kept their hands some distance above it but with none of them touching it (Nielsson, 1922b, p. 452). Neither Einar Kvaran nor Haraldur Nielsson mention where Indridi was placed, and it is unlikely that any research controls were employed on this occasion.

A new control personality now appeared who instructed the sitters to hold séances every evening for a period of time in order to produce further phenomena. This third control said he was Konrad Gislason, the brother of Indridi's grandfather, who in his earthly life had been a Professor of Icelandic at the University of Copenhagen. He was to become Indridi's principal control throughout his career as a medium.

The table experiment was repeated at Einar's house on Monday evening, 13 November (Kvaran, 1906, pp. 20-21). A small table with three legs levitated so high that it "bumped" into the sitters' faces, whilst they touched the table top. The table was also raised when the sitters held their hands together at some distance above it, without touching it. The sitters then tried with a very heavy table, which tilted a few times without being touched and once levitated completely off the floor. Unfortunately, Einar Kvaran describes neither the research controls nor the lighting conditions.

In this period, a small table was abruptly levitated off the floor and up onto another table. This happened twice and apparently without Indridi attempting to make them levitate (Kvaran, 1906, pp. 21-22). The first time, Indridi was sitting by a table with two other people. He was not in a trance and his hands rested on the table. Then another table behind Indridi levitated and landed on the table they were sitting at. Einar reports that the three of them had their hands together, so it was "unthinkable that the medium could have extended his hand behind himself" (*ibid.*, p. 21).

On the other occasion, Indridi was sitting "still as the grave" in a trance state and was speaking with an unfamiliar voice (*ibid.*, p. 21). One of the sitters placed his arm on a small table situated in front of his chair. He noticed that the table started to make movements. He pushed the table down but it was nevertheless "snatched" away. A few moments later, the experimenters heard sounds as if the table had landed on another, bigger table, a fact which was confirmed when the light was lit. When the light was turned off, the table moved, in the same manner, to its original place. "Those who were present assert that Indridi could by no means have transported the table by himself, " writes Einar (*ibid.*, p. 22). Tables also moved on a few occasions during "a brightly lit day" and in the presence of observers. The tables even moved a "great distance" across the floor to Indridi. He was then "expected" to write something automatically, reports Einar (ibid., p. 22), without explaining further what was meant.[1]

Haraldur Nielsson (1922b, p. 452) reports that at first the experimenters had sat in the dark during meetings, but afterwards they tried a red light. The red light seemed to reduce the power of the phenomena to a great extent, so they abandoned it. Haraldur explains further (*ibid.*, p. 452):

> In accordance with the wishes of the controls, who complained of the limiting influences of the light, we gave it up. On the other hand, they emphasized the importance of the greatest possible caution in order to exclude the slightest vestige of fraud on the part of the medium. That is why it soon became a custom that one of us sat down beside the medium and watched him carefully, placing an arm around his waist or holding one or both of his hands.

Most often, either Einar or Haraldur sat by the medium (Thordarson, 1942, p. 97).

The first minute book (5 December 1905 to 6 January 1906) contains the protocols of 14 sittings. Some physical phenomena are described in 11 of them. Direct voice phenomena (that is, voices around but independent of the medium) were most frequent in this period, heard at eight sittings. Knocks were heard at seven sittings; over half of them were loud and heavy. Next in frequency were light phenomena (observed at five sittings) followed by seeing a materialized human being (three times); sensing movement of air (twice); observing movements of objects (twice); the dematerialization of Indridi´s arm (twice); and two sitters were touched by a hand.

---

[1]   This is probably reference to automatic writing which was an occasional feature of Indridi's mediumship.

Direct Voice Phenomena

Direct voice phenomena were a common characteristic of Indridi´s mediumship, namely voices heard somewhere around Indridi or in the room,
that did not come from his throat. In the first minute book the phenomenon is specifically mentioned to have taken place on eight different dates.
On 15 December 1905, Dutch was spoken three times although we are not
told what was said. On two days a particular direct voice speaks, twice
on one occasion; on five different dates the direct voice of a deceased
clergyman, identified as Rev. Steinn Steinsen (1838-1883; abbreviated as
St.St.), was heard speaking. On 16 December he chanted "Our Father"
at the end of the séance. On 18 December Dutch was again spoken independent of the medium, but again the minutes fail to state what the
voice said. On 19 December St.St. sang a hymn at a distance from the
medium and asked those present to join him. On 20 December he did
so again but it is not mentioned whether it was independent of the medium or not; he also sang a hymn on the 4 January 1906.

The First Knocks

Knocks on walls were heard for the first time during the third meeting
in November 1905 while Indridi was in trance (Kvaran, 1906, pp. 22-23;
Nielsson, 1922b, p. 453). The date is not given but, in the first minute
book, knocks are first mentioned on 6 December as "very clear lights
and knocks." The knocks started in the vicinity of Indridi and were
heard on walls or objects and sometimes close to the ceiling. They developed and moved around the room according to the sitters' requests.
The knocks appeared as affirmative or negative replies to questions
from the sitters. Einar states that this phenomenon was checked many
times for fraud and so carefully that the sitters were in no doubt that
Indridi could not have produced it by any normal means (Kvaran, 1906,
p. 22). Unfortunately he does not give any details of how they checked
the knocks, or if other sitters could have produced them. The knocks
were also heard at the same time as Indridi was writing automatically
or speaking in trance.

Later, when the Society started to use the newly-constructed, purpose-built experimental house for the séances, the knocks increased
(Kvaran, 1906, pp. 22-23). They even seemed to come from the ceiling,
which was about ten feet above the floor.

One evening, at the end of a sitting, only Einar and Haraldur were present. They heard very strong knocks as though something was striking the walls (Nielsson, 1922b, p. 453). Indridi was lying in such a deep trance, according to Haraldur, that his heart seemed to have stopped beating, and his pulse was so weak that it could hardly be detected. "Then the strokes [striking sounds] roared on the panels round him and replied very promptly to questions" (*ibid.*, p. 453). Meanwhile not a word came from Indridi's own lips.

Another new phenomenon started during the fourth séance in November 1905 (probably 6 November). Clicking sounds were heard in the air, as when fingers are snapped together, but with a sharper sound. These clicks were heard every evening for some time and they were heard to move all around the room. Indridi was observed to be sitting completely still (Kvaran, 1906, p. 23; 1910, p. 45). Haraldur Nielsson (1922b, p. 453) writes that they had "obtained" peculiar cracking sounds in the air. These sounds moved around the room even though Indridi remained quiet and in the same place.

Light Phenomena

The other phenomenon comprised "lights" with no obvious source, referred to as light phenomena (Kvaran, 1906, p. 23; 1910, p. 45; Nielsson, 1922b, pp. 454- 455). The sitters first saw them manifested as flashing lights or light spots in the air or on the walls in the séance room. The lights appeared to be mostly "tongue-shaped" (Nielsson, 1922b, p. 454). During the evenings that followed, the flashes grew in strength and had different forms and colors—some were white and others reddish. Just before the clearest lights appeared Indridi was heard to groan painfully.

One evening, at Einar Kvaran's home, the sitters counted 58 appearances of lights during a single séance (Kvaran, 1910, p. 45; Nielsson, 1922b, p. 455). Einar writes (Kvaran, 1906, p. 23):

> They [the lights] had distinctly different colors; some were very white; others were more reddish. Once, during an experimental séance at my home, 58 lights were counted. These lights were of various shapes: some of the lights were round, while others were oblong. They were of different sizes: some were small, about an inch in diameter, but others were stripes of light around two to four feet long.
>
> —AUTHORS' TRANSLATION FROM ICELANDIC.

One evening. Haraldur counted more than 60 lights while Indridi was sitting in the middle of a circle of sitters (Nielsson, 1919b, p. 344). Lights in the shape of a tongue with different colors were seen at different locations in the room. The light spots developed into large flashes with a strong reddish tinge, which spread all over one wall of a large room. Nielsson (1919b, p. 344; 1922a, p. 13; 1922b, p. 455) reports that later the whole wall behind Indridi had become "a glow of light" (probably a continuous mass of light). Einar Kvaran (1906, p. 24) writes:

> There were a few times when a light spread across a whole wall behind the medium which was twelve feet wide and ten feet high. Sometimes it looked like a sort of net of light with circular meshes: slightly darker circles around bright flashes. Again, the light was sometimes continuous, similar to the glow from a great fire. These expanses of light were never as white as the small lights were, but were more reddish.

—*Authors' translation from Icelandic.*

Often peculiar clicking sounds were heard accompanying the lights (Nielsson, 1922a, p. 13). The clicks followed one after the other very quickly. Haraldur Nielsson (1919b, p. 344; 1922b, p. 455) also reports that strong gusts of wind would most often blow through the room before the lights appeared. The wind was so strong that the hair moved on sitters' heads, and the pages of notebooks, lying open on their knees, flapped vigorously. Three years later Gudmundur Hannesson (1908-1909, p. 9) also observed a strong wind blowing across the hall. Indridi's controls told him that the gusts of wind had "to accompany the light phenomena."

Einar reports that the guarantee for the authenticity of the light phenomena was as follows (Kvaran, 1906, pp. 24-25):

1. Lamps or equipment that might produce the same kind of flashes, with as much variety as those observed in the Society's experiments, were not available in Iceland. Only one kind of electric lamp which could produce flashes was available in shops: Einar Kvaran owned one of these, but stated that the difference in the flashes was obvious. Indridi had moved into Einar's home before the strongest light phenomena began. Einar Kvaran's wife was responsible for maintaining Indridi's belongings.

2. Einar Kvaran states that he and his wife were familiar with everything that Indridi owned. Indridi had only one trunk, which could not be locked, and therefore he could not hide things from the Kvarans in their own home, and there is no evidence that he tried to do so. (At the time, the séances were being held in the Kvarans' home.)

3. According to Einar, the sitters made a careful body search of Indridi and also searched the room on some of the evenings at which most of the lights were seen. He does not provide any details.

4. Haraldur states (Nielsson, 1922a, p. 12) that when the light phenomena were occurring the sitters "kept a good eye" on Indridi. He does not provide further detail.

Eufemia Waage (1881-1960), daughter of Indridi Einarsson, was present at a sitting in the early period of Indridi´s mediumship. In her autobiography she writes that she does not recall that Indridi said anything memorable in that sitting but "the light phenomena were like stars all over the room. I saw them later on an even larger scale" (Waage, 1949, p. 165).

Light phenomena are described in five of 13 sittings in the first minute book. On some days they occurred many times during the same session. The minutes for 6 December 1905 record: "Very clear lights and knocks." A little later: "Bright light is seen and a dark man in the light. (All see it)." Later, the main control (Konrad Gislason) says: "It was a man by the name of Jensen that you saw [in the light]." "It could not have been the medium that you saw." "Very bright flashes every now and then in the interior of the room (seen by all), flashes with dark dots."

The purported spirit controls were attempting to produce materializations, the lights being a part of that process. The light phenomena continued until eventually, on 6 and 7 December 1905, there appeared for the first time in the light the full form of a man, whose identity was not recognized by those present (Kvaran, 1910, p. 45; Nielsson, 1922b, p. 455). Einar Kvaran (1906, p. 24) describes this in more detail:

> On two evenings one could clearly see a man standing in the light. He was slightly above average height, muscular, well built, with broad shoulders. His back was turned towards us. Now one would naturally think that it was the medium that we saw in the light. I would assert that it was not. I was certain, at least the other time when this vision was seen, that the

medium was in the corner, crying out loudly and screaming, some eight to ten feet from the place where we saw the man standing. The lights, as in all his major phenomena, seemed to cause him much pain. He began to shriek and scream when the lights were coming, and he continued to do so as long as the lights continued. They came in bursts, with small pauses in between, and during the pauses the medium was calm. After the séances he said he felt as if he had been beaten up.

—AUTHORS' TRANSLATION FROM ICELANDIC.

Haraldur reports that many members of the Society had first seen the materialized being, who later identified himself through Indridi as "Jensen," against a strong reddish glow, in the middle of the radiance which appeared on the wall (Nielsson, 1919b, p. 344; 1922a, p. 13; 1922b, p. 455). Haraldur himself saw very distinctly the outline of the head and shoulders of the materialized being. These light phenomena were observed several times, but then ceased around Christmas 1905, and reappeared around Christmas the following year (Kvaran, 1910, p. 46).

The Beginning of Indridi's Levitations

A new phenomenon occurred in November 1905, 10 days after the experiments recommenced after the summer break. Einar describes Indridi's first levitation, which apparently took place in darkness, as follows (Kvaran, 1906, pp. 25-26):

The medium was then in a trance, and suddenly he started complaining that now he was going to be "dragged." He was then "dragged" prostrate back and forth along the floor. ... After a short while we noticed that his neck was resting on the top edge of a small table in front of me. A few moments later another sitter noticed that his feet were resting on the living-room table. We were then allowed [probably by the controls] to light a match, and we all saw him in this position, with nothing else holding him off the floor. As we put out the match, he fell down on the floor, overturning the living-room table as he fell. One sitter noticed that the table righted itself again without anything touching it. The medium complained about the treatment.

—AUTHORS' TRANSLATION FROM ICELANDIC.

During the period when the séances were held in members' homes, Indridi is reported to have levitated sometimes up to the ceiling, which he touched with his head (Kvaran, 1910, p. 45; Nielsson, 1919b, p. 344; Thordarson, 1942, p. 13). Sometimes he even bumped his head harshly against the ceiling and complained about "pain in his head" after sittings (Kvaran, 1906, p. 26). According to Einar, it was difficult at first to observe the levitations of the medium because of the darkness. But the noise, especially when he crashed down on the floor, resulted in complaints from neighbours. At least twice the Society had to find another flat to hold their séances (Kvaran, 1906, p. 26; 1934).

Haraldur Nielsson reports (1922a, p. 12; 1922 b, p. 453) that during a sitting in his own living room, a sofa levitated and was carried around the séance room by invisible powers, while Indridi lay prostrate upon it (probably in a trance). Even in the pitch dark, the sofa did not collide with anything, but was delicately placed over the knees of the sitters, who could then touch the medium. Afterwards, the sofa was brought back to its original location, with the medium still in position on it, as if the "intelligent power" that directed these transported levitations could see in the dark (Nielsson, 1922a, p. 12). Although this occurred in darkness, it is difficult to imagine that Indridi alone could have transported the sofa while lying prostrate upon it.

Einar Kvaran writes (1906, p. 26; 1934) that on one occasion, when the séances were held in Haraldur's home, a sofa with Indridi on it had levitated and come down to rest "on the chest" of one of the sitters, who noticed at the same time that Indridi was lying flat on top of it. The sitter "held Indridi" who stayed in that position until the sofa levitated again and was finally brought back to its original position.

Brynjolfur Thorlaksson states that Indridi was once sitting in a trance state on a small sofa in darkness (Thordarson, 1942, p. 13):

> Then we realized that the sofa with Indridi on it had suddenly been levitated without us being aware of it. The control from the other side, who said he was Konrad Gislason, brother of the medium's grandfather, spoke through Indridi's lips and asked us to feel the sofa with our hands so we could get a sense of what had happened, and to ensure ourselves that no known force was at work. Some of us touched the sofa carefully all over with our hands, under it and around. There was no doubt, the sofa was at the height of our chest and Indridi was on it. We ensured ourselves that the sofa was not held up by any force that we could feel or touch. Thus the sofa remained stationary in

space long enough for all of us to feel it with our hands. Then it slowly moved down to the floor.

—Authors' translation from Icelandic.

Haraldur has described attempts by the sitters to authenticate the early levitations (Nielsson, 1922b, pp. 453-454; see also Nielsson, 1922a, pp. 17-18):

In order to substantiate these phenomena, we placed him [the medium] in a wicker chair, which creaked upon the least movement. We placed this chair at one end of the room and tight rows of chairs all across the room, so that any passage between the chairs was made impossible. Then the sitters — and it must be remembered that we were sometimes 50 or more in number — sat down on all the chairs, the light being put out. Very soon the medium was levitated in the wicker chair a great distance from the floor—the creaking in the chair being heard while it glided, containing the medium, above our heads — and was eventually, rather noisily, deposited on the floor behind the chairs. Then the light was immediately lit and there sat the medium unconscious (in a deep trance) in the chair, in which he seemed to have been sitting immovable during this ... trip [through the air].

On 5 December 1905, the minutes report that Indridi might have levitated: The main control, Konrad, says using direct voice "I got him [Indridi lying flat] almost up but then I had to let him go down because the energy was not sufficient and I was afraid that he might fall on you." What the sitters witnessed is not mentioned. Levitations became increasingly common as will be shown in later chapters.

Around Christmas 1905 Indridi performed some "remarkable" physical exercises or gymnastic feats in a trance state, which were so complex and difficult that Olafur Rosinkrans (1852-1929), who was a gymnastics education instructor, could not repeat them (Kvaran, 1934). The Society members had the lights turned on while Indridi did the exercises (Kvaran, 1906, p. 38). These exercises, unfortunately, are not described in our sources or in the minute books.

CHAPTER 5

THE FIRE IN COPENHAGEN

Interesting mental phenomena frequently occurred in Indridi's mediumship, though physical phenomena were more prominent. Perhaps the most interesting of these took place at a séance in November 1905. On 24 November 1905, a new communicator appeared. He spoke Danish and introduced himself as "Mr. Jensen," which is a common Danish surname, and gave his profession as a "manufacturer." At this time a break was made for the medium to rest, as he had complained of being tired. It seems that the séances often lasted a long time — one of five hours' duration is reported. When the séance resumed later in the evening, Jensen returned. He stated that he had been to Copenhagen and described a fire raging in a factory in one of the streets. About an hour later he said that the fire had been brought under control. Jensen's statements were recorded and a written account was deposited with the Bishop of Iceland.

Copenhagen is over 1,300 miles from Reykjavik. There was no telephone or telegraph communication with Iceland in 1905. Newspapers arrived by ship close to Christmas that confirmed that a fire had indeed broken out on 24 November in a factory at Store Kongensgade 63. The fire was brought under control in an hour, as had been stated during the séance.

None of the sitters recognized Jensen, so he falls into the category of a drop-in communicator (Haraldsson & Stevenson, 1975).

Accounts of Witnesses

Three witnesses, who were present at the séance on 24 November 1905, provided written accounts of the incident in which "Jensen" described a fire in Copenhagen. Haraldur Nielsson (1922b, p. 456) writes:

> The first evening he [Mr. Jensen] manifested himself through the medium he told us that, in the half-hour pause while the medium was being allowed to rest in the middle of the sitting, he had set off for Copenhagen and had seen that a factory was on fire in one of the streets of the city. He told us that the firemen had succeeded in conquering [extinguishing] the fire. At that time no telegraphic connection between Iceland and the outside world had been established, so there were no means of recognizing that event.

> This happened on 24 November 1905. Next day I went to see the Bishop of Iceland, the Right Reverend Hallgrimur Sveinsson [1841-1909], who was my uncle, and stated to him what Jensen had told us and asked him to write it down and be a witness, whether it proved true or not. [This document no longer exists.] At Christmas, the next boat came from Denmark, and my uncle looked with curiosity through the Danish paper, *Politiken,* and to his great content observed the description of the fire. Both day and time were right. About the factory, Jensen was also right. It was a lamp factory in 63, Store Kongensgade [a major street in Copenhagen].

Einar Kvaran (1910, p. 46) gave a more detailed account in a lecture given at the Danish Metapsychic Society in Copenhagen in 1910 and spoke about when Jensen appeared for the first time:

> This person, your countryman whom we have come to like so much, presented himself for the first time as he appeared through the medium in a very distinct and elegant manner. He [Jensen] told us that he had come directly from Copenhagen, and that there was a fire there: a factory was burning. The time was about 9 o'clock when he came. Then he disappeared and came back an hour later.

> Then they [the firemen] had extinguished the fire, he said. We did not have any telegraph at that time, so we had to wait to have this statement verified. But we wrote down his account and kept the document with

the Bishop [who had taken part in earlier séances]. With the next ship [from Copenhagen], the papers brought us the news that there had been a large fire in Copenhagen that evening—in Store Kongensgade, I think it was—where amongst other things a factory had burnt. It also said that at about 12 o'clock the fire had been brought under control. As you know, the time is about 12 o'clock here in Copenhagen when it is 10 o'clock in Reykjavik.

—AUTHORS' TRANSLATION FROM DANISH.

There are some differences between the accounts of Haraldur and Einar. Haraldur mentions that in the half-hour break to allow the medium some rest Jensen told them he had set off for Copenhagen and observed a fire. Einar writes that about 9 o'clock Jensen appeared and said that he came directly from Copenhagen and that there was a fire there in a factory. Then he disappeared and came back an hour later. These differences need not be a contradiction as they may only have had a half-hour break, yet Jensen did not return for an hour. Haraldur writes that he went to the Bishop and asked him to write down a description of the event and be a witness. Einar writes (Kvaran, 1910, p. 46): "we wrote down this account and kept the document with the Bishop." These are minor discrepancies and not of much consequence.

A third witness, Mrs. Gislina Kvaran (1866-1945), Einar's wife, reports that the Bishop of Iceland was chosen to keep a written document about Jensen's statements about the fire until the next ship would arrive from Copenhagen as the Bishop was known to subscribe to *Politiken*, the leading Danish newspaper (Thordarson, 1942, p. 102). It was expected that a fire of any consequence in Copenhagen would be reported in *Politiken*.

We have testimony from these three witnesses, but undoubtedly many more were present. Exactly how many attended on 24 November is nowhere stated, as the minute book containing this sitting is lost. We know that the number of sitters at the séances of the Experimental Society ranged from a small inner circle to up to seventy sitters or more.

To sum up, Jensen not only said that there was a fire that evening in Copenhagen. He also made three specific statements:

1. The fire was in a factory.
2. The fire started around midnight on 24 November 1905.
3. The fire was brought under control within an hour.

Let us now examine how these statements fit the facts as they were reported in the newspapers and by the fire brigade.

Reports in the Newspapers

On the day following the séance, Saturday, 25 November, the two main Danish newspapers reported a major fire in Copenhagen.

The text of *Politiken* follows in an English translation by the senior author:

Factory Fire in St. Kongensgade - Copenhagen's Lamp and Chandelier Factory in Flames

Last night at about 12 o'clock the janitor of number 63 Store Kongensgade discovered that there was fire in "Copenhagen's Lamp and Chandelier Factory," which is located on the ground and first floor of a side-house in the back yard. He called the Fire Brigade and soon fire-extinguishing carriages from Adelsgade Fire Station and the main Fire Station arrived under the direction of Fire Chief Bentzen. The first floor was already ablaze with powerful flames reaching out of the windows and breaking the glass in the windows on the second floor where there is a factory for making cardboard boxes.

The Fire Brigade quickly attached two hoses to fire hydrants. One of the hoses had to go across the street so all tram traffic came to a halt. The water from the two hoses soon subdued the fire but then it was discovered that the fire had gone through the ceiling to the floors above the factory... [There follows a detailed description of the work of the fire brigade.] In about half an hour the fire had been diminished to such an extent that the firemen could remove the hoses across the street to let about a dozen trams pass that had been waiting, after which the hoses were connected again. It became obvious that the fire had caused quite substantial damage. Walls and floors had been burnt out and both stocks and machines of considerable value had been destroyed. There was still fire in some places... Around 1 a.m. some of the firemen and equipment were able to leave but a fairly large number of firemen had to remain at the location for a further hour and a half. The fire is assumed to have started by a breakdown in an electric circuit.

Denmark's second-largest newspaper, *Berlingske Tidende,* gave a shorter report:

> Last night at around twelve o'clock the Fire Brigade was called to Store Kongensgade 63, where fire had broken out in a house in the backyard in the warehouse of the Copenhagen Lamp Factory. The fire had spread considerably when the fire brigades arrived from the Main Fire Station and Adelsgade Station. Still, the firemen managed to get the fire under control in about an hour. The damage was substantial.

Report of the Fire Brigade

In the City Archives of Copenhagen the senior author located Fire Brigade report number 273 about the fire in Store Kongensgade 63. It is handwritten and signed by Fire Chief Bentzen on 25 November 1905. In those days telephones were rare so someone had to run to the next fire alarm, which stood at Dronningens Tvaergade number 31, which is about 320 yards (about five minutes' walk) from Store Kongensgade 63. The fire was thus reported at 11:52.

The fire brigade report is much shorter than the article in *Politiken*, and Bentzen's handwriting is difficult to decipher in some places. It states that the fire was destructive. In the house were three workshops of a lamp factory, two of them for packing with much flammable material. The fire had been fully extinguished at 02:00. After clearing the site the Fire Chief left around 03:00 and the rest of the team at 03:55. At 04:27 they were called again in response to fire alarm 47 because the fire had flared up again. Some firemen and equipment were sent, and by 06:00 they had completed their work. The cause of fire is unknown.

Haraldur Nielsson does not provide the exact time for Jensen's statements about the fire, only that they occurred during a pause for the medium to rest, which would presumably have been late in the séance which took place on Friday evening. The sittings started at eight and lasted up to a few hours. One five-hour sitting is reported. Einar Kvaran writes that it was around nine when Jensen told them about the fire, and then an hour later that the fire had been brought under control. At nine o'clock in Reykjavik the time in Copenhagen would then have been 11:15 p.m., as the time difference between Reykjavik and Copenhagen was two hours and fifteen minutes at that time (Thorsteinn Saemundsson, Editor of the *Almanak Thjodvinafelagsins*, personal communication).

According to the fire brigade they were called at 11:52 p.m. (9:37 Icelandic time). The fire may have been going for a while before it was noticed and it took a few minutes to run to the next fire alarm. Einar Kvaran's statement about the timing when Jensen spoke of the fire must be an estimate, and our records indicate that the fire is likely to have started sometime after 9:00 p.m. Icelandic time. Here, then, we find a reasonably close correlation.

The fire was brought under control in half an hour, according to *Politiken,* and one hour, according to *Berlingske Tidende.* Einar's timing comes quite close as he writes that Jensen came back after one hour and claimed that the fire was under control.

When considering the nature of this case, an important question arises. How frequent were newsworthy fires in Copenhagen at the beginning of the twentieth century? Is it just a fluke of chance that this fire and Jensen's statements took place at the same time? The senior author checked this possibility by examining the frequency of fires reported in *Politiken.* In a four-week sampling period from two weeks before the fire in Store Kongensgade to two weeks afterwards, four fires were reported in *Politiken,* including the fire in Store Kongensgade. According to our sources Jensen reported the fire in the late evening Icelandic time, a little before midnight Danish time. In the four week period examined, only the Store Kongensgade fire started at this time. One fire took place in the late morning and two started in the early evening, at 6:45 p.m. and 7:16 p.m. Danish time.

In the four-week period, only one fire took place in a factory, namely the Store Kongensgade fire. The factory fire gets more coverage in *Politiken* than any other fire during these four weeks; it was the largest fire, and caused the most damage, while the other fires were minor and quickly extinguished.

We can conclude that Jensen not only accurately reported that a fire took place in Copenhagen on 24 November 1905, but also that it started late in the evening Icelandic time. He correctly states that the fire was under control in about an hour. He correctly identifies the fire as in a factory. These are the four features of the fire that Jensen mentions.

CHAPTER 6

ANY NORMAL EXPLANATION?

Could there be a normal explanation for the fact that Jensen - or for that matter Indridi Indridason - described in real time a fire that was taking place some 1,300 miles away? Telephones did not come to Reykjavik until almost a year later, and telegraphy service not until 1918.[1]

The only conceivable explanation that the authors have been able to come up with is that Indridi had a confederate in Copenhagen who set the fire in the factory at a predetermined date and time. He and Indridi would have had to agree upon this several weeks earlier, for communication with Iceland in the winter was limited to about one ship sailing to Copenhagen per month. Furthermore, the confederate would have to see to it that the fire was extinguished within an hour. Both of them risked that it might turn into a major conflagration, possibly with casualties, for the location was densely populated. If they

---

[1] In 1905 there was much discussion in Iceland about whether the country should have a telephone cable connecting it with other countries, or radio communication. The government chose the cable. The Marconi Company set up a station in Reykjavik in the summer of 1905 that was only able to receive telegrams from the powerful Poldhu station in Cornwall that transmitted messages to America. This receiving station distributed some major world news to the newspapers in Reykjavik until it was closed in 1906.

had been caught, he and Indridi would have risked years in prison. It seems reasonable therefore to reject this explanation, besides which there is not a trace of evidence to support it. Furthermore, Politiken writes that the fire was caused by electric failure; the fire brigade lists the cause as unknown. If there had been suspicion of arson, it would have been reported to the police for investigation. Search in police records for this period reveal no such charge.

Are there any other normal possibilities? What about a carrier-pigeon? The problem is the long distance. It takes a commercial jet airplane about three hours to reach Iceland from Copenhagen, usually against a westerly wind. 1,300 miles is beyond the flying capacity of a pigeon and most of the journey is over open sea. Also, there is no indication that Indridi kept pigeons. He kept a horse.

Remote Viewing, Travelling Clairvoyance or Spirit Communication?

Is this a case of clairvoyance by the medium, an out-of-the-body experience with perception of a fire in distant Copenhagen (travelling clairvoyance), or a case of telepathy? As far as is known, Indridi knew no person in Copenhagen who might have felt the need to think of him at the time of the fire.

Was this a case of spirit communication? Let us assume for a moment that Jensen existed as a discarnate entity communicating through Indridi. Then we can ask why should Indridi go to a place to which he had no relationship, where he knew no one and had never visited? Let us compare this with reasons Jensen might have had to observe the fire. He may have felt compelled, during a pause from mediumistic work with Indridi, to return to Copenhagen to observe an event that must have been important to him, and to many people he knew, as it took place in the street where he had lived most of his life. Jensen would have had a much stronger motivation than Indridi to follow and report on the development of this fire.

The Role of Jensen in the Mediumship of Indridi Indridason

Jensen soon became an important figure in the mediumship of Indridi and later attempted to materialize, that is, to make himself visible.

At many sittings Jensen was seen by sitters appearing in a "luminous, beautiful light-pillar," usually very briefly but several times during the same séance and at various locations in the hall. This "pillar of light" would first appear in the darkness, and after that Jensen would appear in it. The "pillar of light" was larger than Jensen and emitted light in such a way that Jensen and Indridi could sometimes be seen side by side at the same time. At the same time, both of Indridi's hands were being held by a witness to exclude the possibility of fraud. It is reported that, at times, when Jensen was not visible, his hands could be touched, or sitters felt him touch various parts of their bodies.

Brynjolfur Thorlaksson describes that once, when he was playing the harmonium, his hands were carefully touched, so softly, that he was able to continue playing. At the same time he heard whispered into his ear in Danish (Thordarson, 1942, pp. 102-103):

> "Continue. Don't be afraid. It is me Jensen." My hands were held for a while. At the same time I heard that Haraldur Nielsson was talking to the control through the medium, and I also heard at the same time that a voice was speaking through the trumpet that was kept in the room. On this occasion we were in the small experimental room.
>
> —AUTHORS' TRANSLATION FROM ICELANDIC.

Brynjolfur states that the sitters often felt that Jensen touched them when he had materialized. At another sitting at the home of Einar Kvaran, Brynjolfur suddenly felt something coming into his arms (*ibid.*, pp. 100-102):

> Indridi was in trance. Then I suddenly felt something come into my arms. I spontaneously grasped it with my hands. I felt that it was a foot of a man. It was dark in the room so I could not see the foot with my eyes. But I touched it again and again all the way up to the knee. Higher up I did not feel appropriate to go. I felt that on the leg were stiff hairs like on corpses. After a while the foot moved slowly higher and higher. I followed it up as far as I could stretch without rising from my seat, but then rose and held it as high up as I could. It then moved out of my hands. The foot was neither warm nor cold to touch. This was Jensen's foot we were told by Jensen himself or the control.
>
> —AUTHORS' TRANSLATION FROM ICELANDIC.

The light appearances seemed to be particularly painful to the medium and, while in trance, he could be heard moaning and screaming with pain. That topic will be discussed in more detail later.

CHAPTER 7

SWEDENBORG AND THE FIRE IN STOCKHOLM

Jensen's description of the fire in Copenhagen through Indridi's mediumship is remarkably similar to the vision of Emanuel Swedenborg (1688-1772) of the great fire in Stockholm in 1759, but there are also important differences. The Swedish scientist and seer is reported to have described a fire that raged in Stockholm during his visit to Gothenburg (Broad, 1950, 1969; Haraldsson & Gerding, 2010). The case became so well known that the German philosopher Immanuel Kant (1724-1804) asked an English friend, whom he held in high esteem, to investigate this case along with three other cases. His friend, who is not identified by name, was a merchant who sometimes visited Gothenburg and Stockholm. His report to Kant is lost but Kant describes this famous case in a letter, dated 10 August 1763, to a friend who asked him about the case, Miss Charlotte von Knobloch. The relevant passage reads as follows:

> The following occurrence appears to me to have the greatest weight of proof, and to place the assertion respecting Swedenborg's extraordinary gift beyond all possibility of doubt. In the year 1759, towards the end of September, on Saturday at four o'clock p.m. Swedenborg arrived at Gothenburg from England when Mr. William Castel invited him to

his house, together with a party of fifteen persons. About six o'clock, Swedenborg went out [not stated if out of the house or only out of the room], and returned to the company quite pale and alarmed. He said that a dangerous fire had just broken out in Stockholm, at the Sodermalm, and that it was spreading fast. He was restless and went out often. He said that the house of one of his friends, whom he named, was already in ashes, and that his own was in danger. At eight o'clock, after he had been out again, he joyfully exclaimed, "Thank God! The fire is extinguished three doors from my house." The news occasioned great commotion throughout the whole city, but particularly amongst the company in which he was. It was announced to the Governor the same evening. On Sunday morning, Swedenborg was summoned to the Governor, who questioned him concerning the disaster. Swedenborg described the fire precisely, how it had begun, and in what manner it had ceased, and how long it had continued. On the same day the news spread throughout the city, and as the Governor had thought it worthy of attention, the consternation was considerably increased, because many were in trouble on account of their friends and property, which might have been involved in the disaster.

On Monday evening, a messenger arrived in Gothenburg who was sent by the Board of Trade at the time of the fire. In the letter brought by him, the fire was described precisely in the manner stated by Swedenborg. On Tuesday morning the royal courier arrived at the Governor's with the sad news of the fire, the loss which it had occasioned, and houses it had damaged or ruined, not in the least differing from that which Swedenborg had given at the time when it happened, for the fire was extinguished at eight o'clock.

—ENGLISH TRANSLATION FROM TROBRIDGE, 2004, PP. 228-229.

News arriving in Gothenburg with a messenger from Stockholm verified Swedenborg's description in the same way as the Jensen (Indridi) account was confirmed when the next ship brought a *Politiken* to Reykjavik. In both instances, normal communication of any kind was not possible. The fire in Sodermalm in Stockholm was described in the newspaper *Stockholms Posttidningar* on 23 July 1759, and in the Gothenburg newspaper *Hvad Nytt i Staden* on 30 July. This was the largest fire in Stockholm for many years, and destroyed some 250 houses. It was far more destructive than the fire in Copenhagen.

The fire started about half a mile away from Swedenborg's home, and was extinguished less than 300 feet from his house, which stood where Hornsgatan 41-43 is now. This distance is known because Maria Church, which is very close by, was destroyed. Where it used to stand is now a public park.

The date given for the fire in Kant's letter differs about a month from the actual date as reported in the newspapers. The Cambridge philosopher and former President of the Society for Psychical Research (SPR), Charlie Dunbar Broad (1887-1971), wrote an excellent paper on the case, its strength and weaknesses, which was published as a *Proceedings of the SPR* in 1950 (1950, 1969). Another former SPR President, John Poynton (2004, pp. 262-268), has written an interesting essay review of a book about Kant and psychical research.

The senior author made an attempt to improve upon Broad's findings by searching in archives and libraries in Gothenburg (with the help of psychologist/parapsychologist Adrian Parker) and Stockholm and by meeting with Swedish experts on Swedenborg, such as Inge Jonsson, former Rector of Stockholm University, and Rev. Olle Hjern of the Swedenborg Church in Sweden. No new documents were located, and none have been found for a long time.

There are some obvious similarities between the cases of Jensen (Indridi) and Swedenborg. Both men tell of two or more observations of the fire with some time in between. In their last observation, both report that the fire has been brought under control. In both instances many observers were present, fifteen with Swedenborg and presumably many sitters with Indridi, with their exact number not given. In both cases, those present were so impressed that they selected two highly placed individuals to bear witness in the event that the vision of a distant fire should prove true. The witnesses were the Bishop of Iceland and the Governor of Gothenburg. Both groups had to await the arrival of news from afar: the group in Reykjavik, from Copenhagen, over 1,300 miles away; and the group in Gothenburg, from Stockholm, which is 245 miles distant.

In both cases, the location of the fires must have been of utmost importance to the percipients (assuming that the discarnate Jensen was one of them). In Swedenborg's case the fire threatened his home and property. In Jensen's case the fire took place very close to houses where he had lived during his lifetime, in fact all his life, and where he must have had many close friends.

The two cases also differ in important ways. Indridi was in trance and one of his communicators described the fire. Swedenborg was apparently in his normal state of consciousness. We should, however, take notice that Swedenborg wanted to be alone and undisturbed as he went outside to receive his impressions of the fire. Perhaps he had to enter an altered state of consciousness when he may have presumably communicated with discarnate spirits, in which case, we come close to the situation of Indridi.

Alternatively, could this be a case of telepathy by Swedenborg? We do not know if anyone was living in Swedenborg's house while he was away. Like Jensen, Swedenborg never married, so possibly there was no one in the house who might become aware of the approaching fire and with whom Swedenborg might have communicated telepathically. Obviously he had neighbours, but they were probably more concerned with their own property than his. This makes the telepathy interpretation unlikely, but there is no way to decide what kind of perception this might have been, such as clairvoyance or telepathy, if it was Swedenborg's own perception. What we know for certain is that later in life Swedenborg had a reputation for claiming to communicate with spirits of the deceased.

As a result of his prolific writings, which were translated into English and many other languages, Swedenborg is often considered an important forerunner of the modern Spiritualist movement. He had considerable influence, particularly in the United States and in Great Britain, where churches were founded in his name that still exist. In the United States his writings became well known and to this day are still in print. He influenced such persons as American philosopher and psychologist William James (1842-1910), whose father was a Swedenborgian.

CHAPTER 8

THE SEARCH FOR EMIL JENSEN

Who was the mysterious Jensen? Was he a figment of the imagination in the mind of Indridi Indridason, or had he been a real living person? The only information given in the account of Haraldur Nielsson (1922a) is that Jensen was a manufacturer (in Danish: "fabrikant"). Einar Kvaran (1910) describes him as a clothing manufacturer ("klaedefabrikant") and a native of Copenhagen which, he writes, was easily judged from his "genuine Copenhagen accent." That is all we know from those who wrote about Indridi and his phenomena. About Jensen, Einar (Kvaran, 1934) wrote that we never came "to know anything about who he was when he was living." After Jensen's first appearance on 24 November 1905 he appeared frequently associated with the light phenomena and attempts to produce materializations. However, not a word is found about his personal history or identity.

Unexpectedly the newly-discovered minute books revealed interesting details about Jensen. The minutes start with a sitting on 4 December 1905, ten days after the sitting in which the fire in Copenhagen was described. According to the minutes, Jensen appears again at a sitting on 11 December 1905. Then he makes several highly specific statements about his life. Apparently in response to being asked, Jensen says that his Christian name is Emil, and he gives other details regarding his personal life. The exact Danish text reads as follows:

Det (mit Döbsnavn) er Emil. Mit Navn: Emil Jensen, ja! Jeg har ikke Börn. Ja, (jeg var Ungkarl). Nej, (jeg var ikke saa ung naar jeg (döde). Jeg har söskende, men ikke her i Himlen.

In the senior author's translation:

It (my Christian name) is Emil. My name: Emil Jensen, yes! I have no children. Yes (I was a bachelor). No (I was not so young when I died). I have siblings, but not here in heaven.

After these statements the medium greets someone and speaks of eating beans (Icelanders sometimes jokingly refer to Danes as bean-eaters). Then he moans and screams in pain and says, "do not do it, do not do it." The minutes continue, "very bright lights on and off, a man appears in one of them." This is not described further. Einar and Haraldur mention that the light phenomena caused much pain to the medium.

Apparently no attempt was ever made to verify if any person had lived in Copenhagen who fitted the description that was given on that occasion. We can only speculate about the reasons for this. Copenhagen is far away from Reykjavik and required a major sea voyage to reach. Also, Copenhagen was at this time a major city and it might not have seemed feasible to trace someone who might have lived an indeterminable time ago and carried a very common name. Were these few sentences in the minute book quickly forgotten and never looked up again? Or, were the sitters already at this time so convinced through prior experience that everything that came from Indridi was so grounded in reality that it needed no verification?

After more than a century the question remained unanswered; had there lived in Copenhagen any Emil Jensen who was a manufacturer? Or, had there perhaps been several of them? Was there any connection between such a person or persons, if they had existed, and the location of the fire that was described when the communicator Jensen first appeared on 24 November 1905?

In June 2009, the senior author was able to spend a day in Copenhagen. At the Royal Library there exists the *Kobenhavns Vejviser* [Copenhagen Business Directory], which was published annually in the nineteenth century. It lists professionals and business people in alphabetical order according to family name, profession, Christian name and address. The author looked up the volume for 1890.

Jensen is one of the most common surnames in Denmark. Hundreds of Jensens were listed, including several manufacturers of that name, but only one manufacturer had the Christian name Emil. And his address? Store Kongensgade 67, which is two doors away from number 63 where the fire broke out. This seemed to be more than a mere coincidence. It verified that a manufacturer by the name of Emil Jensen (ca. 1848-1898) had in fact lived in Copenhagen, and, even more remarkably, had lived in Store Kongensgade 67, close to the house where the fire started.

Later that year the author searched census documents in the *Landsarkiv* in Copenhagen. In 1885 Thomas Emil Jensen, single, 37 years old, born in Copenhagen, is listed as manufacturer and coffee merchant. At that time he was living with four single sisters at Store Kongensgade 68, again close to number 63 where the fire broke out. He was head of the household. Five years earlier he had lived at Store Kongensgade 40 where his father ran a business, F. Jensen & Son, selling spices (Danish: "urtekraemmer") for some thirty years. In 1880, Emil Jensen had been living with three unmarried sisters and Edvard Julius Jensen, which inquiries revealed to be his brother.

The census record of 1860 showed that his parents lived at that time at St. Kongensgade 40 with seven children, four daughters and three sons, Lorenz Ferdinand, Thomas Emil and Edvard Julius. Emil Jensen is last registered in 1898 at Fredriciagade 16, which crosses Store Kongensgade and is only some 300 yards away from the house where the fire broke out. The records show that from the age of eight until his death in 1898 Emil Jensen had lived at Store Kongensgade or in streets crossing Store Kongensgade.

His certificate of burial obtained from the City Archives states that he died on 3 August 1898, single, aged 50, had been born in Copenhagen, and was a manufacturer by profession. He was buried by his brother, Rev. Lorenz Ferdinand Jensen, at Assistens Kirkegaard (churchyard) in Copenhagen.

Documents in the Assistens Kirkegaard office show that Emil Jensen had been buried in a family grave. His four sisters were buried there after him; Louise Emilie in 1908, Anna Sofie and Lovisa in 1935, and Julie Caroline in 1936.

What about his brother Edvard Julius Jensen? He was four years younger than Emil. In 1885 he had married and moved to Havnegade

43, and was registered as a coffee merchant and chocolate manufacturer. He died in 1923 and thus survived his brother Emil. His older brother Lorenz Ferdinand became a clergyman who served for many years at the Trinitatis Church in the center of Copenhagen. He died in 1925. A document of the probate court ("skifteret"), written when Emil Jensen's estate was divided, lists his brothers and sisters, states that he had no children and shows that his siblings were all alive when he died.

The identification of Emil Jensen proved to be 100 percent accurate, as was the description of the fire in Copenhagen that was detailed earlier. The only item that is not perfectly verified is that Einar (Kvaran, 1910) and Haraldur (Nielsen, 1922a) state that Jensen was a manufacturer of clothes. Danish documents register him as a manufacturer and coffee merchant. Nowhere is it specified what he manufactured. He seems to have been well off, for he left a considerable estate to his siblings.

Do we know anything more about Jensen? Military records ("Laegdsrulle" in the Landsarkiv in Copenhagen) show that for health reasons he was deemed unfit for military service. The military records give his height at 66 inches and chest at 29 inches, which shows that he had been a very thin man. He died of liver cancer, according to his certificate of burial.

Einar Kvaran (1910, p. 46) writes that they were told that "Jensen would be the leader in the attempts to produce materialization phenomena because he had obtained knowledge of such experiments from other places." It is not explained if this refers to some knowledge from the time Jensen was living or post-mortem experiences through other mediums. We do not know about the interests and cultural background of Jensen's family apart from them being merchants and manufacturers. For example, did the family have an interest in Spiritualism that came to Denmark in the 1880s (Kragh, 2008).

The search for relatives came quickly to a dead end; Emil Jensen and his sisters had no children. His brothers married. The clergyman, Lorenz Ferdinand, had no children, while Edvard Julius had one son who became a prominent lawyer and married but had no child. The fact that one of the brothers became a clergyman shows that someone in the family had spiritual interests, although this does not imply that he had any interest in Spiritualism. Jesper Vaczy Kragh who wrote a paper on the history of the Spiritualist movement in the Nordic countries did not recall that he came across the name of Emil Jensen when researching the early history of Spiritualism in Denmark.

CHAPTER 9

DISAPPEARANCE OF INDRIDI'S ARM

Perhaps the most mysterious phenomenon observed with Indridi Indridason began on 18 December 1905 when the sitters heard some cracking sounds in his arm while he was in a trance state. At Einar Kvaran's home the next day, Indridi, whilst awake, wrote automatically about the serious concern the controls had about the experimental séance that was to be held the following evening. The controls stressed in the automatic writing that the sitters would have to be very calm and quiet otherwise the medium's life could be in danger. An "operation" would be carried out on him but he was not to have any knowledge about that beforehand so he would not be worried. At the séance on the evening of 19 December, Indridi's left arm became invisible. The left sleeve of his jacket became empty. Einar was invited by the control to feel carefully with his hands. Indridi's arm had become intangible (Kvaran, 1906, pp. 27-32; 1910, p. 45).

Then Einar describes what happened at the séance the following evening (20 December). After the usual séance opening, a song from the sitters and a prayer from the control, the control went away for a while. Here is Einar Kvaran's description, based on notes taken during the séance, beginning with the medium's greeting (1906, pp. 29-30):

"Hi! I'm glad to see you come. But what are you going to do with all those knives? — No, no, no!" (Goes into the cabinet). "No, no, this is not allowed."

The control's voice: "You be careful!"

Now for a while one could hear cries of pain from the medium coming from the cabinet. Then he comes out of the cabinet and says, as if very unhappy:

"When are you coming back with it?"

Then the medium came to me (I sat at the back of the hall), handed me the empty left sleeve of his jacket and said with the control's voice: "Take hold here, carefully! You can touch with caution." I touched, but could not find the left arm.

The control: "Take the jacket and be careful! Take it from the right side! [Probably, start by taking the jacket off the right shoulder.] I will take him outside; the air is more refreshing there. [Probably, take Indridi out of the séance room.] I am afraid that, if it becomes too hot, he will bleed."

The medium then went out into an empty room at the front of the hall and stayed there for a while. Then he came back in and went into the cabinet.

Then I was called up by the control's voice: "Would you see if his nose is bleeding?" I asked if I could then light a match. "Yes, but you may not have the light on for a very long time."

I lit a match and saw that it was not bleeding. The medium was lying on his right side on a mattress inside the cabinet. I checked again to see if I could find the arm. But the result was the same.

The medium: "Ah, where are you going with it? Where is it?"

The control: "Check now carefully whether you can see any phenomenon in front of you; perhaps someone will be able to see something waved; my relative's arm [the control had claimed to be the brother of Indridi´s grandfather], for example."

48

We searched carefully around us in the hall, but didn't see anything. However, two sitters felt a cold, soft hand touch their faces.

I was again invited to search the shoulder, and I did it as thoroughly as I could, but did not find the arm.

The control: "In time, you will see this in full light . . ."

—AUTHORS' TRANSLATION FROM ICELANDIC.

The next evening this same phenomenon occurred again, and also one evening later during the same winter, much to the surprise of the sitters. When the phenomenon occurred on the evening of 20 December, five men searched many times for the missing arm by feeling Indridi's upper body all over. They did this repeatedly, and matches were lit many times during the search, but no one found the arm (Kvaran, 1906, p. 31). Three sitters out in the hall felt a hand touch their faces at the same time as Indridi was lying in the cabinet. Haraldur Nielsson (1919b, p. 344) was one of the five who searched Indridi that evening. The arm had disappeared entirely, he reports, and it was not found even though a light was lit and Indridi's body was carefully searched (Nielsson, 1922a, p. 19).

Haraldur states that seven persons observed the phenomenon the third evening that Indridi's left arm disappeared (*ibid.*, 1922a, p. 19). They shone light all around Indridi while the empty sleeve hung down. They were permitted (probably by the controls) to touch and feel him all round the shoulder. They were not allowed to undress the shoulder and see it bare in the light.

A description of this phenomenon is recorded in the first minute book for 18 and 19 December. On 20 December we read the most detailed description:

> ... E.H. (Einar Hjorleifsson Kvaran) steers his hand up to Indridi's shoulder and finds the arm missing. – Haraldur Nielsson. Come. Carefully. Feel here. Higher up. There it is. (H.N. hand is steered; feels that the arm is missing. Bjorn Jonsson – Carefully. So. Here it is. Yes. (You may light the light). But for heaven's sake be careful. A little higher; he feels that the arm of the medium is missing, and that is also seen when the light is lit. – See if he is bleeding! (Not bleeding). Your wife, my friend [to Einar Kvaran]. I control her [hand]. You may light

the light. (She feels the same; that the arm is missing). Now all of you take a seat and pay attention to determine whether you see something. There is one medical doctor here, let him come. Same conditions. The light can be lit. (Steers his hand – Hinrik Erlendsson)[1] and then he (H.E.) senses by touching that the arm is missing, and it can be seen [when light is lit].

Are you quite sure? How many are you? (Five had felt that the arm was missing). Now you should all sit down and examine. (Sk.Th. (identified only as a young man), B.J. (Bjorn Jonsson) and Mrs. G.H. (Gislina Kvaran, Einar's wife) feel that a cold hand touches their faces.)

—AUTHORS' TRANSLATION FROM ICELANDIC.

The description in the minute book is somewhat like a telegram. Einar says that he observed the arm's disappearance a second time, and became more convinced: Indridi stood on the floor and Einar felt from Indridi's "shoulder down along his side and back and the same on his front" (Kvaran, 1906, p. 32). He also felt "all around him and high and low over the torso." He thought that with such careful checking he would have noticed the arm if it had been there. All the seven witnesses signed a document at the end of this séance, stating that they had not been able to feel or find Indridi's arm and were prepared to certify this under oath.

Einar Kvaran reports (*ibid.*, p. 32):

This phenomenon occurred once much later, one winter evening quite unexpectedly. Then it was again inspected by seven men, and several times with a light lit. I was one of those and can report about it myself, that I then got greater certainty than before. The medium stood on the floor. I stroke with my hand from the shoulder downwards, at the side and at the back, and also in front [down his chest]. I also touched and felt with my hand around his body, and low around his chest and back. It would be outright ridiculous to think that I would not have felt the arm with such a thorough touching if the arm had been there in its usual state, except if I had at that time been influenced by some hypnotic means that caused some sensory misperception. Then all

---

[1] Hinrik Erlendsson (1879-1930) was a medical student at this time and received his medical license in 1912.

the other six would have been influenced in the same way. We all signed at the end of the meeting a declaration that we had not been able to feel or sense the arm in any way, and that all of us were ready to affirm this under oath.

I am not sure which would be more mysterious, that we all underwent the same gross misperception at that time, or that the arm had in fact become unperceivable.

—AUTHORS' TRANSLATION FROM ICELANDIC.

Brynjolfur Thorlaksson writes that he was one of the seven who searched for Indridi's left arm and signed the document that they were willing to confirm under oath (Thordarson, 1942, pp. 14-23). He further states "This event drew much attention and caused considerable discussion at the time and was considered one of the most mysterious phenomena that occurred at the meetings with Indridi."

Haraldur Nielsson (1919a, p. 75) reports that he was one of those seven who searched Indridi while he stood in full light without his left arm being visible to any of the people present. Half an hour later, the arm reappeared on Indridi. Haraldur helped Indridi to get his clothing on afterwards, "as the controls had pushed his shirt, waistcoat and jacket up above the shoulder on the left side [probably while "replacing" it], the arm hanging down bare" (Nielsson, 1919 b, p. 344).

Indridi's main control personality, Konrad Gislason, said that the levitations, light phenomena, physical exercises and dematerialization experiments were preparations for the materialization of human forms (Kvaran, 1906, p. 38; Nielsson, 1919a, p. 19; and 1922b, pp. 455-456).

From the text, it is not clear how far Indridi was undressed while the sitters were searching for his left arm. We are not informed whether it was his jacket sleeve or only his shirt sleeve that hung down empty. It would have been easier to feel and try to find the arm if Indridi had only been wearing his shirt, but with or without a jacket, it should have been easily felt and ascertained.

Reports of dematerializations of a medium's body are extremely rare in the literature of physical mediumship. Alexander Aksakof (1832-1903), the well-known Russian psychical researcher, reports (1894) extensively on the case of the dematerialization of the lower part of the body of the medium Madame Elizabeth d'Espérance (1855-1919), that occurred in December 1893 in Helsinki, Finland (for further discussion, see Carrington, 1906-1907, and Hyslop, 1907). Reportedly the light was sufficient for the eleven persons who were present to see, and five persons verified by passage of hands that Madame d'Espérance's body from the waist downward had disappeared. Recently some new documents have been found in the archives in Gothenburg where Madame d'Espérance lived for some time (Adrian Parker, personal communication). A few more cases of this kind can be found in Fodor (1966, pp. 115-116). This is an extremely infrequently reported phenomenon in the history of Spiritualism.

CHAPTER 10

HEALING, OLFACTORY (ODOR) PHENOMENA AND SURGICAL-LIKE OPERATIONS

In February 1906, Indridi Indridason suddenly became seriously ill (Kvaran, 1910, p. 46). Our sources do not tell us what the problem was. It was decided to stop the materialization experiments. The Society turned to healing experiments (Kvaran, 1906, pp. 40-41). These experiments commenced with attempts to heal Indridi. The controls were then asked if other people could be healed. The answer was negative unless the person could fall into trance. A little later the controls offered to do healing attempts on people in a waking state. The controls stressed that these were only an attempt as they lacked experience and did not know if they would succeed. According to Einar Kvaran, the condition of some patients improved, others not and the results were variable.

Indridi disliked the healing experiments and participated reluctantly. He had no belief in himself as a psychic healer and thought that this would be turned against him (*ibid.*, p. 41). In association with the healing attempts, some strange phenomena took place. One of them was light taps, such as a doctor might make during his examination. They were sometimes heard on Indridi's chest. Those present held both his hands, but the taps or thumps continued. Similar thumps on his chest were heard while he lay in a trance very ill in his bed.

It also happened that the control personality, called "the Norwegian doctor," would, so the sitters thought, let clear knocks be heard in the bedrooms of those sitters he claimed to visit at night. This personality later revealed at séances what had happened, though these incidents were reportedly known neither to the medium, nor to other sitters beyond the people who had been "visited" (*ibid.*, p. 37).

In February 1906, with Indridi very sick in bed, a strong, fragrant odor was experienced coming from his head. Einar writes that Indridi could "not possibly" have had with him any substances that could have emitted this fragrant smell (Kvaran, 1906, pp. 40-42). The odor from Indridi's hands and arms was sometimes so strong that it spread over the whole experimental hall and, when he touched the sitters' faces, the odor would linger there for a good while. Indridi was carefully searched many times before the séances when the fragrance came forth, to rule out the possibility that he had brought some chemical perfume with him, but nothing was ever found. Each and every sitter experienced the odor, sometimes twenty to thirty sitters at the same time. Because of its fragrant nature this olfactory phenomena resembles the "odor sancti" - the odor of sanctity - reported around some Catholic and Indian saints, among them Sathya Sai Baba (1926-2011) (Thurston, 1952; Haraldsson, 2013)

Many other phenomena occurred during healing experiments with Indridi. For instance, in February 1906 (Kvaran, 1906, p. 42), Indridi was in a trance state and was massaging the back of one of his patients when Kvaran and other members saw some material or substance covering most of the patient's back (we are not told how the sitters were able to see the substance). It looked like "dried dew; in some places it was whitish grey but in other places it had a greenish gloss" (ibid., p. 42). Einar Kvaran asserts firmly that Indridi "did not have any chemical like that on him and would not have had any idea as to how to obtain it."

Our sources describe in detail one healing operation during this period and we shall review it briefly (*Fjallkonan*, 1906, p. 38). Indridi probably always "operated" in darkness. Before the operations he first went into a trance, within one or two minutes. The following operation took place at the beginning of March 1906. Present, besides Indridi and the patient, were Bjorn Jonsson, Ragnheidur Bjarnadottir and Ingibjorg S.

Palmadottir. The patient, Jon Jonsson, had been medically diagnosed as having stomach cancer (*ibid.*, p. 38). In the middle of the "operation" the sitters were allowed by the controls to turn on a light and bring it to the patient. They thought they saw a hole in his abdomen, nearly as large as a fingertip, and out of the opening flowed brownish pus. Indridi removed some brownish blobs from the wound and threw them into the stove. A little later a light was turned on again. The wound still seemed open, but it was smaller than before. A few minutes later the light was again turned on, but no trace of any opening or cut could be seen on the patient's abdomen. This operation was done without any equipment or tools, and many symptoms of the illness were reported to disappear. The healing attempts on Jon Jonsson took about three or four weeks. During that time no medically trained doctor attended him, since he was expected to die "imminently" (*Isafold*, 1906, p. 63). The patient Jon Jonsson died on 16 March 1906. It was disputed in the local newspapers whether his death was caused by the cancer or by the pneumonia he caught shortly before his death.

In his 1906 article, Einar Kvaran states that the personalities of Konrad Gislason and the Norwegian doctor were as different as any two unrelated living persons tend to be. Their voices and way of speaking sounded completely different as well as the language they spoke (Norwegian and Icelandic). The Norwegian was gentle and cordial with a good sense of humor. Though they sometimes expressed differing views, they spoke respectfully about each other. This occurred to such an extent that the Norwegian said on at least one occasion that he would take no responsibility for what Konrad was doing and would not be present or the planned task would be too difficult for the medium. It seems that the doctor was right. Konrad´s eagerness to produce phenomena was sometimes greater than Indridi´s strength and health permitted.

Once when a patient was being treated, Konrad called "the Norwegian" inadvertently by his name. This was heard by a patient who heard the doctor´s name "Danielssen" called from the empty cabinet when the medium was out in the hall. Later the Norwegian told some sitters about some events in his life and they were found to be correct. Daniel Cornelius Danielssen (1815-1894) had been a prominent physician and a scientist in Norway.

Indridi claimed to have often seen in a waking state his controls and other deceased persons that appeared at the séances. Leading members of the Experimental Society were able to trace one photograph of Danielssen. It was placed so that Indridi would discover it but without telling him why it was there. When he saw it, he spontaneously re-marked, "Here is a photo of the Norwegian doctor."

One gets the impression when reading the various papers by Einar Kvaran and Haraldur Nielsson that the initiative for producing the var-ious phenomena originated to a greater extent from Indridi's controls, primarily Konrad Gislason, than from the leading sitters. Einar reports that Konrad, for example, actively brought in communicators (deceased persons) who he believed could produce good proof of identity. Proof of identity is covered in greater detail in a later chapter.

Einar reports that the communicators were many and all had their personal characteristics: "Some seemed to be in close cooperation with K.G., others appeared to seek prayer for themselves, others to greet us briefly, and some K.G. brought in to bring us proof of their memory of events in their earthly life. The voices of some we immediately rec-ognized, among them people that the medium had never met in his life. The medium also, whilst in trance, correctly described deceased persons, that he told us were present, and we know for certain that he had never met" (Kvaran, 1906, p. 38).

Many sittings with Indridi took place in this house where Einar Kvaran
lived for some time.

The First International Congress for Psychical Research in Copenhagen, 1921, where Haraldur Nielsson presented a paper on Indridi´s mediumship. He is recognizable by his beard in the middle of the second row. This photograph provided courtesy of the IGPP Archives in Freiburg, Germany; it is from the archives of Albert von Schrenck-Notzing (1862-1929) who annotated the names of some conference participants.

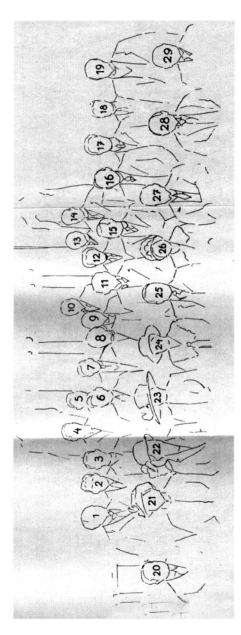

Numbered sketch of participants at the First International Congress for Psychical Research in Copenhagen, 1921.

1) Le Chevalier Clément de St.-Marcq, Brussels, 2) Dr. H.J.F.W. Brugmans, Groningen, 3) Rev. Charles Drayton Thomas, London, 4) Mr. Mélusson, Lyon, 5) Mr. Maurice Schaerer, Brussels, 6) Dr. Hereward Carrington, New York, 7) Prof. Viktor Mikuska, Prague, 8) Prof. Haraldur Nielsson, Reykjavik, 9) Dr. Sydney Alrutz, Uppsala, 10) Dr. Thorstein Wereide, Oslo (in 1921, Kristiania) 11) Prof. Oscar Jaeger, Oslo, 12) Mr. René Sudre, Paris, 13) Director Carl Vett, Copenhagen, 14) Rector Uno Stadius, Helsingsfors, 15) Dr. Mackenzie, New York, 16) Mr. Jules Magnin, Geneva, 17) Dr. Niels Christian Borberg, Copenhagen, 18) Mr. William Henry Salter, London, 19) Department Head Selboe, Oslo, 20) Dr. Zeehandelaar, Amsterdam, 21) Mrs. Mikuska, Prague, 22) Mrs. Helen de G. (Verrall) Salter, London, 23) Mrs. Juliette Bisson, Paris, 24) Miss Simmonds, London, 25) Dr. Walter Franklin Prince, New York, 26) Miss Felicia R. Scatchherd, London, 27) Dr. Albert von Schrenck-Notzing, Munich, 28) Engineer Fritz Grunewald, Berlin, 29) Dr. Gustav Geley, Paris.

Prof. Haraldur Nielsson lived on the second floor of this house where many sittings with Indridi took place. With furniture banging on the floor, the sessions became so loud that other tenants complained and they had to move the sittings elsewhere.

Store Kongensgade (Great Kingstreet), from the left, number 63 where the fire broke out, 65 (red house), and 67 where Emil Jensen had lived on the second floor.

We were unable to locate a photograph of Emil Jensen (ca. 1848-1898) but found one of his older brother Lorenz Ferdinand Jensen (18??-1925) who was a clergyman at the Trinitatis Church in the center of Copenhagen.

Stereoscopic photograph of the experimental room showing the net that isolated Indridi from the sitters. It was one of the precautions taken by Prof. Gudmundur Hannesson to prevent the possibility of fraud. A table and other furniture have been tipped over by the psychic force.

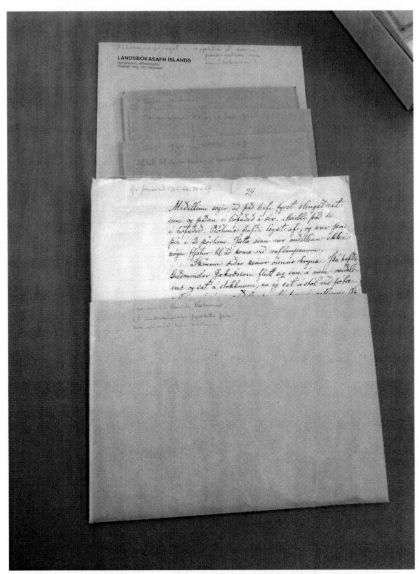

Handwritten notes accompanying the minute books.

Indridi Indridason photographed with the broomstick on 6 December 1907, when he appears to have resorted to fraud, whether conscious or unconsious.

Indridi Indridason (1883-1912). His mediumship started in 1904 and came to an untimely end in 1909 because of illness.

Indridi Indridason (sitting) with a relative.

Map of Copenhagen showing Store Kongensgade where Emil Jensen lived and where he and his father had a store. "A" shows number 63 where the fire broke out, and "1" shows the house where Emil Jensen died in 1898.

CHAPTER 11

PROOF OF IDENTITY

During the winter of 1905-1906, Indridi´s main control, Konrad Gislason, stated that the purpose of the sittings was to enable the sitters to see and speak to him and other communicators. The more impressive phenomena, he said, like the levitations, the lights and the disappearance of the arm, were preparations to make this possible. In February 1906 the medium became sick, and the controls stated that he was in danger of losing his mediumistic ability. For some time after this no light phenomena could be shown in spite of many attempts. All attempts to produce materializations and other physical phenomena were put on hold until the medium had regained his health.

Instead emphasis was on bringing in spirit communicators who would speak of their memories so that their accuracy could be checked by people who knew them best. Such "proofs of identity" have played an important role in research about mediumship and survival. The argument is that if people survive death they should retain their memories, personality and individual characteristics. Einar Kvaran writes about these séances for proof of identity: "Evening after evening we were told about matters that the medium could not have had any inkling about in a normal way; about farms and landscapes, local names, events, small things in the possession of deceased people, and so on. Most of the content of these communications has been found correct when checked, the accuracy of some still remains unknown and a very small number were proven incorrect " (Kvaran, 1906, p. 39).

Sigmundur Gudmundsson's Memories Verified by his Widow

A detailed account of one such case is given in the minute book for 10 to 14 October 1907. A list is attached with 41 statements given by Sigmundur Gudmundsson (1838-1897), a farmer in Fjardarhorn in Gufudal County and a skilled smith of iron and wood. He lost his way in bad weather and died of exposure in the wild on his way over Kollafjordur heath on 2 December 1897. Sigmundur appeared at most séances recorded in the minute books, almost as frequently as Konrad Gislason. His statements were given at séances in October 1906 and concern his memories of various events in his life, things he had made, his and his wife's possessions and things they had in their home. The statements were later checked by his widow Gudny and her responses to each statement were written down. That list accompanies the second minute book.

Of the 41 statements given by Sigmundur, 25 were confirmed as correct by his wife. Many of these were quite specific. For example, Sigmundur describes in detail what clothes he had on when he died. Also that he still had some sign of life when he was found. He correctly stated the farm at which his daughter had died, and so on. Six items his wife partially verified, five she could not assess or was not sure about. Five statements she rejected and thought they were wrong.

Brynjolfur Thorlaksson writes that Sigmundur appeared at almost every séance he attended. He describes Sigmundur as particularly memorable; always ready to help out with things, bright, with a good sense of humor, most likeable, had a pleasant effect on all present, was exceedingly articulate in his thinking, speech and in the way he spoke. Brynjolfur states this was also the case with many other Icelandic and foreign personalities that appeared regularly at Indridi's sittings. "It was very convincing to interact with them and observe the distinct personality traits that each of them had, and the great continuity of these characteristics day after day and year after year" (Thordarson, 1942, p. 53). Here is another example from the second minute book (3 February 1908):

> Thordur from Leira greets. (Thorgr. Gudmundsen asks him if he remembers when they were in Hotel Island with a Frenchman – does he remember him?)

The man with the black beard? (Thorgr.: Yes.)

Small man in a leather jacket. (Thorgr.: That is right.)

(Thorgr.: Do you remember the color of his eyes?) They were brown.
(Thorgr.: Quite right.) He had little hair on his forehead, particularly
on the right side. (Thorgr.: Do not remember.)

(Thorgr.: Do you remember what refreshments you gave us?) I gave
you more than one.

 Don't you remember his watch? It could be opened on both sides,
you pressed a button to open it. (Thorgr.: Do you remember its color?)

It was golden colored, was it not? (Thorgr.: No.) It had a dark steel like
color. Now I remember it; I wished it had belonged to me. (Right, says
Thorgr.) The chain was silvery.

His waistcoat was black with dots and borders at the sides. It had
a collar, different from what we have on our waistcoats. Do you
remember his boots? (Thorgr. No.) They protruded so long for the toes.
Do you remember his ring? (Thorgr.: No.) He put it on his forefinger,
or he took it off and put in in his purse. It had two stones.

—Authors' translation from Icelandic.

A second kind of proof of identity is reported in Brynjolfur's memoirs about Rev. Sigurdur Gunnarsson (1848-1936). A séance was held
in the smaller experimental hall and was mostly devoted to contacting
Rev. S. Gunnarsson's deceased wife, Soffia Emilia Einarsdottir (1841-
1902). At one time there was a long silence. Then Rev. S. Gunnarsson
expressed his great astonishment. He told the other sitters that "his
wife's hand had materialized. He touched it thoroughly all over and
clearly felt a knot or scar that she had had on one of her fingers. The
scar had been on the same hand, the same finger and on the correct
place on the finger" (Thordarson, 1942, p. 104).

A third kind of proof of identity was reported when a sitter recognized a deceased friend through his voice, manner of speech, choice
of words, and shared memories. Such was the case when the composer Sveinbjorn Sveinbjornsson (1847-1927) attended a séance on 14

September 1907. The minutes state that Sveinbjorn immediately recognized the voice of his old schoolmate Rev. Steinn Steinsen without being told who that person was. Rev. S. Steinsen addressed him very warmly and there followed a long conversation between them. In the end they sang a duet together.

CHAPTER 12

MATERIALIZATIONS AND APPORTS

During the winter of 1906-1907 the Society experimented mostly with apports, light phenomena and materializations, which reached their climax while other phenomena were set aside (Nielsson, 1924a, p. 234).

Einar Kvaran (1910, p. 47) and Haraldur Nielsson (1922b, p. 456) report that shortly before Christmas 1906 sittings were being held in two rooms in Kvaran's house (one fairly large room and a small adjoining bedroom). During sittings in the large room, the smaller séance room began to fill with a very strong whitish light. In this light appeared a human being that purported to be the discarnate Mr. Jensen. He first appeared between the curtains (probably curtains between the rooms) in the small room, and shouted, in a genuine and typical Copenhagen Danish accent, "Ka' De se mig?" ("Can you see me?") (Kvaran, 1934; Nielsson, 1922a, p. 20). The control personalities had said they required the small room for their own use. Einar's wife and Brynjolfur Thorlaksson said that Jensen always asked when he appeared, "Can you see me?" (Thordarson, 1942, pp. 102, 109). Einar Kvaran (1910, p. 47) continues:

> Then Jensen became visible in the light. In the New Year he showed himself in the living room, where we sat. He was dressed in a very fine

white robe, which reached down to the floor. The light radiated from him and we saw him in various locations in the room. Sometimes he stood very close to one of us. Once he stood on a sofa and behind his shoulders was something like a tiny sun on the wall. This was a very beautiful sight. Sometimes he stood on the chair back behind the medium. Once he sat with the medium on his [Indridi's] knees. He could not stay more than a few moments each time, but he showed himself several times at each séance.

—AUTHORS' TRANSLATION FROM DANISH.

Einar reports that on one occasion Jensen appeared eleven times in one hour (Kvaran, 1910, p. 47). He tells of an occasion when Jensen appeared and stood upright on a sofa, which was next to Indridi's chair (Kvaran, 1934). The light that radiated from this materialized being was quite bright, but somehow it did not penetrate far into the room, with the result that only people sitting closest to the entity could be seen in the light. On one occasion, Jensen stood behind the chair in which Indridi was sitting. In the light from the materialized being the sitters could clearly see Indridi in a trance state. Haraldur Nielsson (1922a, p. 20) writes that Jensen had:

... shown himself after the New Year in the living room, where we sat with the medium among us—do not forget that! The medium was in a very deep trance. The new visitor was dressed in very fine white drapery, of which many folds hung down to the floor; and the light was radiating from him. We saw him at different places in the room. Once he stood on a sofa, and behind him was a red light, which was similar to a little sun, with whitish light streaming out from it. This sight I shall never forget. Frequently he managed to appear seven or eight times the same evening in different places in the room. Many times we saw the medium and this materialized being simultaneously. But this extraordinary visitor could not be visible for more than a few seconds each time. When he had finished showing himself he tried to touch a few sitters with his hand, arm or foot, and he always allowed us to touch his materialized body before he dematerialized it again.

—AUTHORS' TRANSLATION FROM DANISH.

Unfortunately, we are not told how Jensen disappeared or "dematerialized." Brynjolfur Thorlaksson described the materialization of Jensen (Thordarson, 1942, p. 99):

> ... it always appeared as a luminous, beautiful light-pillar just taller than the average height of a human figure and slightly broader. Inside this light we saw a human form but it was not clear enough, for example, for the facial expression to be distinctly seen. This light-pillar was very white but with a tinge of blue. It was very luminous but did not flicker. However, it did not radiate much light. We saw the medium when the light-pillar stood near where he was sitting in a trance although otherwise there was darkness in the room.

> —AUTHORS' TRANSLATION FROM ICELANDIC.

The appearance of the light-pillar lasted only briefly each time and was always accompanied by a low buzzing sound (*ibid.*, pp. 99-100). Our sources say that Jensen often touched the sitters when he materialized (*ibid.*, p. 100).

Thorkell Thorlaksson (1869-1946), Brynjolfur Thorlaksson's brother, is reported to have seen the materialization of Jensen, but only during one séance at Einar Kvaran's home (Thordarson, 1942, p. 100). He saw Jensen five times the same evening but just for a brief period each time. The light-pillar had a color very similar to moonlight but was translucent at the edges, where folds could be seen as on cloth. Jensen seemed to be of average height but "hardly as thick" as an average man. His figure did not emit much light, but Indridi could be seen when the pillar was close to him. Jensen became visible in different places in the séance room and once on a sofa with Indridi. Our sources do not include any discussion of the differences or similarities between the physical appearance of Jensen and Indridi.

Einar reports that at one séance forty people simultaneously saw Jensen appear a number of times (Kvaran, 1910, p. 46). Three witnesses were invited to attend a séance one evening in 1907 (Nielsson, 1919b, p. 344; 1922a, p. 22; 1922b, p. 458): Hallgrimur Sveinsson who was Bishop of Iceland, the Magistrate of Reykjavik, and the British Consul. The Magistrate later became one of the five Supreme Court Judges in the country. He undertook to examine the two rooms and the medium to prevent fraud. Unfortunately, no description is given of how he actually conducted his investigation. Forty people attended and "many of them" had to stand. Amongst them, the three "highly esteemed men in whose evidence people could trust" (Nielsson, 1919b, p. 344) saw Jensen appear eleven times that evening in bright, luminous light. Haraldur writes that the three reliable witnesses were unable to find any indication of fraud (Nielsson, 1922a, p. 22).

The Bishop asked for a séance to be held in his own house, and séances were held at his home from time to time during a three-year period. The sittings were held in the bishop's library, and there the various phenomena occurred with even greater ease. Sometimes the control personalities brought Indridi, walking in a trance state, directly from the séance room to the bishop's home. At such times Indridi was always under Haraldur's close attention (Nielsson, 1922b, p. 459). The Bishop declared later that he was completely convinced that what he had observed was genuine.

Haraldur quotes from his diary to describe the following events which occurred on 4 February 1907 at 8 p.m. (Nielsson, 1922b, pp. 457-458):

> First Jensen showed himself three times, seated himself with the medium, sitting on his knees. I was sitting this evening myself in the foremost row and saw them both, so that I could discern them, especially the two heads and Jensen's arms as well. Then he appeared right in the very corner close by the door between the rooms. He was clearly to be seen in white drapery stretching his arms along the walls. Then he was seen still more distinctly beside the stove; then clearly on top of the sofa; next most distinctly by the window at the other end of the room opposite the stove, close by my cousin, Miss Sigridur Bjornsson. Finally just above the medium, standing on tiptoe on the back of his chair, so that Jensen's head nearly reached the ceiling.

A little later during this same séance another being appeared, in the doorway, but only the upper part of its body was visible. Haraldur saw his white covering very distinctly. At this point several of the sitters felt as if someone touched them. Haraldur felt as if he was being pushed below his knee. This was followed by a firmer push. Haraldur leaned forward and felt at his knee a man's bare foot, which was slightly cold. He grasped it around the toes and examined it, especially the big toe and the nail on it. The foot then levitated and Haraldur followed it as far as he could stretch himself while still remaining seated. After the foot had disappeared, Haraldur rested both hands on his knees. He then felt a man's foot step on both his hands. He felt the sole of the bare foot; the foot was cold and rather clammy. Finally Haraldur's chin was scratched by a foot or a hand and he felt as if two toes touched his cheek-bone. In his description Haraldur Nielsson does not mention where Indridi was situated while this was happening.

Einar Kvaran (1910, pp. 48-49) writes that sitters had on occasion spoken with the materialized beings, touched them and been embraced and kissed by them. However, it is not stated whether these "conversations" with the materialized beings were of a responsive nature. Einar (Kvaran, 1934) says that these materializations lasted for a few weeks altogether. The lights that accompanied the materialized beings disappeared after the beginning of 1907, according to Brynjolfur Thorlaksson (Thordarson, 1942, p. 4). It was thought at this time that Indridi's poor health was the reason for the deterioration of his materialization ability. After this period it seems that complete human beings never appeared again, but parts of human forms were often seen and felt. Brynjolfur (*ibid.*, p. 104) reports an example of a typical materialization that predominated from this point onward. Rev. Sigurdur Gunnarsson was once at a séance with the inner circle in the smaller hall of the experimental house. A hand materialized and was recognized by Rev. S. Gunnarsson as that of his deceased wife, Soffia Emilia Einarsdottir. He claimed that the hand had a scar on the same finger of the same hand, and in the same place, as his wife had had. The hand touched Sigurdur Gunnarsson and then the voice of his wife reportedly spoke to him in the direct voice.

Apport Experiments

Brynjolfur Thorlaksson says that during the winter of 1906-1907 members had special sittings in Einar's home which they called "apport séances." Sitters sat by Indridi and controlled him while he was in trance and the room was in darkness. Sometimes objects mysteriously appeared in the room seemingly teleported from other locations in Reykjavik. Brynjolfur attended only one such séance, during which a viper preserved in a bottle of spirit was, he reports, transported through matter. Sitters heard the sound of something being placed on the table which stood in the room. A light was immediately turned on and the sitters saw a bottle with the viper in it. After three days they managed to find the owner, who reported that the viper had belonged to a small collection which was kept in the attic of the owner's house. The relation, if any, of the owner to Indridi is not known. According to Haraldur, this type of phenomenon was frequently observed and it appears that Indridi became an apport medium at this stage (Nielsson, 1919b, p. 350; 1922a, pp. 23-24).

One evening that winter, after Indridi had fallen into a trance, the controls told the sitters that they could transport an object from any house in Reykjavik through the walls and roof, and then bring it onto the table in the séance room. Haraldur reports (Nielsson, 1922a, pp. 23-24):

> After the medium had gone into trance and was therefore unconscious, we first selected the house where the object was to be brought from, to exclude the explanation that he [Indridi] had brought the object with him. We allowed the controls to choose between the house of a well-known medical doctor and the bishop's residence. The controls chose the house of the doctor because the medium had often visited the home of the bishop. Immediately afterwards we heard a very peculiar knocking sound, the like of which I had never heard before, nor have I since then. There followed a short pause, during which the controls informed us that they had now got the object out through the roof of the doctor's house. After a pause the knocking sound was heard for the second time, and shortly thereafter a large bottle containing a few bird specimens [preserved] in spirit [alcohol] landed on our table. The doctor was immediately contacted by telephone and asked if this was his property; but he answered, no. The medium, who had come out of the trance state, again fell into a trance, and one of the controls claimed assuredly that this *was* correct [Haraldur's emphasis]. He [the control] had himself taken the bottle from a yellow-painted clothes chest which was located in a room in the doctor's house, where an old man had been sitting engaged in conversation with two other gentlemen. The doctor was given this information, and by closer investigation it was found that the description was indeed correct. The doctor's father-in-law had been sitting in his room, where the clothes chest was, engaged in conversation with two strangers. The bottle belonged to a relative of the doctor and was now missing from the chest.
>
> —AUTHORS' TRANSLATION FROM DANISH.

From the report it seems that the sitters had selected the house from which an object was to be fetched, but the nature of the object was not decided. It would have been interesting to know if Indridi had ever visited the doctor's house and, furthermore, if the clothes chest in question had, in fact, been yellow as the control had claimed. Unfortunately, these details are not included in the report.

One evening Indridi was himself reportedly taken through a wall into another room, which was locked and in darkness (Nielsson, 1919b, p. 350). This phenomenon is mentioned nowhere else in our sources and little information is given about it. Rev. Jakob Jonsson (personal communication, 1984) remembered that Haraldur Nielsson described this incident in a lecture at the theological faculty at the University of Iceland. The Italian medical doctor Professor Pietro Tarchini (fl. 1880s-1950s or beyond) reports (1947) a similar incident from a séance where the sitters thought that an (unidentified) Italian medium had been dematerialized and apported from one place (the cabinet) to another (the séance room).

Manifestation of the "Monster Beast"

Animal appearances or materializations are extremely rare in the history of mediumship and Spiritualism. One such case is reported in relation to Indridi. The case of Indridi's animal manifestation is described in the memoirs of Brynjolfur Thorlaksson (Thordarson, 1942, pp. 92-96).

The organist Brynjolfur Thorlaksson and Indridi were both interested in horses and loved riding. Brynjolfur had a horse kept at a stable in the outskirts of Reykjavik. In the fall of 1907 they agreed that Indridi would take care of the horse and could ride it in return whenever he wanted. Below is a slightly shortened account by Brynjolfur of a deformed creature that followed them one bright summer night.

One late evening when the night was bright,[1] Indridi ran into Brynjolfur by chance as he was on his way home from feeding the horse. They walked together towards Indridi's house. Suddenly they heard hoof-clatter as if a young horse was about 50 meters behind them. They looked behind and saw following them a creature the size of a young horse, about one to four years old. It looked like a young horse but at the same time like a calf—and yet it was neither or both. It looked like a deformed creature, a mixture of horse and calf. The head was a combination of both animals. The creature had shorter legs than a young horse normally has, but its step sounded like that from a horse's hoofs.

---

[1] For about two months in the summer the nights do not get dark in Iceland.

It had a tail but not like a horse. It had a lot of hair but not a horse's mane. The animal was dark and ugly. Brynjolfur and Indridi felt very uncomfortable as they saw this creature lumbering behind them, especially as it was the middle of the night and they were alone in the street.

They hurried to Indridi's home, where the séances were held. As they were about to enter the house Brynjolfur looked back and saw the creature right behind them. It lifted its head and looked at them. There was a ladder standing upright, leaning against the northern wall of the house. As they entered the house three things happened at once: Indridi immediately fell into trance; the ladder levitated and fell to the ground away from the house; and the monster disappeared. The ladder fell in this direction which was against the law of gravity; it looked as though the ladder had been thrown at the monster.

Indridi's control reported that there was nothing to be afraid of; he would see to that. Brynjolfur asked what it was all about. The reply was that he would be told later. Then Indridi woke up from his trance and Brynjolfur walked back to his own home.

A séance was held shortly afterwards for the inner circle and Indridi fell into trance. Then they heard the clatter of horse hooves and felt shivers going through them. They heard a peeping or whistling sound, as when steam is released from a steam engine. Then the sound of the horse's hooves stopped. The controls said that this was a case of a man who had hanged himself in a horse's stable and after his death was able in some way to use material from animals to make contact with the physical world.

At later séances the sitters heard these hoofbeats a few times and they were always followed by the same whistling or peeping sound. The controls said this was because they were dematerializing the monster. The monster seemed to have no evil intentions; it just wanted to join them, but neither the sitters nor the controls wanted that. After a few séances the beast disappeared completely. (Thordarson, 1942, pp. 92–96).

Thorbergur Thordarson, who recorded Brynjolfur's memoirs, made some enquiries about this incident. He reports that Brynjolfur's brother, Thorkell, remembered that his brother had told him about this shortly after it had occurred. He also recalled having heard the horse's hooves and the whistling sound at séances. Another sitter, Kristjan Linnet (1881-1958), recalled Indridi complaining that he would sometimes become aware of the beast in the lobby.

This incident occurred spontaneously in the spring of 1908 and not during a séance as was the case with the eagle in the mediumship of

Franek Kluski (1873-1943) or the "ape-man" and the dog with Jan Guzyk (1875-1928). Both of these Polish mediums were investigated by French physician and psychical researcher Gustav Geley (1860-1924), among others (Claudewitz, 2010; Weaver, 1992).

CHAPTER 13

VIOLENT DISTURBANCES AND THE PHOTOGRAPHY EXPERIMENT

Indridi Indridason and the Experimental Society experienced violent psychokinetic attacks, particularly in December 1907. Some of these phenomena occurred under good lighting conditions while Indridi was not in a trance.

These events were recorded in the second minute book immediately after they occurred, and the events were attested to by witnesses and signed by the President and Secretary of the Society. Sometimes they were further corroborated in written testimony obtained from members who had observed particular phenomena. Haraldur Nielsson (1924b) and Einar Kvaran (1910) wrote reports on these violent phenomena which are therefore well documented. During the winter of 1907-1908, the number of sitters at séances was sometimes as high as seventy.

Visit to the Westman Islands

At the end of September 1907, Indridi visited a clergyman living in the village on the Westman Islands off the southern coast of Iceland.

One day while he was out walking with the clergyman's daughters, he twice told about seeing a dead man, about whom he made some mocking remarks. Reportedly he saw a man in his shirt-sleeves, with a belt around his waist, first in connection with a lady they had met, and then when they passed a certain house in the village. The lady lived in that house and her husband had committed suicide the previous autumn by drowning himself in the sea. Before doing so, he had taken off his hat, coat and waistcoat, because these garments were found on the shore (Nielsson, 1930, p. 171; Thordarson, 1942, p. 24). The medium was reportedly ignorant of this incident when he visited the Westman Islands.

In the newspaper *Reykjavik* (1906a, p. 185), in the 20 October 1906 issue, we found the following announcement:

> SUICIDE. Jon Einarsson, around fifty, who came back home in the spring from America after nearly one year's stay there, drowned himself in Westman Islands on the ninth of this month (his clothes were found on the shore, but he had disappeared).

—Authors' translation from Icelandic.

After the medium's return to Reykjavik, strange disturbances started in the rooms which the medium shared with a theology student, Thordur Oddgeirsson (1883-1966), as well as during séances. For instance, in the night following the 3 October meeting, the light was turned off in their rooms in the middle of the night, and Indridi claimed to see the man in the shirt-sleeves whom he had seen in the village of the Westman Islands (Nielsson, 1925, p. 91; 1930, p. 172).

At the beginning of the sitting on 5 October the main control requested, through Indridi's automatic writing, that a prayer should be offered for "a certain person who had slipped into the séance" (second minute book, p. 28). The minute book reports several times that before the medium awakens from trance voices are often heard around him (direct voice phenomena).

On this occasion, after the medium had woken up from trance, many sitters had left and only six people remained. They sang some hymns and went into the smaller room and sat in the front row. Then rustling of the curtains was clearly heard by all present. The medium described the "guest" saying he was standing there wearing a striped shirt and black trousers, with a narrow belt around his waist. A prayer was said for him during which the medium said he saw the man move to the center of the floor. He was standing calmly with his head facing down. When the prayer was over, the medium said that the guest had left nodding his head to all of them to say good-bye. He disappeared through the middle of the wall. This man was Jon Einarsson, the person they had prayed for at the beginning of the séance.

After this prayer the disturbances stopped for about two months. Haraldur reports (Nielsson, 1925, p. 92):

> After this we got levitation phenomena on a larger scale than we ever had before. On the 21st of October the medium was carried in a wicker chair above the heads of the sitters, who sat in two tight rows. Phenomena of the same kind occurred repeatedly. Likewise the harmonium, time after time, was taken away from the organist, while he was playing it in the dark, and shifted out on the floor. Sometimes it was jogged along while at the same time the keys were touched or played upon by an invisible force.

The levitation of the wicker chair is confirmed in the second minute book on 21 October (p. 44):

> Furthermore, the medium in the wicker chair levitated above the heads of the sitters and came down behind Mrs. Lovisa Jensen and Mrs. Kristin Simonarson who sat in the second row. A light was lit immediately after this occurred and it was seen that the row of chairs had not been moved, so it would not have been possible to squeeze Indridi's wicker chair between the other chairs. Apart from that we heard him in the air especially when his chair hit the floor.

—AUTHORS' TRANSLATION FROM ICELANDIC.

Before this levitation occurred, the minutes report: "Fairly strong light lit up the pulpit. The harmonium had, at the request of K.G., been moved closer to the rows of chairs, and was three times taken away from Brynjolfur Thorlaksson while he was playing on it, and his neck was touched" (*ibid.*, p. 44).

The Fiasco of the Photography Experiment

Towards the end of the sitting on 2 December: "Danielssen speaks about conducting an experiment by taking a photograph of the medium with a magnesium light to find out if they [the controls] succeed in making themselves visible in the picture" (second minute book, p. 63).

On 5 December we read that the previous day an experiment had been conducted to photograph the medium by magnesium light but it failed as the hall became filled with smoke; attention had not been paid to clear the hall with enough fresh air (second minute book, p. 64).

On 6 December 1907 an attempt was made to photograph the medium with a flash light to see if Danielssen (one of the controls) would appear on the photograph. Only the photographer was present, which was thought to be all right, since it was the first experiment of that kind. This was a marked deviation of the usual procedure to have several people present and to let one or two persons sit at Indridi's side to hold him and watch him closely.

During the photo session the photographer Magnus Olafsson (1862-1937) said that he had noticed an unpleasant influence, he had felt as if "power" was being drawn from him and that he was losing consciousness (Nielsson, 1930, p. 173). He heard choking sounds coming from Indridi while the photograph was being taken and Indridi's voice sounded somewhat strange. The negative showed an arrangement of drapery on a pole but the circumstances pointed to a possible unconscious fraud on the part of Indridi. He seemed to have slipped out of the room during the interval of darkness, got a bed sheet from a cupboard and slung this on a curtain pole to imitate drapery. Afterwards he attempted to get away and rid himself of something that he had hidden beneath his clothes, which was "obviously the sheet." However, it is reported, that Indridi seemed to have no idea of what had happened.

After conferring with Einar Kvaran, it was decided not to investigate the incident, to avoid embarrassing the medium. Indridi was told that the experiment had not been a success, and he was asked to give a sitting to three or four members of the Society. Indridi wanted to see the negative, but was told that it had been broken accidentally, in order "to keep his mind at ease" (Nielsson, 1924b, p. 151).

At the séance on 7 December, the day after the photography attempt, the doors were closed from the inside as usual so that no one could get in (Nielsson, 1925, pp. 92-94; 1930, pp. 176-178). This séance, which lasted five and one half hours, took place in darkness, but some light seems to have come from a fire burning in the stove. The sitters who stayed through this séance were Julius Olafsson, Haraldur Nielsson and Einar Kvaran, who held Indridi's arms or had both arms around him all the time. Indridi was in a trance state throughout the séance.

During this séance the controls said they had discovered that the person who had committed suicide had played a dirty trick on them and had interfered with the photography experiment. They said that "Jon" was now at the séance, in control of "the power" and in the worst of tempers. They further stated, "Heaven knows how this sitting may end, as Jon is now a semi-materialized ghost" (Nielsson, 1925, pp. 92-93). Then the curtains in front of the cabinet were roughly drawn aside, so that the rings were heard rattling on the pole, and loud noises were heard on top of the cabinet. Indridi was moved between Einar and Haraldur on the front bench. He then suffered convulsions and was thrown into Einar's arms. Einar noticed that he was trembling all over. Julius Olafsson was sitting very close to Einar on the other side. The wicker chair in which Indridi sat was thrown about on the floor, and a persistent, tumultuous noise was heard on the cabinet roof. Indridi's chair was repeatedly jerked about and finally turned upside down with Indridi "thrown out of it" onto the floor (ibid., p. 93). Haraldur reports (Nielsson, 1924b, pp. 152-153):

> After a pause an attempt was made to tear off my hat [gentlemen wore hats at that time], and something touched the brim of Mr. Kvaran's hat. I then took off my hat and held it in my right hand. In my left hand I had a stick, on which I was leaning. This stick was then caught and for a while pulled at, so as to get it behind me to the left. While this was being done, I had my right hand on the back of the wicker chair, and felt that the medium was sitting in it, and at the same time Mr. Kvaran was holding down his arms in the chair. I then shifted the stick into my right hand, taking the hat in my left. The leg of my trousers was then taken hold of at the back, a little above the knee, and my overcoat pulled at with considerable force.

A considerable noise was heard on the cabinet top. The sitters' chairs were once more thrown out on the floor. The medium shouted to Haraldur to go to Julius Olafsson, who had gone inside the cabinet to take care of the chairs. When Haraldur came inside they heard something being thrown and crashing down with a great noise. Haraldur and Julius lit a match and saw a coal shovel on the floor under the front bench, but the scuttle was lying on the second bench. It seemed that the coal-scuttle, full of coal, had been thrown right onto the spot where Haraldur had been standing (Nielsson, 1922b, p. 461). Indridi never went into the cabinet, but stood outside, and Einar had put both his arms around him. (This seems to have taken place in the small experimental room. No exact description is given of the cabinet or its use in our sources.)

Reflections on the Photography Experiment

Now back to the photography experiment. Haraldur Nielsson reflects on it in notes accompanying the minute books:

> Why did the medium do this foolish attempt to deceive when the photograph was taken? I say foolish because the fraud was bound to get known quickly as indeed it did.

> For almost five years we conducted experiments with him, and however closely we and other very skeptical people watched him, we never found any attempt to deceive us apart from this one incident. Was he at this moment overtaken by some madness, or suggestive influences, so that he was no more his own master? Or, had Jon got hold of him and was able to let him perform this fraud to throw suspicion on him and get us to have no faith in him? That would have been the surest way to destroy all our research work? Did Jon get the overhand over the Norwegian doctor without the doctor being aware of it when the power was taken from the medium? Had the medium perhaps been in trance? Nobody knows, but the rattling sound would point in that direction. The rattling sound, we were told by the controls, was Jon's characteristic as he had drowned. If that was the case Jon had caused the medium to fall into trance...

> This [incident] suggests that mediums should be treated with more care than is sometimes given, particularly by very skeptical investigators. We are certainly dealing with forces that are controlled by intelligences. These intelligences may be good or evil. Perhaps the conditions that we create can sometimes be such that it will be easier for the evil forces to get hold of the medium...

It is important to remember that on this occasion the medium was without any of the support and sympathy that he was accustomed to be surrounded with. If we seriously start to seek the causes of this tragedy, I would not be surprised that it lies in our ignorance [of mediumship]. In this research we find ourselves on a treacherous ground. If we are not careful we may cause great harm to the medium. We must not surrender, but we must avoid the dangers and learn what they are...

—Authors' translation from Icelandic.

CHAPTER 14

DESTRUCTIVE ASSAULTS

Our main sources regarding the violent phenomena that took place in Indridi Indridason's living quarters are three papers written by Haraldur Nielsson (1924b; 1925; 1930). These are mostly based on accounts written in the Society's minute books — and "they were all exceptionally well attested [to] by witnesses, as it was not thought sufficient merely to have the record of them written in the minute book and signed by the President and the Secretary of the Society; but confirmation in writing was obtained from a number of persons who were especially connected with the phenomena" (Nielsson, 1924b, p. 148). Haraldur personally witnessed some of them.

On the evening of 7 December 1907, Indridi and Thordur Oddgeirsson had gone to bed in the experimental house. A lamp was burning on a table between the beds. Suddenly a plate, which had been standing on a bookshelf in the front room, was thrown onto the floor (Nielsson, 1930, p. 179). It came down in the inner room, the bedroom, just inside the curtains that enclosed the room. Indridi's bed was pulled about one foot away from the wall. Indridi was terror-stricken, and Society members had to stay with him at night for some time after this happened, and all regular sittings stopped.

Einar Kvaran stayed with Indridi and the theology student during the night of 8 December. He lay in Indridi's bed by the north wall while Indridi and Thordur Oddgeirsson occupied the other bed (Nielsson, 1930, pp. 179-181). The doors were carefully locked. A lamp was burning on a table between the beds. (There was no electricity in Reykjavik at this time). Indridi fell into a trance and through him the main control said that "Jon" had gone to get power and this was very serious. The control ordered the light to be turned off, as it would do Indridi's controls more harm than Jon, who now had a more compact body than they had. Indridi then woke from the trance and wanted to get a light, but the light was not lit. One of Thordur's slippers, which had been under his bed, was thrown into a hand-basin which stood in the room. The other slipper landed lightly on Einar's blanket. Haraldur writes (Nielsson, 1924b, pp. 154-155):

> Next, the ends of the bed in which the medium and Mr. Oddgeirsson were lying (Mr. Oddgeirsson with his head nearest to the window and the medium with his head at the other end of the bed) were raised and lowered alternately and the bed shaken. The medium was lying on the side farther from the wall. He shouted that he was being dragged out of the bed, and was very terror-stricken. He implored Mr. Oddgeirsson to hold onto his hand. Mr. Oddgeirsson took his hand, pulling with all his might, but could not hold him. The medium was lifted above the end of the bed against which his head had been lying, and was pulled down onto the floor, sustaining some injuries to his back from the bedstead. At the same moment a pair of boots, which had been under Mr. Oddgeirsson's bed, were thrown at the lamp, breaking both the glass and the shade.

Indridi was dragged head first through the curtains that enclosed the room and along the floor into the front room. He tried strenuously to hold onto anything he could, and both Einar Kvaran and Thordur Oddgeirsson pulled at his legs, but he was still pulled along. Finally they managed to "get under his shoulders, which they had great difficulty in lifting" (*ibid.*, p. 155), and brought him back to the bed. Thordur sat down on the side of the bed in front of him. Indridi's legs were then lifted so forcefully that Thordur could not weigh the leg down. Einar grasped the other leg but could not force it down either.

At this point all three left the experimental house and went to Einar's home, where some activity continued during the night in spite of all the lights being on (Nielsson, 1930, p. 181). A small piece of wood from a cigar box was lifted from the floor and moved four to six feet in the air. A book which had been lying on a table was thrown at a hanging lamp which was burning in the drawing room. Nobody was in there but the doors were open between the drawing room and the dining room, where all three of them sat. The book continued from the lamp to a card table standing by the far wall of the room and hit a small lamp which stood there. The book knocked the shade off the lamp, knocked down two photographs which had been standing on the table, and finally fell on the floor. A plant pot which was standing in the unoccupied drawing room was shifted a few inches. The hanging lamp swung to and fro for a while. Knocks were also heard on the walls of both rooms.

The next evening (9 December), a few members of the Society had agreed to meet in the offices of Bjorn Jonsson before going to the experimental house to keep a watch over Indridi (Nielsson, 1925, p. 96; 1930, pp. 181-182). Before the others arrived, Bjorn Jonsson was alone in his office, inside which an oil lamp was burning. Indridi was alone in an adjacent room, where another light was burning, and the door between the rooms was open. Suddenly Indridi entered the inner office where Bjorn was, saying that he had seen "Jon" coming through the window. At that very instant two chairs standing at a large desk were thrown through the open door from the adjacent, unoccupied room into the office. Then Indridi said he saw Jon by the far window of the adjacent room beside a high book case which was there. Immediately afterwards a large volume was propelled from the top shelf of the book case.

Later the same night (around 11:30 p.m.), Haraldur Nielsson, Gudmundur Jonsson (who later became a well-known writer in Denmark and Iceland and changed his name to Gudmundur Kamban (1888-1945)), Gudmundur Jakobsson (1860-1933) and Bjorn Jonsson went with Indridi to the experimental house (Nielsson, 1930, p. 181; 1925, pp. 96-97). After Indridi was in bed, he went into a trance, but after a short while, when the controls had spoken through him, he came out of the trance. During that night a small table standing between the beds at the head of Indridi's bed was lifted up and fell on his bed, making a loud noise. It had apparently smashed against the wall and had broken into two pieces. Indridi's bed was shifted away from the wall, even though Gudmundur Jakobsson sat on the edge of it and Haraldur sat on a chair by Indridi's feet and leaned forward, pressing on the bedstead with both hands. According to Haraldur (Nielsson, 1925, p. 97), the foot of the bed was shifted "the width of a hand," but the head board much more. A cardboard box fell down in the inner room at the feet of Gudmundur Jonsson, who was sitting close to the threshold. Indridi said that the cardboard box had been under a couch in the outer room. At the same instant, the lid of the box fell down on Thordur Oddgeirsson's bed, in which Bjorn was lying. No other phenomena took place that night.

The next night (10 December), Brynjolfur stayed in the experimental house (Nielsson, 1930, pp. 182-184; Thordarson, 1942, pp. 24-32). Thordur Oddgeirsson and Indridi went to their beds but Brynjolfur lay down on a couch in the front room. Indridi fell into a trance, and through him the controls said that during the day Jon had collected considerable "power." The controls ordered that no lights should be turned on. Indridi then came out of the trance. Two candlesticks which had been standing on the harmonium in the front room suddenly fell to the floor. A brush, which was under a chest of drawers in the same room, was thrown into the inner room. Indridi screamed that Jon was there. Brynjolfur then came in and lay on top of Indridi on the bed. The table between the beds lifted up onto Thordur's bed.

Then the situation calmed down for a while and Brynjolfur returned to the couch in the front room. Again Indridi shouted that Jon was coming. Brynjolfur came into the doorway between the rooms and received a splash of water in his face, while simultaneously a water-bowl fell in front of his feet. It had stood under the wash-stand four to six feet from the foot of Indridi's bed. Brynjolfur went to Indridi, who lay kicking in his bed asking Brynjolfur to hold him down. Brynjolfur again laid himself on top of Indridi. At the same time a chamber pot from under Indridi's bed was thrown into the outer room. The bed in which the two of them were lying suddenly moved about a foot from the wall, although Brynjolfur pushed with his foot with all of his might against the other bed. At the same time he had to use all his strength to hold Indridi down on the bed. Thordur came to help, but the table between the beds levitated high up and came down on his shoulders. Thordur caught hold of one of the legs of the table and held onto it while he went back to his bed and pulled the quilt over his head. He then received continuous knocks on his head from the table top.

Then they lit an oil lamp which stood on the chest of drawers between the washing tables in Indridi's bedroom, and also three candles in the front room. At this point they had decided to leave the house. Brynjolfur was standing in the doorway between the rooms and Thordur was sitting on the couch in the front room. Indridi was standing up on his bed and beginning to dress. Brynjolfur was looking at Indridi and saw him suddenly flung down on the bed. Brynjolfur rushed to him but at the same time a bowl, which had stood on the chest of drawers in the bedroom, flew towards him. It did not hit Brynjolfur, but according to his account it went past him. It altered its direction, and took a direct line to the southeast corner of the outer room where it smashed against the stove located there. Then Brynjolfur went into the outer room and stood there. Again Indridi started to put on his trousers, and according to Brynjolfur (Thordarson, 1942, p. 31):

> Indridi was starting to dress again and was putting on his trousers, but I walked into the outer room and stood there. Then Indridi screamed for help once more. I ran into the bedroom to him. But then I saw a sight that I shall never forget. Indridi was floating horizontal in the air, at about the height of my [Brynjolfur's] chest, and swaying there to and fro, with his feet pointing towards the window, and it seems to me that the invisible power that was holding him in the air was trying to swing him out of the window. I didn't hesitate a moment, but grabbed around the medium where he was swinging in the air, and pushed him down onto the bed and held him there. But then I noticed that both of us were being lifted up. I screamed to Thordur Oddgeirsson and asked him to come to help.

> —AUTHORS' TRANSLATION FROM ICELANDIC.

Haraldur Nielsson reported the same incident in his paper (1925, p. 99):

> The medium again started to dress, and having got his trousers on, he once more screamed for help. Mr. Brynjolfur [sic; should read Mr. Thorlaksson] had been standing in the outer room, but now rushed to the medium and saw him balancing in the air with his feet towards the window. Mr. Brynjolfur took hold of him, pulled him down onto the bed and held him there. He then felt the medium and himself being lifted up. Mr. Brynjolfur shouted to Mr. [Thordur] Oddgeirsson to help him. Mr. Oddgeirsson went into the bedroom, but a chair was hurled at him and fell beside the stove in the outer room. Mr. Oddgeirsson moved aside to avoid the chair and went on into the bedroom. Mr. Brynjolfur was then lying on the medium's chest. Mr. Oddgeirsson lay down on the knees of the medium, whose whole frame was in motion on the bed. Then a bolster, which was under the medium's pillow, was thrown into the air; it fell on the bedroom floor. Simultaneously the candlesticks which were in the outer room came through the air and

were flung down in the bedroom. Then all three of them stood side by side and walked backwards out of the room in order to be able to defend themselves against more assaults. Oddgeirsson held the lamp with the light in his left hand and had his right arm around Indridi's left arm. Brynjolfur held his left arm around Indridi's right arm. Then they all saw a hand-basin, which had stood on a washing-table in the bedroom, come flying straight towards them nearly a man's height off the floor. Suddenly, when it came into the outer room, it altered its direction and flew past them and broke into pieces on the stove. Then they all rushed out. Finally, they closed the outer room, but Indridi said he saw Jon take a water-bottle and throw it at Oddgeirsson, who went out last. (The next morning, Oddgeirsson's water-bottle lay in pieces on the floor). It was 2.30 a.m. when they left the house and went to Kvaran's home. Soon after they arrived there, small things were thrown down from the walls, and a table made small movements, but no violent disturbances took place.

The second minute book gives a detailed description of the violent phenomena that started on 7 December 1907 and lasted until 6 January 1908.

On ten of the eleven days in which séances were held during this period, there were movements or levitations of objects, some of them quite destructive and that would have required much force. On six days, the sitters felt touches or tugs as if from materialized hands or limbs. On five days, knocks were heard in various places. On four days the medium was levitated or thrown around, and on four of the eleven days direct voice phenomena were heard. Some of these phenomena occurred more than once or even often each day. Usually several different phenomena were observed each day. On 4 January 1908 the destructive disturbances reached their climax when around fifty occurrences were observed and recorded in the minutes.

CHAPTER 15

RETURN TO ORDINARY SÉANCES

In spite of the violent phenomena, the Society attempted to hold an ordinary séance in the hall on 16 December 1907; the previous one had been on 5 December (Nielsson, 1925, pp. 99-100). On 16 December, Indridi was carefully controlled all the time. A small table was hurled from near where Indridi sat all the way to the stove, where it broke into pieces. The minutes describe how the desk of the pulpit and the steps leading up to it, both firmly held by nails, were torn up and flung out onto the floor. Immense force was needed to achieve this. This presumed poltergeist activity was highly destructive and violent. The minutes report that this could not possibly have been done by the medium for he was watched the whole time by sitters who sat beside him.

On 30 December, the wooden steps up to the pulpit were torn up again. The carpenter, Sveinn Sveinsson, had firmly nailed down the steps after they were torn up on 16 December. The minutes include a written declaration signed by the carpenter describing how he had done this. One board under the steps to the pulpit was nailed into the wall with two three-inch long nails and further fastened with a strip of wood. The other board under the steps was nailed down onto the pulpit with one four-inch long nail.

Thordur Oddgeirsson wrote a declaration in the minutes stating that, since the steps had been torn up at the last sitting, it occurred to him to examine how well the steps had been fastened. He writes that he tried to pull them up with great force but they were unmovable. (second minute book, pp. 98-99)

Gudmundur Jonsson declares that the President of the Experimental Society had asked him before the séance started on 30 December to examine how well the steps had been re-fastened: "I pulled at it firmly but it was unshakeable" (second minute book, p. 99).

Out of fear, Indridi stayed at Einar Kvaran's home during the night of 17 December. Present were Indridi and Einar and four other people. Brynjolfur and his brother, Thorkell, arrived later in the evening. Indridi went into a trance, and from his throat were heard choking sounds. The spirit control asked for the lights to be turned off. Einar Kvaran reports in the second minute book (pp. 86-91) that the intruder, Jon, had at times gained control over Indridi's body and spoke through him in his strong, heavy voice. Haraldur writes that Jon had mumbled and groaned and started to swear at Indridi, whom he spoke of "as a trained instrument which he should like to use at his pleasure" (Nielsson, 1925, pp. 101-102). But, above all, he said, "he should have liked to be able to kill him and to do all possible harm to those in the so-called upper world" (*ibid.*, pp. 101-102). Then the controls seem to have found some means of expelling Jon. A kind of buzzing sound was heard around Indridi when the sitters thought Jon was leaving him (Thordarson, 1942, p. 41). When Jon had been driven out of Indridi, the control personalities said that they had poured some substance onto Indridi's forehead in order to diminish Jon's influences. The sitters touched his forehead and said it felt wet, but as if from an oily substance.

One incident occurred one evening when Brynjolfur and Indridi visited Bjorn Jonsson in his editorial office. Bjorn invited them to take a seat, which they did quite apart. Then he opened a drawer in his desk and took out two apples and gave one to each. As Brynjolfur was beginning to eat his apple, it is suddenly thrown out of his hand across the room and is smashed on the wall, and the rest fell on the floor. Shortly afterwards a chair moves up to the ceiling which was fairly high from the floor. Then Brynjolfur says to Indridi "Let us go" and they left hurriedly. Jon was considered responsible for these pranks (Thordarson, 1942, pp. 59-60).

One night (probably sometime after the 17 December séance), Engilbert Gislason (1877-1971) and the brothers Thordur and Pall Oddgeirsson (1888-1971) stayed with Indridi (Nielsson, 1925, pp. 102-103). An oil lamp was burning in the bedroom and there was candlelight in the outer room. In this light the following phenomena took place (Nielsson, 1925, pp. 102-103):

> The medium had got into his bed when the manifestations began. The first incident was that a tea-cup, which had been standing on Thordur Oddgeirsson's washing-table, was lifted into the air and thrown down again with such force that it broke into tiny fragments. Engilbert Gislason, who was standing in front of the medium's bed, observed that the medium had his hands under the quilt when the cup was broken. After a little while, the medium warned them that Jon was present and was preparing to throw his (the medium's) water-jug. Engilbert then went to the washing-table and took hold of the jug, which was standing in the hand-basin. The jug was then turned round in his hand with considerable force. After a while the medium again said that Jon was moving about, and at the same moment the medium's bed was pulled away from the wall six inches or more. When the bed was pulled out, Thordur Oddgeirsson was sitting on his bed opposite the medium's bed, but Engilbert Gislason and Pall Oddgeirsson were standing at the foot of the former's bed.

During an ordinary séance on 30 December, Jon was heard to speak around Indridi using direct voice for the first time (Nielsson, 1925, p. 103; 1930, pp. 188-189; Thordarson, 1942, p. 43). The steps up to the pulpit were pulled up, although they had been securely nailed to the wall after the séance on 16 December. Three men had unsuccessfully tried to pull them up. Now they were completely torn off. Einar Kvaran and his wife both witnessed this incident. A waterbowl moved from a shelf over the pulpit and poured water over one sitter and into his pockets. Then the waterbowl was put on a small table in front of Einar and his wife. A bell was taken off the same shelf and flew around ringing, all over the hall, even close to the sitters' faces. One sitter was touched with a cold hand, and several others felt a touch.

During a séance on 2 January 1908 (Nielsson, 1925, pp. 103-104), a medical doctor from the Westman Islands who had known Jon personally was present. Indridi was closely controlled the whole time and he had both hands resting on the left shoulder of the physician, who sat just in front of him. Knocks were heard on the wall and on the harmonium. Benches, which had been piled up close to the pulpit before the meeting, were thrown on the floor with great commotion. A bell was rung and at the same time it touched the doctor's head. A chair on which one of the sitters was seated was pulled out of the row of seats. A table which was under Einar Kvaran's watch moved many times. Once Einar had great trouble in retaining hold of it, and once he felt the shape of two hands on it. Haraldur Nielsson's head was touched many times, and he felt fingers, as if a hand was coming from behind where the pulpit was. A pile of benches were heard being pushed about (this occurred five times). One bench came down on Einar's shoulder and on the knee of another sitter as they sat in the front row, and from there started to push against the doctor on the other side. The doctor's chair rolled as if moved by waves. Lastly both Haraldur and the doctor felt a hand touch them.

The disturbances continued and reached a climax on 4 January 1908 (Nielsson, 1925, pp. 104-105; 1930, p. 189; Thordarson, 1942, pp. 43-44). The chair on which Indridi sat was thrown to the floor, and Indridi was lifted up while both Einar and the doctor were controlling him. When sitters were singing a hymn, it sounded as if a human foot was beating time on the floor near Indridi. Some of the sitters heard footsteps and whispering behind the rows, and many of them saw a big flash of light. Just after this, the chair under the medium was broken. Gudmundur Jonsson went up to Indridi to observe him more closely. Indridi clasped both his hands around Gudmundur's hands. Then a rod from the back of Indridi's chair was thrown up high in the air. Indridi's chair was put back together, and he was seated in it. Haraldur continues (Nielsson, 1924b, p. 161):

> While both the medium's hands were being closely guarded, the very chair on which he was sitting was totally demolished, and some of the fragments thrown at a big hanging lamp in the hall. The lamp broke into pieces — shade, glass and oil-vessel—the fragments falling down on Bjorn Jonsson's head.
>
> Other pieces flew against the east wall of the hall. Bjorn Jonsson then left, along with a few other sitters. A very heavy bell which had stood on a shelf over the pulpit, rang repeatedly at different places in the hall over the heads of the sitters, and eventually fell down a short distance from the door of the materialization room. Those who sat

by the harmonium said that they felt it being moved. Several sitters reported being touched, and one of them touched what appeared to be a hand. Various other objects were thrown around the hall.

After this eventful séance, Indridi went with some friends to the restaurant at Hotel Island (Nielsson, 1925, p. 105; 1930, pp. 189-190). During the evening, Indridi walked out into the courtyard, without a hat and coat, and did not return. His friends wondered what had happened to him and went out into the courtyard to search for him, but could not find him. At about 11:30 pm, about the same time he disappeared, he arrived in a trance state at Einar Kvaran's home without his hat and coat, speaking with the voice of the "Norwegian doctor." Later that night there was a séance with Einar's family and Gudmundur Jonsson. At this, Jon apologized for his behavior. From that moment onward he was at peace with Indridi, and he became one of his most powerful controls. After the sitters had conversed with Indridi's controls, Indridi emerged from the trance and wondered where he was.

We also have Thorkell Thorlaksson's account of this and, according to Thorbergur Thordarson, there was an account in the Society's minute books. All three sources agree that Indridi had gone out to the courtyard alone (Thordarson, 1942, pp. 52-53). Thorbergur reports that the minute books report that the main control, Konrad Gislason, had described this incident, saying that the controls had brought Indridi "prostrate" in the air from the yard and over the wall, in order to give Jon an immediate opportunity to be reconciled with the members of the Society (ibid., p. 53). A healthy man could have run the distance between Hotel Island and Einar's home in a few minutes.

Brynjolfur Thorlaksson describes this somewhat differently (Thordarson, 1942, pp. 45-47). He reports that with Indridi, Jon Fjeldsted (1878-1932), and Thorkell Thorlaksson, he had been at Hotel Island; they had all gone out to the yard at the south side of the hotel because the table they were sitting at began to move and the cups nearly fell off. First they had tried to keep it down, but they could not control it. In the yard, Indridi disappeared from the group without anyone noticing. The yard was surrounded by high walls on three sides, the hotel itself being on the fourth side. The yard was illuminated by light from the hotel windows, and everything was clearly visible. The only door through the wall was locked, but the hotel door was located in such a position that they would all have noticed if Indridi had gone through it. Indridi had not been seen to go through any door. Brynjolfur's account must be given less credibility than Haraldur's and Einar's as it is recorded from memory a third of a century after the events took place.

They went to Einar Kvaran's home to announce Indridi's disappearance, only to be informed that Indridi had already arrived in a trance state at nearly the same minute as they had noticed his disappearance from the yard. Indridi claimed that he was not aware of anything until he emerged from the trance at Einar's house.

It is often mentioned in the minute books that Indridi saw various communicators and knew the controls by sight, similar to what one reads in William Crookes' notes recording his sittings with Daniel Dunglas Home. Home claimed he often saw the various communicators, and those who moved objects, and touched or pulled the sitters. The sitters sometimes saw spirit hands, but not the full body. In a later chapter, we will compare the mediumship and phenomena that took place at Home's and Indridi's sittings. There are a great number of similarities.

CHAPTER 16

JON BECOMES PEACEFUL

In the end Indridi's spirit controls seem to have found some means of controlling Jon. A kind of buzzing sound was heard around Indridi when the sitters thought Jon was leaving him. When Jon had been driven out of Indridi, the control personalities said that they had poured some substance onto Indridi's forehead in order to diminish Jon's influence. Some sitters touched his forehead and reported that it felt wet as if by a foam-like oil (second minute book, p. 90).

We also read that Jon was in the end pacified through help from the spirit of Rev. Hallgrimur Petursson (1614-1674), a famous Icelandic religious poet. In the minutes for 3 February 1908, Hallgrimur Petursson brings greetings from Jon and adds that he has "brought Jon one level up from the lowest black pit. He was now in lighter spirit. For a while he suffered intolerable fits of remorse and regret over having committed suicide, and for having used his connection with this group for destructive purposes and to harm people." Hallgrimur said he watched over Jon like "a mother over her sick child" and he asked if he could bring greetings to Jon from the sitters.

After that Jon and Rev. H. Petursson could sometimes be heard talking to one another, Hallgrimur from the lips of the medium and Jon using direct voice. At the sitting on 11 March Jon speaks briefly as he swings the trumpet in all directions: "Greetings, I will come later." Hallgrimur Petursson says Jon is feeling better now is making rapid progress, but must not be connected much to the earthlife, lest his earth memories come flooding back. On 23 March he is back and carried the music box around. After that he appears more often and helps and works with the controls. He is particularly diligent in moving the trumpet, music box, fiddle, bow, and zither that are now placed in the hall, also the large table and the iron stand on which the large trumpet rested. Jon became the master at moving objects and a great friend of the medium. We read in the minute books: "Sometimes Jon got into rather long conversations with us." Sometimes Jon mentioned the disturbances that he caused. For example, he once told Kvaran: "I gave you proof when I was dragging the medium away from you, but because I got into this (mediumistic) contact, I am now feeling better, and thanks to that good man [Hallgrimur Petursson]."

The history of Jon in the mediumship of Indridi is in some ways similar to that of Runolfur Runolfsson (1828-1879) in the mediumship of Hafsteinn Bjornsson (1914-1977). When Runolfur (nicknamed Runki) first appeared, he created a major disturbance, swearing and verbally abusing the sitters (without physical phenomena however) until a man that he said was living in his neighborhood attended a sitting. He told him his leg was missing and was in his house. The sitter was ready to look for it if he revealed his name. In the end he did, and the leg was found in a wall in the house.

The leg was buried, and Runolfur became Hafsteinn Bjornson's principal control, an outspoken and distinct personality who became much liked by the sitters (Haraldsson & Stevenson, 1975). Like Jon, Runolfur had suffered a tragic death. He had been drunk and fallen asleep on the beach on his way home; the tide washed him out and he drowned.

The senior author conducted an extensive survey of spontaneous encounters with the dead through in-depth interviews with 450 persons who had reported such encounters. Deceased individuals who had died violently, namely by accident, murder or suicide, were particularly prone to appear and seemed to actively seek contact with the living. See *The Departed Among the Living* (Haraldsson, 2012c).

Indridi Identifies Jon Einarsson's Photo

When things had calmed down, the medical doctor in the Westman Islands obtained a photograph of Jon from his family. In a statement dated 14 March 1908 (attached to the second minute book), he wrote:

I placed the photo on a page in my photo album, among photos of seven other men, young or middle aged (Jon had looked rather young in spite of being around fifty). I then invited the medium to my home and told him I wanted to know if he could recognize a photo of Jon. I first showed him some photo albums, but when we got to page in the album with Jon's photo, I pointed to one or two photos and asked the medium if this was Jon. He replied, "No.". He then looked quickly at the whole page, placed his finger on Jon's photo and said: "This photo resembles him most, but it is not quite as he looked when I have seen him."

CHAPTER 17

CONTROLS AND COMMUNICATORS

As with most trance mediums, there appeared various communicators (trance personalities) in Indridi's mediumship, some of them frequently or almost at every sitting. These controls were known as "stjornendur" (plural form) in Icelandic, which means conductors or rulers. Other communicators appeared only once or a few times. The controls were seen as the organizers of Indridi's mediumship and remained in close contact with the leaders of the Experimental Society, such as Einar Kvaran and Professor Haraldur Nielsson. Contact between the leaders of the Society and the controls was either verbal through the medium in trance or sometimes by automatic writing or by direct writing. This is how it was planned and determined what kinds of phenomena and communications would be attempted. The minute books reveal that these attempts seem primarily to have been initiated by Indridi's controls. The attempts seemed particularly proof-oriented and to be directed towards producing a variety of different phenomena. The genuineness of Indridi's trance was tested time and time again by pricking him with pins on sensitive areas of his body. There was no reaction. He was in deep trance.

The minute books reveal that in 15 séances during the period from 4 December 1905 to 26 January 1906 eleven control communicators appeared: Konrad Gislason (1808–1891) at every séance; Rev. Steinn Steinsen (1838-1883) at fourteen; and Emil Jensen (ca. 1848-1898) at six; three trance personalities appeared two or three times, among them one who spoke Dutch; four appeared only once; and "disruptive entities" are mentioned a few times without further description. All the séances started with prayer and the singing of hymns. Einar Kvaran states that in the beginning the sitters did not plan or want such religious involvement. It developed at the request of the controls. Some of the singing was led by the deceased Rev. Steinn Steinsen, sometimes singing "outside," as it was described in the minute books. "Outside" is the direct translation from Icelandic and intended to mean around or near and independent of the medium.

Two years later, in another sample of 15 séances in the second minute book, covering the period from September 1907 to February 1908, there appeared on average nine communicators per séance. Konrad Gislason was at every séance, as was Sigmundur Gudmundsson (1838–1897); Rev. Steinn Steinsen appeared eight times. There were two foreigners: a Norwegian doctor, Daniel Cornelius Danielssen (1815-1894), who was present at almost every sitting and had become one of the controls, and a French lady Madame Maria Felicia Malibran (1808-1836) with a magnificent soprano voice. Jensen was also present and appeared three times in these 15 séances.

The controls had a variety of backgrounds and the frequency of participation of each at the séances changed over time, perhaps because of the particular phenomena that were being produced at the time.

In the minute books there is much talk about the power or energy that is needed for the communications: the need to gather and collect energy; addressing the lack of energy; that the energy has been stolen by undesirable entities; that the controls needed to build the energy for the next séance; that the energy is strong or weak; etc. Similar statements about "power" are found in William Crookes' description of his sittings with Daniel Dunglas Home (Crookes, 1874; Medhurst, 1972): "The power is not strong;" "the power is going;" "we are unable to do more;" "we find we have no more power;" and "... is getting more power over you...." Sometimes at the end of séances we read, "We have no more power."

The Three Classes of Communicators

In his great classic, *Human Personality, and its Survival of Bodily Death*, F.W.H. Myers (1903, vol. 2, pp. 226-227), who had been one of the founders of the London-based Society for Psychical Research, divides communicators into three classes:

A. A group of persons recently deceased.
B. A group of personages belonging to generations more remote, and generally of some distinction in their day.
C. Spirits who give such names as Rector, Doctor, Theophilous and above all Imperator. Their constantly avowed object was the promulgation of certain religious and philosophical views; and the physical manifestations are throughout described merely as a proof of power, and a basis for the authority claimed for the serious teachings.

In Indridi's mediumship the communicators fall easily into these three categories, particularly A and B. For Class C, Indridi's controls do not carry such grandiose names as found with some English-speaking mediums. Their identities, for some only reluctantly or partially revealed, is not as easily or convincingly verified as for class A.

Prominent among those in class A are those who had died violently and prematurely, either by accident, murder or suicide. It is interesting that at least two persons who died violently figure prominently in Indridi's mediumship. They are the very disruptive Jon from the Westman Islands who committed suicide, and Sigmundur who died of exposure. The French singer can be added to this list for her untimely death, aged only 28 years, shortly after falling off a horse, and thus torn away from a brilliant career at an early age.

In the mediumship of American mental medium Mrs. Leonora Piper (1857-1950) we also find that those who died violently figure prominently, and this was also the case in the mediumship of the Icelandic mental medium Hafsteinn Bjornsson (Haraldsson, 2009). A recent extensive survey of 450 personal spontaneous encounters with those who have died showed that those who die violently appear much more frequently in spontaneous apparitional experiences (30%) than is the frequency of violent deaths in the general population (9%) (Haraldsson, 2009; 2012). In the case of children who claim to remember a previous life, the figure is even higher depending upon the country, with from

61 to 77 percent of children speaking of memories of a violent death (Haraldsson, 2012, p. 228; Stevenson, 2001, p. 165).

CHAPTER 18

DIRECT VOICE PHENOMENA -
SPEAKING AND SINGING

irect voice phenomena were a prominent feature of Indridi Indridason's mediumship, voices speaking as well as singing "outside," that is, voices that would be heard away from the medium and not coming from his mouth. This is reported by our six main sources: the two minute books; by Gudmundur Hannesson, Haraldur Nielsson, Einar Kvaran and Thorbergur Thordarson; and by Sigurdur Haralz (1901-1990), the eldest son of Haraldur Nielsson, who observed this phenomenon in broad daylight and without Indridi being in trance.

In the first minute book (4 December 1905 to 6 January 1906) direct voice phenomena are reported on nine of twelve days in which some phenomena occurred, sometimes more than once during a séance. On four occasions the voices were heard singing. Voices are reported in 22 of 36 days in the second minute book (9 September 1907 to 2 February 1908), and on eleven days there is singing.

Haraldur reports that one evening 26 different personalities, each with its own personal characteristics, had spoken through or independent of Indridi, who was in a deep trance (Nielsson, 1922a, p. 17; 1924a, p. 234). Haraldur also describes independent voices occurring in full light in 1909 (Nielsson, 1925, p. 108):

It was an afternoon in 1909. I was sitting with the medium on a sofa in my own drawing room. We were deep in conversation about some irrelevant matter when, all of a sudden, we heard the voice of "Jon" coming as if from just below the ceiling. That was the only time I ever heard him speak in full daylight.

One night in 1909, Haraldur slept in Indridi's bedroom to observe him while asleep. Before the men went to sleep they chatted a little with Jon and two of Indridi's other controls. Indridi was not in trance during the conversation. They sat in Indridi's room, a light burned in the outer room, and the door was open between the rooms. Before they went to sleep, Jon promised he would wake them at a certain time next morning. At that precise moment the following morning, Haraldur woke up hearing Jon's voice shout, "Aren't you going to wake up?" (Nielsson, 1930, pp. 193-194).

Brynjolfur Thorlaksson recalls, as already reported, that two personalities sang "together" independent of Indridi, "Ak, vad vårt liv är eländigt" (a Swedish song, "Oh, how miserable our life is") (Thordarson, 1942, p. 87). Thorkell Thorlaksson and Kristjan Linnet were at this séance and remembered this particular song when interviewed by Thorbergur Thordarson.

Einar Kvaran (1910, p. 48) states that voices had spoken and sung at a distance from Indridi. The voices even sang the same melody together "at the same time," one being a powerful baritone voice and the other a beautiful female voice.

Haraldur reports on the direct voice phenomena (Nielsson, 1919b, p. 350):

I have often heard two voices speaking or singing loudly, while I was sitting alone with the medium inside the net [enclosed space] . . . holding both his hands and talking with the control.

Sometimes the control spoke through the medium while the voices were singing, but more often he was silent while the singing was going on but started speaking the moment it ceased.

The independent voices very often sang beautifully, especially three of them, writes Haraldur: "we could sometimes hear two voices singing simultaneously: the soprano voice of a lady and the bass voice of a man" (Nielsson, 1922b, p. 459).

Sigurdur Haralz

In 1985 the authors were able to interview two people who had met Indridi. One of these was Sigurdur Haralz, Haraldur Nielsson's oldest son who was born in 1901.[1] He told us he still remembered very clearly two occasions when many independent voices were heard around Indridi. Indridi was at a farm in the country to visit his fiancée, Jona Gudnadottir, who was Haraldur Nielsson's niece. Sigurdur was spending the summer at the farm. On the first occasion, Indridi was alone in the room where he was to sleep. Sigurdur described it as follows:

> Indridi was to sleep in the living room... He was alone in there, the only person. We knew he was alone. Then many voices started talking. The people of the farm were in the kitchen when they heard Indridi in the living room. ... The voices spoke as grown-ups. Direct voice phenomena were heard around Indridi in the room where he slept. He was alone in there. This happened probably in the evening before he went to sleep. ... These voices bid him goodnight. They joked with Indridi and answered each other. We heard the words. The door between us and Indridi was closed.

The second incident occurred in broad daylight. The morning after his arrival Indridi was standing on the lawn in front of the farmhouse, "probably to get some fresh air" after the night. Three people were present besides Sigurdur Haralz: Gudny Nielsdottir (1856-1947); Thorsteinn Bjarnason, a worker on the farm; and Gudny's husband. Suddenly there on the lawn all around Indridi voices started to speak to him. The voices bid Indridi good morning and asked how he was. Some of the voices were joking with Indridi, teasing him jokingly but happily, and other voices seemed to be answering each other. Most of the voices spoke one after the other, each with different characteristics. Some voices spoke simultaneously. Sigurdur did not hear any female voices; most of them were Indridi's "closest controls." Their speech lasted only a few minutes. Sigurdur was of the view that no ventriloquist could have produced these voices.

---

[1] Sigurdur and his brother Jonas, sons of Haraldur Nielsson, adopted the surname "Haralz."

CHAPTER 19

THE FRENCH SINGER AND "MUSICA TRASCENDENTALE"

Let us now turn our attention to the purported trance personalities of foreign birth who appeared frequently at Indridi Indridason's séances: the "French singer," the "Norwegian doctor," and the Norwegian composer Edvard Grieg (1843-1907).

Sometimes the French singer was heard joining the sitters when they sang a hymn at the beginning of their meetings. For 14 September 1907 the second minute book records that the French singer and the Icelandic composer Sveinbjorn Sveinbjornsson sang together, "O Sanctissima." She sang independently of the medium's vocal chords. The deceased Rev. Steinn Steinsen often led the singing at the beginning or early in the séance, and she often sang with him, both independently. Another example of two "otherworldly" voices singing at a distance from the medium and at the same time occurred on 3 October 1907: Konrad Gislason asked for music to be played (on the harmonium), then they heard singing by voices of invisible beings, such as the French singer and others. It seems that the French singer was sometimes keen to sing at the séances: on 23 January 1908 the minute book reports that "the French singer asked for permission to sing but was not allowed to do so" (presumably by the main controls).

Sometimes a choir was heard singing, as if far away. The vigorous and healthy skeptic Gudmundur Hannesson reports that at the beginning of a séance on 8 June 1909, the sitters were singing a hymn with the accompaniment of the harmonium when "an extra feminine voice was heard." On 11 June, "while music was being played so that the medium would fall deeper in trance, there sang (outside) first a bright feminine voice... and then a strong male voice." Once, for a short while, Skafti Brynjolfsson and Gudmundur heard them "sing at the same time ... Both voices were heard very close to me" (Hannesson, 1924a, pp. 217, 223). This phenomenon was not restricted to the séance room. Indridi sang sometimes in the Cathedral choir, and Brynjolfur, who was a music teacher as well as an organist in the Reykjavik Cathedral, reported: "I, as well as the rest of the choir, sometimes heard strange voices singing with them. Some of the audience also heard this. Once, one of the churchgoers said to me after the service: "You were not quite alone today; there were more than the choir singing" (Thordarson, 1942, p. 89).

The minutes report an interesting incident after a séance on 25 September 1907. Some sitters used the trance personality of the French singer to test ingeniously the accuracy of Indridi's statements about the movements of deceased persons he claimed to see. This provides further evidence of xenoglossy at the séances:

After the meeting I.I. [Indridi], Brynjolfur Thorlaksson and Thorarinn Th. Gudmundsson went to Hotel Island where they drank a cup of chocolate, etc. There they met Brynjolfur's brother, Thorkell, who joined them. From there they all went up to the experimental house. Brynjolfur played a few tunes on the harmonium and they chatted for a while. Then one of them suggested that they go into the smaller hall to see if anything would happen.

They sat down on the bench in the first row. As soon as they had sat down the curtains to the cabinet were drawn so that all could hear. Brynjolfur held both of Indridi's hands while sitting on his left side with his leg placed around Indridi's legs. Thorarinn sat to Brynjolfur's right side and held his arm, and Thorkell sat next to Thorarinn. Next Brynjolfur requested that the curtains be moved again, and they were drawn back and forth a few times. As this happened, Indridi said that he saw the Norwegian doctor standing between the curtains. A little later he said that he saw the French singer standing between the cabinet and a chimney that stood close by.

Then it occurred to them to ask Thorarinn to address her in French and get her to do something that the rest of them, who did not understand French, did not know about. He did that. Then Indridi said: "Now she bows down."

Then Thorarinn said: "This is correct. This is what I asked her to do." Thorarinn spoke to her again. Then the medium said: "Now she walks towards us, and has almost reached us when she suddenly turns around and walks to the Norwegian doctor in the cabinet, as if he was calling her."

Thorarinn responded: "This is not quite what I asked her, because I asked her to walk behind us." But as this happened the medium saw Sigmundur stand right behind us.

Next they heard that a chair or a table was thrown on the floor just inside the door or in the cabinet ... (violent movements, etc., follow).

—AUTHORS' TRANSLATION FROM ICELANDIC.

Brynjolfur also describes this incident in his memoirs and adds that "Thorarinn was convinced that no deception had taken place, neither by Indridi nor anyone else. He spent the night as Indridi's guest and they talked into the night" (Thordarson, 1942, pp. 73-78).

The French lady sang rather frequently, spoke sometimes in French, and tried also to speak in English and German. Few Icelanders spoke French in those days but there was much interest in testing her French. On 17 September 1907, the minutes relate that the Icelandic linguist Geir T. Zoega (1857-1928) took part in a séance. He addressed the singer in French and "apprehends that she understands him. He hears clearly French words and phrases in her speech, though he could not hear whole sentences."

On 25 September, the French lady "speaks to Thor Gudmundsson, who hears French words and sentences, and in addition observes, as a French speaker, that she understands him." On 13 January, "The French lady sings a little. Thor Gudmundsson and E.H. [Kvaran] converse with her, both in French and English, and check carefully that she understands both languages. She then tries to repeat a few Icelandic words." This description indicates responsive xenoglossy (Stevenson, 1984).

The minutes that have survived reveal nothing about her identity, other than that she was a French singer. The organist Brynjolfur

Thorlaksson describes an incident that in his view threw light on her identity (Thordarson, 1942, 79-81):

> At a meeting of the inner circle we heard a male voice speak French at a distance from the medium that we had never heard before. It seemed that his words were not directed at us but to someone on the other side. At the same time we heard some other voices around the medium, but rather unclearly. We did though discern among them the voice of the French singer and heard her suddenly scream in distress. It seemed as if there had been an uproar or disagreement of some kind. We did not distinguish individual words except at one time a male voice said "Madame Malibran."

> We asked the control what had happened. The answer was that the man, who had used the name to address the woman, was Malibran, and he had been the husband of the French singer who had also been there. They had not seen each other since their passings. He had learnt about her whereabouts and came to the meeting in order to get her to go with him, but she had refused. That was the cause of the uproar. More we were not told.

> None of those present had the faintest idea about "Madame Malibran" and her husband. The next day some of us looked for the name in some encyclopedias. Unexpectedly, we found that in America (USA) there had been a wealthy French plantation owner by the name of Malibran. He had married the singer Maria Felicia who was of Spanish descent; she was born in Paris 1808 and died in Manchester 1836. He went bankrupt three months after they married; she divorced him and returned to Europe.

—AUTHORS' TRANSLATION FROM ICELANDIC.

Brynjolfur adds that none of them had the faintest idea about Mr. Malibran, nor did they expect Indridi to have any idea. Nevertheless, they found that there had indeed been a celebrated mezzo-soprano singer named Maria Felicia who sang leading roles in opera houses in Paris, Naples, London and New York. She was born in Paris of Spanish parents; her father was one of Rossini's favorite tenors and she trained as a singer from an early age. While in New York it is reported that she hastily married Francois Eugene Malibran, a man 28 years her senior, whom she left a year later. She died in Manchester in 1836. Biographies (for example, Bushnell, 1979) have been written about her because she was considered one of the greatest opera singers of the nineteenth century.

There is no obvious way for us to verify anything regarding the French singer. It seems odd that Mr. Malibran was looking for his former wife who had died more than seventy years earlier. According to Bushnell's biography about her, Francois Eugene Malibran was born in Paris in 1781 of a French father and Spanish mother. He died in 1836, the same year as Maria Felicia.

Another incident is reported by Brynjolfur (Thordarson, 1942, p. 88):

> Once in the middle of the day, as often occurred, Indridi was at my home. While he was there I played on the harmonium a melody by Chopin. Indridi sat to the left of the harmonium. I expected that Mrs. Malibran knew the melody that I was playing for I heard her humming it around Indridi. Then I saw him falling into trance... I heard many voices, both of men and women singing behind me, but especially to my right with Indridi being on my left. I did not distinguish individual words, but the voices I heard clearly, both higher and lower voices, and they all sang the melody that I was playing.
>
> This singing differed from ordinary singing as it sounded more like a sweet echo. It seemed to come from afar, but was at the same time close to me. No single voice was discernible except the voice of Malibran. I always heard her distinctly.
>
> —AUTHORS' TRANSLATION FROM ICELANDIC.

Direct voice phenomena are known in the literature, with mediums such as D.D. Home (Dunraven, 1924) and Mrs. Emily S. French (1831-1912) (Randall, 2010). However, singing and music are rare. Indridi is perhaps the most extraordinarily-gifted medium able to demonstrate direct singing of many voices simultaneously. A few similar cases are reported in the early history of Spiritualism. One example is described in a letter written by Charles Partridge about "the spirit room" of Jonathan Koons (1811-1893) in Ohio (Coleman, 1861):

> I attended three public circles (open without charge to all comers) in the spirit-house of Mr Koons — a house or room a little distance

from his residence, built expressly for the purpose. The presiding spirit is an Indian named John King... After the circle is formed the door and windows are shut, and the light extinguished. Instantaneously a tremendous blow was struck upon the table by a large drumstick, and immediately the bass and tenor drums were beaten rapidly, like the roll-call on the muster field, making through the hills a thousand echoes. This continued for five minutes or more and, when ended, King saluted us through the trumpet, and in an audible voice... Presently we heard, as it seemed, human voices singing in the distance, in so low a tone as to be scarcely distinguishable; the sounds gradually increased, each part relatively, until it appeared as if a full choir of human voices were in our small room singing most exquisitely. I think I never heard such perfect harmony — so captivating was it that the heart-strings seemed to relax or to increase their tension to accord with such heavenly sounds. It seemed to me that no person could sit in that sanctuary without feeling the song of "Glory to God in the highest, peace on earth, and goodwill to all men," spontaneously rising in the bosom and finding expression on the lip.

(COLEMAN, 1861, PP. 49-50).

Another example is found with the medium Mary J. Hollis:

As soon as the room was darkened, "the birds began to sing!" I never heard such singing — the many voices blending in perfect harmony, clear, loud, musical, and bewitching. It was a love-feast of celestial melody, which we, one and all, enjoyed to the full capacity of our appreciation. This charming concert continued for about twenty minutes, unassisted by a human voice, until it suddenly ceased, and Mrs Hollis seemed to be surrounded by a multitude of spirit-voices, speaking quickly, confusedly, and in an undertone... A spirit-voice began to chant a part of the Episcopal service, and then improvised a rhapsody that was indescribably sweet and beautiful. This musical manifestation continued for about ten minutes. (Wolfe, 1874, p. 292).

And finally, an example from a London medium named Mrs. Everitt:

The sitting was terminated by the singing of a hymn by three or four soft, gentle voices, purporting to be "direct" voices, which sounded as if they proceeded from the top of the room close to the ceiling. They were certainly not the voices of any of the company present. It was one of the most beautiful and touching manifestations I ever experienced. (Bennett, 1907, pp. 34-35)

Similar reports are found in the German literature on mediumship, such as in *The Para-normal: Personal Experiences and Deductions* (1939) by Countess Nora Wydenbruck (1894-1959) (Peter Mulacz, personal communication).

Singing or music is, on rare occasions, heard by patients shortly before they die along with experiences of visions (Hyslop, 1918). The senior author reports a case experienced by Stefan Sörensson (1915-2010), a retired acquaintance who had held a high administrative position at the University of Iceland. He had been an amateur singer all his life, singing in various choirs. This is how the incident, which occurred early in 2010, was reported by his wife:

One morning when I woke up he told me that he had heard such extraordinarily beautiful singing. I woke up around seven in the morning and he asked me, "Did you hear the beautiful singing?" Because of this strange question I wondered if he was confused, although there was no other sign of it and had not been earlier. I understood this happened just as he was waking up, perhaps in a dream. "Such beautiful magnificent singing," he said. He had never heard such beautiful singing in his life. He was singing and there were many people around listening. "I thought there might have been a choir," he added. I went to the kitchen to make coffee. Then we sat up in bed reading. He appeared in good health but three to four hours later he unexpectedly collapsed and died instantly.

Is this a case of deathbed *hearing*? Had some unconscious part of him become aware of his impending death? Or, were "some forces on the other side" already approaching him, which means that they were aware of his impending death? Or, is there perhaps a more mundane explanation: two unrelated events occurring together by chance? It is interesting to speculate about this. His wife does not believe the last interpretation is valid and found his experience a very meaningful event. The Italian psychical researcher Ernesto Bozzano (1943, 1982) wrote a book about the subject and called the phenomena "musica trascendentale." Scott Rogo (1970, 1972), himself a musician, also wrote an interesting two-volume book on what he termed "psychic music."

Painting of Emanuel Swedenborg (1688-1772) in the Swedish Academy of the Sciences, of which Swedenborg was himself an early member.

The "French singer" was a frequent communicator with a magnificent soprano voice; she was believed to have been the celebrated opera singer Maria Felicia Malibran (1808–1836), who is the subject of this sketch.

The great Norwegian composer Edvard Grieg (1843–1907) was a communicator at some of Indridi´s sittings. He appeared at Indridi's seances within days of his death. Particularly interesting was the interaction between Grieg and the living Icelandic composer Sveinbjorn Sveinbjornsson.

Rudi Schneider (1908-1957) was a famous Austrian physical medium whose phenomena were investigated by several prominent European psychical researchers.

Einar Hjorleifsson Kvaran (1859-1938) was a prominent editor and writer. He started the investigation of Indridi's mediumship; he was the principal founder of the Experimental Society and its President.

Haraldur Nielsson (1868-1928) was Professor of Theology at the University of Iceland. He was one of the prinicpal investigators of Indridi's mediumship and one of the founders of the Experimental Society.

11. des. 1905   **17**

[handwritten manuscript text]

Minutes of the Experimental Society where Jensen makes several
statements about his life that were verified over a century later.

Einer Nielsen (1894-1965) in trance, seated in a cabinet during a séance
with ectoplasm draped over his lap and down to the floor. Holding his
left hand is Prof. Haraldur Nielsson. We gratefully acknowledge the IGPP
(Freiburg, Germany) for providing this photograph.

Daniel Dunglas Home (1833-1886) is history's most famous physical medium. Many scientists, kings, and famous writers were among the great number of people who had sittings with him. We gratefully acknowledge the IGPP (Freiburg, Germany) for providing this photograph.

A drawing of Daniel Dunglas Home while levitating.

CHAPTER 20

THE NORWEGIAN DOCTOR AND THE COMPOSER EDVARD GRIEG

Let us now turn to another frequent foreign communicator who was one of Indridi´s controls. The "Norwegian doctor" is first mentioned in the available minutes on 23 January 1906. He "speaks often in a distinct Norwegian," and "several characteristics of the Norwegian language were very striking in his speech." He was involved in healing attempts that are vaguely described and impossible to assess. In the 1907-1908 minutes he appears at most sittings. Not much is written about what he said except that he is sometimes asking about the health of various persons. He was, along with Emil Jensen, involved in the production of materializations and light phenomena. Einar Kvaran (1906, pp. 36-37) wrote about him:

> We could not get him to say who he was. Then it so happened at a healing session in a private home that Konrad Gislason, inadvertently, mentioned his name. He quickly started to speak about something else as if to cover his mistake. Only one person noticed the name... At another séance in the experimental house a patient lay on a bench in front of the cabinet in the smaller hall while the medium was in the main hall in a trance. Then the patient said: "Now I know the name of the Norwegian doctor." He heard him being called from the cabinet

(which was empty)... He and the man who had heard the name earlier compared notes; it was the same name. The Norwegian doctor then called one of them into the cabinet, and admitted to the name, but asked that it not be revealed and told him about a few events from his life. It has all proven correct. The medium in his waking state has often seen the doctor as one of the many invisible communicators that he is in touch with. He says he knows what they look like as clearly as the people around him on a daily basis. In this city, there exists only one photograph of this doctor, as far as I know, and it is impossible that it could have come into the hands of Indridi.

—AUTHORS' TRANSLATION FROM ICELANDIC.

Brynjolfur Thorlaksson says that identification of the Norwegian doctor happened in the office of Bjorn Jonsson. Bjorn was paging through a book when Indridi dropped in. The photograph was in the book. As soon as he saw the photo, he said, "This is the Norwegian doctor" (Thordarson, 1942, pp. 68-69).

This doctor's name was Daniel Cornelius Danielssen, born in Bergen, Norway, in 1815 and died there in 1894. He became head of a leprosy hospital, and among other achievements made pioneering discoveries in the treatment of leprosy, initiated the establishment of a scientific academy, and founded a national theatre in Bergen. He was a prominent man in Norway during his lifetime, a member of the city council for 38 years, and in the Norwegian parliament for several terms of office. He was made a member of the Royal Swedish Academy of the Sciences.[1]

The appearances of the French singer and Danielssen raise the question of whether xenoglossy occurred at Indridi's séances. The evidence for it is there, in the minute books and other sources. Was there also evidence of xenoglossy of the responsive type, meaning that the control not only spoke in a foreign language but also responded to questions in that language? Apparently this was the case with the French singer. Yet the descriptions about the Norwegian doctor leave us wanting more information. In his case, detailed evidence for responsive xenoglossy is lacking.

Jensen was the third control who spoke in a foreign language, in his case in Danish. Haraldur Nielsson writes about Jensen's speech (Nielsson, 1922a, pp. 14-15):

---

[1] Norway and Sweden were in union at that time.

As you certainly understand Jensen had great difficulties as he had to speak in a foreign language through the medium. The medium had never learned any language other than Icelandic... but Jensen succeeded remarkably well and although the words came sometimes a bit distorted from the lips of the medium, it sounded often like the best Copenhagen dialect.

—AUTHORS' TRANSLATION FROM DANISH.

Edvard Grieg

We will now continue discussion of xenoglossy and independent direct voice singing by a communicator who was not a control personality. The famous Norwegian composer Edvard Grieg (born 1843, died 4 September 1907) appeared several times according to the minute books. On 14 September 1907, ten days after Grieg's death, Konrad Gislason says that Grieg is present and asks the living Icelandic composer Sveinbjorn Sveinbjornsson to play a lullaby for him, which he does. In some ways Sveinbjorn is similar to Grieg though he did not reach such fame as Grieg did. They were contemporaries but Sveinbjorn lived for twenty years after Grieg died. They never met but had at least one mutual friend, the Norwegian composer Johan Svendsen (1840-1911), with whom Sveinbjorn once played music, so Grieg must have known about Sveinbjorn. In their musical compositions, both turned increasingly to their respective national heritage of folk music and melodies in their lyrical pieces.

Later the same evening Grieg speaks through the medium and talks for 15 minutes with the organist Brynjolfur Thorlaksson. Grieg tells Thorlaksson, among other things, that Rikard Nordraak (1842-1866), who composed the Norwegian national anthem, had influenced his music, which he learned only after he "returned home" (died). Grieg sang a melody, *Nu löftes laft og lofte*, through the medium. Jon Mannsåker of Norway has informed the senior author (personal communication) that "this song is in fact a lullaby (Norwegian: "vuggevise") written by Henrik Ibsen (1828-1906) in his historical play *Kongs-Emnerne*. Edvard Grieg composed the melody for it in 1866, the first text by Ibsen for which he had composed music. It is considered one of the best lyrical pieces by Grieg, and was composed after the birth of his only child Alexandra. So it is reasonable to see this song as very dear to Grieg."

At the next séance Grieg appears again, speaks a few words and thanks Brynjolfur for their previous séance visit. On 25 January 1908 he appears and says he had always been interested in Icelanders. This seems reasonable for there were traditionally strong cultural ties between Norway and Iceland, and both countries were struggling at this time to achieve national autonomy, within the unions with Sweden and Denmark respectively.

Grieg is known to have spent three years in Copenhagen where he would have met some Icelanders. Grieg as well as Sveinbjorn studied music in Copenhagen and Leipzig, but Grieg a few years earlier than Sveinbjorn. On 5 February he appears again and speaks of two well-known Icelanders he knew in Copenhagen. He asks one sitter (a good singer) to sing for him a certain Icelandic song (*Thu blafjallageimur*), which he does. The sitters then hear two voices singing softly around Indridi which they believe to be Grieg and Steinn Steinsen. Brynjolfur refers to this and more incidents with Grieg in his memoirs (Thordarson, 1942, pp. 86-87):

> I became acquainted with the personality who said he was Edvard Grieg once when I sat with Indridi after a séance and while he was waking up, which always took a long time. Someone always stayed with Indridi until he was fully awake, when most of the sitters left at the end of the séance. This was often left to me and I was not allowed to light up a lamp until he was awake.

> On one occasion the control said to me: "A man is there that you would like to meet." The control left and through the medium an unknown voice spoke in Danish with a Norwegian accent: "God aften, jeg er Edvard Grieg" (Good evening, I am Edvard Grieg). I replied that it was an unexpected pleasure to speak to Edvard Grieg. We talked for a while back and forth. Among the things we spoke about was the Norwegian composer Nordraak, who composed the Norwegian anthem.

> "He was rather young when he died," I said.

> "Yes, he did not live long," Grieg replies in Norwegian, "he was only 24 years old. I know now that he often inspired me after he went over to the other side."

This, I felt, was strange for I did not know how old Nordraak had been when he died. And as far as I could gather Indridi did not even know that Nordraak had ever existed and still less that he died at the age of 24.

—Authors' translation from Icelandic.

Direct Writing

Brynjolfur reports another incident involving Grieg. Once he was alone with Indridi in his apartment, playing the harmonium while Indridi hummed the melodies. He knew that sometimes direct writing took place. While Indridi was sitting in the living room, he decided to place on a table in Indridi's adjacent bedroom a piece of paper he tore out of his pocket book. He placed a pencil on the top of it and went back to the room where Indridi was sitting (Thordarson, 1942, p. 84).

> We listened and after a short while we heard the pencil fall on the table. I went into the bedroom to fetch the paper and the pencil. On the paper had been written: "Edvard Grieg."

> I had never seen Grieg's handwriting so now I was very curious to know if it looked like what was written on my paper. Somewhere — I do not remember where — I succeeded in digging up Grieg's signature. It was exactly the same writing as on the paper I had torn out of my pocket book.

—Authors' translation from Icelandic.

On this same occasion when Brynjolfur was playing the harmonium he heard the French singer sing in a low voice independent of Indridi, who was not in trance. Brynjolfur then tore another page from his pocket book, placed it on the table in Indridi's bedroom where no lamp was lit, and went back to Indridi in the living room. Then both of them listened until they heard a sound as if the pencil had fallen on the paper. Brynjolfur went into the room and saw that the pencil was no longer on the paper where he had left it, but beside the paper. On it was written "Singa sola mina vina" (in broken Norwegian/Danish/Icelandic which might mean, "Sing alone my friend," or "I sing alone for my friends"). The handwriting was large and beautiful with upright (vertical) letters. The senior author found in Bushnell's biography an example of Madame Malibran's handwriting; it appears large but not straight.

Brynjolfur recalls (Thordarson, 1942, pp. 84-85):

> At the next meeting of the inner circle Einar Kvaran, Haraldur Nielsson and I were talking about what had been written on one of the papers in Indridi's bedroom. Then one of them said that if Madame Malibran has written this on the paper, it seems that some Scandinavian had helped her, for it resembled Scandinavian languages. Then from around the medium came a reply, and we recognized the voice of Grieg for he had often been at our meetings before: "Det var mig" ["It was me"].

—AUTHORS' TRANSLATION FROM ICELANDIC.

The minute books and Brynjolfur's memoires do not mention any statements that Grieg made about his life which could be checked, and the handwriting sample is lost. The quality of Grieg's Norwegian is not mentioned, but it can probably be assumed that it was correct. Educated Icelanders, like Haraldur Nielsson, Einar Kvaran and Brynjolfur Thorlaksson, certainly knew the sound of Norwegian very well because all of them had received some of their education in Copenhagen, where there were also many Norwegian students. Norwegian and Danish are closely related, and the spelling at that time was very similar, but the pronunciation was and still is very different. Therefore, we may have here another case of xenoglossy; according to the witness reports, it seems reasonable to assume that it was of the responsive type.

A few other communicators appeared at the séances who spoke foreign languages. A Dutchman is mentioned a few times. He was asked if he spoke German, "no, only Dutch" was a reply somehow made clear to them. The minute books mention at least two personalities who spoke English (John King and Hall), but not much is written about them, only a few short sentences. The medium described John King as a very large man with a powerful voice. He spoke independently of the medium's vocal chords at three séances at least. The recorder assumed that John King was English. A control by the name of John King is mentioned in the mediumship of Jonathan Koons (see above) and Eusapia Palladino. In fact, according to Arthur S. Berger and Joyce Berger (1991, pp. 225-226), "almost every nineteenth century medium seems to have had a

John King control…. In the 1920s and 1930s John King was still around helping Gladys Osborne Leonard and Etta Wriedt." The Bergers add that "Spiritualists theorized that 'John King' was either a pseudonym for a group of controls or was a symbol of power."

CHAPTER 21

ANALYSIS OF INDRIDI'S PHENOMENA

The two surviving minute books describe 59 sittings with Indridi that took place from December 1905 to January 1906 and from September 1907 to February 1908. These records offer a unique opportunity to analyze the frequency of the various phenomena that occurred. The 59 records vary in length and have an average of 664 words.

Physical phenomena took place in 47 of the ordinary sittings which were usually attended by a large group of people who sat in rows of benches. Twelve sittings were for specific purposes, mostly for proof of identity where deceased people would be questioned about memories of their physical life that would then or later be checked for accuracy. Healing sittings were also conducted, as were sittings for discussions with the controls. In those kinds of sittings, physical phenomena rarely occurred, which was not, in any way, considered a failure.

Indridi was a relatively consistent medium in terms of performance. When he was sick, no séances were held, and they were stopped for a while during a period of violent poltergeist-like assaults that were blamed on Jon Einarsson (ca. 1856-1906) who had committed suicide on the Westman Islands.

In the 47 ordinary sittings, a total of at least 456 phenomena are mentioned, some described as occurring frequently. This averages 10 phenomena per sitting, though sometimes over forty were recorded.

It is highly unusual in physical mediumship that direct voice is the most common phenomenon. Spirit voices were recorded in 77% of the ordinary sittings recorded in the minute books. The voices were heard coming from different locations in the séance room. Each voice had its own characteristic and way of speech. The voices might be high- or low-pitched or whispers in the ear of a particular sitter, and they could be softly spoken or as though shouting, and either male or female. They were in most cases recognized by the sitters as voices of deceased people that they had known but were mostly unknown to the medium. Most of them only spoke, but a few also sang. They might address particular sitters and would respond to questions. A few spoke in a language not known to the medium; French, Norwegian, Danish or Dutch.

Next in frequency was the inexplicable movement of objects which occurred at 55% of the sittings. These movements were of various kinds: objects sliding across the floor, or furniture being lifted and carried through the air to another place; sometimes it looked as if they were thrown from one place to another. At other times objects tilted or rose into the air and levitated completely. Some of these movements were responses to requests made by the sitters, such as moving things from one place to another.

Raps or knocks were common (in 38% of the sittings), some of them made on demand. Also frequently reported was the experience of being touched or pulled as if by an invisible hand (36%).

Light phenomena were common (28%), including in different colors and shapes, and some star-like. One sitter described it as: "The lights were like stars all over the room" (Waage 1949, p. 165). At other times a cloud or a bright pillar of light was observed, sometimes as high and broad as the average man. It sometimes would move around the room at great speed. This pillar would emit enough light for Indridi to be easily seen, sometimes near and sometimes further away. Seeing a human figure in this cloud of light occurred about every seventh sitting. The human figures would always appear in a cloud or pillar of light. There were no reports of ectoplasm in Indridi's mediumship.

Levitations of the medium were frequent (26%), and once he levitated in a wicker-chair across rows of sitters.

Comparatively rare were gusts of air as if from an invisible mouth (9%), and the playing of musical instruments without any human hand being involved (6%). Dematerialization of Indridi´s left arm was observed three times and this was checked by several people by carefully touching Indridi´s shoulders, chest and back.

We discovered a letter dated 29 October 1906 that Matthias Jochumsson (1835-1920), a famous Icelandic poet and clergyman, wrote to an old friend, Georg Brandes (1842-1927), who was professor of literature at the University of Copenhagen and famous for his literary and social criticism. Matthias Jochumsson lived in Akureyri in Northern Iceland but in 1906 spent some time in Reykjavik where he met his friends Einar Kvaran and Haraldur Nielsson and attended some séances with Indridi. The relevant portion of Matthias´s letter reads as follows (Jochumsson, 1940, pp. 411-412):

> I was taken by surprise by highly interesting séances that turned my normal beliefs and concepts upside down [in Danish: "konfunderede mine vante begreber"]... A young man by the name of Indridi Indridason was causing a great uproar in the town [Danish: "gor furore in byen"]. The presentations that he made in front of my eyes were quite overwhelming... He lends the spirits his voice. He only knows his mother tongue and Danish, but through his mouth is spoken English, French, etc., yes even singing takes place with known voices. Rev. S. Steinsen sang for me a song that reminded me of the one he had sung for me and my wife in July 1870 when we visited his parish home [manse]; sung with his vibrant, particular voice. This man [Steinsen] died some ten years before Indridason was born. I ask myself, like Professor Crookes: "Am I – are we all crazy? Or what – what is this?" I have no answer. I have been a vehement denier of such things, but now I declare myself agnostic.

—AUTHORS' TRANSLATION FROM DANISH.

Our other sources tell that Rev. S. Steinsen frequently sang using direct voice at Indridi´s séances, and sometimes joined the sitters when they sang hymns at the beginning or during séances.

CHAPTER 22

D.D. HOME, THE WORLD'S MOST FAMOUS PHYSICAL MEDIUM

We will now compare Indridi Indridason's phenomena with those witnessed in Daniel Dunglas Home's mediumship and discuss their similarities and differences. D.D. Home is considered the greatest physical medium of all time and became world famous. Born near Edinburgh on 20 March 1833, he was adopted by an aunt, and accompanied her to America when he was nine years old.

In his autobiography, *Incidents in My Life*, Home (1863 & 1872; re-published 2007) describes experiences of visions he had in his early teens, such as the distant death of a friend who appeared to him "as in a cloud of brightness, illuminating his face with a distinctness more than mortal" (*ibid.*, p. 19).

Soon extraordinary phenomena, such as raps and movements of large objects, at the sitters' request, were occurring in his presence and people began to request sittings with him. Already in March 1851 a newspaper reported on extraordinary séances that usually took place in full light (*ibid.*, p. 27). Home was only eighteen and through the newspapers his manifestations "were becoming public all over the New England States" (*ibid.*, p. 27).

In 1855 Home moved to England where he held numerous sittings, some of them for famous personalities of that time. His fame spread and he held séances for kings, queens and emperors in several countries, for famous writers, poets, scientists, and hostile skeptics. An interesting report exists about sittings he had with skeptics in Amsterdam (Zorab, 1970) During his lifetime he held sittings in many European cities, including London, Florence, Paris, Amsterdam, Geneva, St. Petersburg and Baden Baden.

Home often held sittings in houses and hotels he had not previously visited and those were as successful as ones held where he had been before. He held sittings for believers, the curious and skeptics; the composition of the group had apparently little or no effect on the phenomena produced. Rarely did Home have anyone with him who could be considered a potential accomplice. Whatever the composition of the group, sometimes Home's sittings failed in the sense that no phenomena whatsoever occurred, which must have been embarrassing for him. Viscount Adare writes (Dunraven, 1870, 1924, 2011):

> ...he never took money for séances and séances failed as often as not. He was proud of his gift, but not happy with it. He could not control it and this placed him sometimes in very unpleasant positions (2011, p. 7).

In 1876, at the age of 43, Home stopped giving séances but continued to travel widely with his second, Russian-born wife Julie de Gloumeline. He died in Paris on 21 June 1886 of tuberculosis, aged 53. Home's mediumship covers some twenty-five years compared to Indridi's five years.

Daniel Dunglas Home wrote his autobiography, *Incidents in My Life*, in two volumes (first and second series). His second wife, who survived him and is often referred to as Madame Home, wrote two books about her husband, *D.D. Home: His Life, His Mission* and *The Gift of D.D. Home*, published in 1888 and 1890 respectively.

Many books have been written about Daniel Dunglas Home by admirers and critics alike, the latter searching vigorously for arguments and evidence to explain his feats in normal ways. Two have appeared since 2000, Peter Lamont's *The First Psychic: The Peculiar Mystery of a Notorious Victorian Wizard* (2005), and Patrick Waddington's *Knock, Knock, Knock! Who Is There? Or how chiefly British luminaries were or were not bamboozled by the "spirit medium" D.D. Home at London, Ealing and Florence in 1855 and what they made thereof thereafter* (2007).

One book must be mentioned that argues strongly and fairly in favor of the genuineness of Home's phenomena, *The Shadow and The Light: A Defence of Daniel Dunglas Home, the Medium* by Elizabeth Jenkins (1982).

Two sets of writings are particularly valuable for comparing Home with Indridi as they contain detailed first-hand records of a large number of Home's séances. They are comparable with the records of Indridi's sittings in the Experimental Society's minute books.

The first is *Experiences in Spiritualism with D.D. Home* by Viscount Adare (1841-1926), later 4th Earl of Dunraven, with introductory remarks by his father, the 3rd Earl of Dunraven (1812-1871). It describes 78 sittings that took place in 1868 and 1869. It was first printed for private circulation among friends in 1870, then published in the *Proceedings of the Society for Psychical Research* in 1924, and reprinted in 2011 by White Crow Books. The author writes in his preface that "the phenomena which are here recorded, occurred at all times and seasons, under all sorts of conditions – in broad daylight, in artificial light, in semi-darkness, at regular séances, unpremeditatedly without any séance at all, indoors, out of doors, in private houses, in hotels, at home and abroad - and it is probable that to this extent these experiences are peculiar" (2011, pp. 6-7).

What follows is one of the late Earl of Dunraven's reports of these sittings.

Séance No. 55. 3 March 1869

This séance was held in Adare's room. Present – Mrs. Wynne, Adare, Mr. Home, and myself. Soon after we were seated, Mr. Home went into a trance. He got up and walked about, remarking that the influence was good, and that Mrs. Wynne's influence was very pleasant. He went to the door, opened it, and said, "Ah, here is that strange spirit that came to Ashley House – Thomas, your father's friend – he is very eccentric; he says he wants to recall some conversation with your father." I said, "I hope he will do so." Adare observed that if he exhibited the same curiously abrupt and undecided manner that he did at Ashley House (*vide.* No. 44), he would probably say nothing, at any rate this night. Home said, "Oh, that was his manner; he is very eccentric." He then walked up to Mrs. Wynne, and made passes over her head, and held it between his hands, and told her that her circulation was bad (which it is), and that her liver was out of order.

He pointed to me saying, "Your influence is very good for physical manifestations; you must not think that you are any impediment to their occurrence." I had been fancying that probably my presence was rather adverse, and consequently I was unwilling to attend the séance; but I had not mentioned this to Home. He then gave Adare directions about the table. "You will place it near the window; your father will sit next to Daniel, you on his other side, then Mrs. Wynne, leaving a vacant space next to the window." We then commenced talking about his having had apparently some idea of going out of the window last night (*vide*. No. 54), and were discussing as to whether there was any real danger in his doing so; some saying they would be nervous, while others, myself amongst them, said we should feel no anxiety whatever as to his safety; upon which he remarked, "They will take care and see when the conditions are right; there need be no fear." He then spoke about one of the séances which had been held when he was not present, and said, "We do not approve of it at all; it is all wrong; the whole thing is in confusion. That sentence about B. and the wicked devil is not right; there is no wicked devil in that sense. We do not wish to enter into any explanation, we only tell you that it is all wrong." Turning to Mrs. Wynne, Mr. Home said, "John says he is coming to you tonight, and that he wants to try and put his hand in yours." Soon after this he sat down and awoke. He spoke during his trance in a loud whisper.

We took the table over to the window and seated ourselves as we had been directed. We soon heard a number of very delicate raps, like a continuous stream of little electrical sparks, which lasted for a short time; they were barely audible without placing the ear close to the cloth which covered the table. We then felt vibrations, and heard raps of different kinds, chiefly on the table, but some dull sounds like knocks, occurred elsewhere. We had extinguished the candles, but the fire gave sufficient light to see near objects well and distant ones faintly. In the recess of the window was a large box or chest with papers and other things lying upon it; one could see them, without being able clearly to distinguish what they were. The alphabet being called for, the following messages were given, with short intervals between them, during which there were frequent raps: *"God be with you. Your father Thomas Goold. You must not think we fear the cross, we love it, we also love God." "We are allowed to pray for you and watch over you."* Soon after several loud raps or knocks were heard, and the name "John Wynne" was spelled out.

About this time there were movements and sounds about the papers on the box, and Mrs. Wynne's dress was touched. Presently we had the following message: *"Could you but know the reality of my identity, and the unaltered and unalterable love I bear you, I well know it would be a source of joy to you. I have not sent you messages, for the reason that you could have no means of distinguishing the certainty of my personality."* I then said, "To whom is this message sent," and the answer was, *"You, my own."* I added, "I should like to know the name of the spirit," and was answered, *"Augusta."* At this point some interruption seemed to occur. Mrs. Wynne's dress was visibly and audibly moved about, and Mr. Home several times saw a hand; the slight sounds about the papers on the box recurred. Presently, Mr. Home's feet were moved and placed upon mine; strong movements of his arms and legs took place; his hands appeared to be drawn about in different directions, and rather violently agitated. After these movements had ceased, he said, "I feel a hand on me, pressing against my chest; and now it has, I think, taken the flowers from my button-hole." The idea came into my mind that perhaps these flowers were intended for me; I quietly laid one hand open upon my knee. Almost immediately a flower was placed very delicately in it. I then felt another flower, and tried to grasp the hand holding it, but did not succeed; it seemed to vanish, leaving the flower in my hand. Some curious manifestations now took place. The cloth on the table was lifted up, fully six inches, as by a hand. This occurred along the side next the window several times. Mr. Home saw the hand.

Mrs. Wynne became nervous, which was to be regretted, as she might probably have felt the hand as had been told her at the commencement of the séance. There were vibrations and tilting of the table, and various kinds of raps. Presently, the alphabet was called for, and the following given: *"Even should we be taken to a distant heaven, would it not be our greatest joy to fly as the..."* Here the message stopped; and we heard a rustling sound about the box in the window, which lasted two or three minutes. Adare said, "I am sure I know what this means." My hand was on my knee. I suddenly felt something touch it, which I laid hold of, and drew out from under the table; it was an arrow. We then recommenced the alphabet; and the word *"descends"* was given, thus finishing the sentence: *"as the arrow descends."* During this manifestation, as also when the flowers were being placed in my hand, Mr. Home was sitting quite still, with both his hands on the table. A sheet of paper was lying on the edge of the table next to the window, on which a pencil was placed. We presently saw the pencil moving about on the paper. Mr. Home saw the fingers holding it. Adare noticed it also, more than once, but of an undefined form. We now heard something moving upon the box by the window, and a heavy substance fell near Adare's feet. Some of us at the same moment perceived a decided smell of brandy. Adare said, "I know what it is." The following message was then given: *"You must not take stimulants for your cold."* Adare asked if he was to take none at all. The answer was by two raps, meaning, *"perhaps"* or *"a little."* Afterwards we found that it was Adare's flask that had been thrown under the table. On examining it no brandy appeared to have escaped. Soon after this a curious manifestation occurred about the table, just like the sound and motion of the vibration on board a steamer. This was succeeded by the following message: *"We deeply regret, but we have no more power. God abide with you."* During this beautiful séance, which lasted nearly two hours, the table was twice raised up from a foot to eighteen inches. The messages were spelled partly by raps and partly by tilts of the table. I was touched on two occasions, rather delicately, on the knee. The whole séance was quiet, soothing, and very impressive. D. [Dunraven]

The second is *Crookes and the Spirit World: A collection of writings by or concerning the work of Sir William Crookes, OM, FRS, in the field of psychical research*, compiled by R.G. Medhurst. This book contains detailed notes by Crookes on 24 sittings he had with Home in 1870-1872. Most of them were first published in the *Proceedings of the Society for Psychical Research* in 1889-1890. In 1874 Crookes had written *Researches in the Phenomena of Spiritualism* which describes experiments with and observations of Home. Sir William Crookes was one of the most famous scientists of his time and the material in his *Researches in the Phenomena of Spiritualism* were first published as a series of articles in the *Quarterly Journal of Science*. One sitting follows as an example of these records:

Tuesday, April 16th, 1872.—Sitting at 20, Mornington Road. From 8:50 p.m.

Present: Mr. D.D. Home (medium), Mr. Serjt. [Serjeant] Cox, Mr. and Mrs. Wm. [William and Nellie] Crookes, Mr. and Mrs. Wr. [Walter and Carrie] Crookes, Mrs. Humphrey, Mr. F.G. [Francis Galton], in the following [clockwise] order: Mr. G., Mrs. Wr. C., Mr. D.D. Home, Mrs. Wm. C., Mr. Wm. C., Mrs. H., Serjt C., and Mr. Wr. C.

On the table were flowers, an accordion, a lath, a bell, paper, and pencils.

Phenomena.—Creaks were heard, followed by a trembling of the table and chairs.

The table gently moved from Mr. Wr. Crookes to Mr. Home.

Raps were heard on different parts of the table.

Mr. F.G. was under the table when the movements were going on. There was vibration and knocks on the floor. The table moved six inches from Mr. F.G. to me; and there was a strong trembling of the table.

A shower of loud ticks by Mr. F.G. was heard, and thumps as of a foot on the floor.

The table trembled twice at Mr. F.G.'s request; then twice and a third time after an interval. This was done several times.

The table became light and heavy. Mr. F.G. tested it, and there was no mistake.

There were strong movements of the table when Mr. F.G. was under it.

Mr. Home's chair moved back six inches.

The accordion was taken by Mr. Home in the usual manner and sounded. Mr. F.G. looked under, whilst it was expanding and contracting.

We were speaking of the music, when a message was given.

"It comes from the heart. A hymn of praise."

After which beautiful sacred music was played.

The bell was taken from Mrs. Wm. Crookes, and tinkled under the table for some time. It was thrown down close to Mr. F.G., who took it.

The accordion laid down under the table by Serjt. Cox and played a few notes, when all hands were on the table. Mrs. Wm. Crookes put her feet on Mr. Home's. A big hand pushed Mrs. Wm. Crookes's feet away. The accordion played and then pushed into Mr. F.G.'s hand. Mr. F.G. held it for some time, but there was no sound, and it was given to Mr. Home.

Mrs. Wr. Crookes' dress was pulled around, while Mr. F.G. was looking on. Mrs. Wr. Crookes put her feet touching Mr. F.G.'s.

The accordion played in Mr. Home's hands. He said he felt a touch, on which there were five raps, and a message came:—

"We did."

"The Last Rose of Summer" was played exquisitely. Mr. Home then put the accordion down. There was quietness for a minute, followed by movements of the table, and a message was given:

"We have no more power."

CHAPTER 23

BASIC DIFFERENCES BETWEEN THE MEDIUMSHIP OF INDRIDI INDRIDASON AND DANIEL DUNGLAS HOME

The lives and mediumship of Indridi Indridason and Daniel Dunglas Home differed in many ways. Let us look briefly at the major differences:

- Control personalities played an important role in Indridi's mediumship, but little if any role with Home.
- Indridi's séances were held in darkness or near-darkness although phenomena also occurred spontaneously in full light. Home's sittings were usually conducted in normal light. In this respect Home was unique among mediums.
- Indridi was always in trance during his sittings and it usually took him a long time to wake up to full normal consciousness. Home was sometimes in trance but often not, or in a very light trance.
- Communications with deceased persons or spirits was much easier with Indridi, and mostly through trance speech, direct voice phenomena, or direct or automatic writing. With Home, communications or messages came primarily through the alphabet (planchette) or raps, seldom through trance speech and rarely through direct voice phenomena.

- With Home, communications or messages were short and telegram-like style. They were generally much longer with Indridi and played a greater role. Blank séances, when nothing happened, were infrequent with Indridi, and more common with Home.
- Home's arms sometimes became cataleptic or rigid but there is no mention of that with Indridi.
- There was a period of violent poltergeist assaults with Indridi, but nothing of this sort was reported with Home although undesirable influences were sometimes mentioned.
- There were several cases of spirit controls speaking in foreign languages (xenoglossy) with Indridi, but none reported with Home.
- Indridi's mediumship lasted only five years (1904-1909). Home's mediumship lasted 25 years (1851-1876). Indridi had a short life and died at the age of 28, whereas Home was aged 53. Both died of tuberculosis, a widespread disease in the nineteenth and early part of the twentieth century.
- The majority of the phenomena occurring with Indridi also occurred with Home and vice versa.
- Some of Indridi's phenomena are not reported with Home, such as apports, the disappearance of his arm, and surgery-like operations.
- With Home, we also find phenomena that were never reported with Indridi. Most famous was the astounding earthquake effect (trembling of the floor and room), handling of burning coal, and strange heat radiating from his hands.

Quantitative differences in the frequency of various phenomena

In other ways these two physical mediums differed rather significantly. The many phenomena that appeared with each varied however quite markedly in their frequency. To provide a better understanding we took the 24 sittings described by Crookes in *Researches in the Phenomena of Spiritualism* and combined them with 24 sittings described by Dunraven, by randomly selecting 24 of the 79 sittings in *Experiences in Spiritualism with D.D.Home*.

In that way we obtained 48 Home séances to compare with Indridi's 47 séances reported in the minute books. Let us see what the analysis reveals, but first a few words about our sources described in the previous chapter. Crookes, the scientist, is more succinct, yet more thorough in his description of the physical phenomena, whereas the Earl of Dunraven gives a more general description. It is also possible that Home approached these two sets of séances somewhat differently, as one was for a highly respected scientist and the other for friends.

Movements of objects were more common with Home. They took place at 81% of the séances, but at only 55% of Indridi's séances. Most other kinds of physical phenomena also occur more frequently with Home such as raps, gusts of air, odors, playing of musical instruments, touches by invisible hands, and more. There are however two major exceptions. Direct voice phenomena are the most common phenomenon with Indridi as they occur at 77% of the sittings. With Home direct voice is relatively rare; it occurs at 8% of the sittings but sounds of other kinds occur at 33% of the séances. Levitations of the medium are also more common with Indridi, reported at 26% of sittings but at only 8% with Home. The appearance of lights was comparable, at 28% of sittings with Indridi, and 31% with Home.

	Indridi Indridason	D.D. Home
Raps or knocks	38%	67%
Gusts of air	9	23
Movements of objects	55	81
Playing of musical instruments	6	44
Levitation of medium	26	8
Light phenomena	28	31
Materializations	15	46
Touches/pulls as if from invisible hands	36	60
Direct voice phenomena	77	8

Table 1. Comparison of the frequency (percentage of sittings) of various major phenomena occurring at Indridi Indridason's 47 séances and Daniel Dunglas Home's 48 séances.

These are the physical phenomena. The mental phenomena are much harder to assess in a qualitative manner. We did not attempt such an assessment but refer the reader to the chapters on the fire in Copenhagen and proof of identity where such phenomena are described. There is little of this sort with Home. In that respect, Indridi was a more versatile medium.

We recall that F.W.H. Myers placed communicators in three groups, people recently deceased, people belonging to generations more remote and generally of some distinction in their day, and spirits referred to by such names such as Rector, Doctor, Theophilous and above all, Imperator. With Indridi we find the first two categories, with the third category missing or rarely mentioned. In Home's mediumship the third is completely missing, and so are distinct personages from a previous generation. With Home the physical phenomena are prominent.

Home was carefully investigated by William Crookes; Indridi was just as thoroughly investigated by another highly respected scientist, Dr. Gudmundur Hannesson. He tested and investigated Indridi in numerous sittings through a whole winter. However, before we get to that, let us look at two other physical mediums, the Austrian Rudi Schneider and the Danish Einer Nielsen.

CHAPTER 24

RUDI SCHNEIDER AND EINER NIELSEN

L et us compare Indridi Indridason with two other famous mediums: the Austrian Rudi Schneider (1908-1957) and the Danish Einer Nielsen (1894-1965). Like Indridi, and unlike Home,
both had active control personalities and held séances in darkness or
in semi-darkness.

Ectoplasm played a great role in the mediumship of Rudi Schneider
and Einer Nielsen but was not observed with Indridi and Home. Ectoplasm was mysterious in the way that it extruded from the mediums'
bodily orifices, and from it partial or full human figures were formed.
Shortly after its manifestation, this mysterious substance vanished
without a trace.

Rudi Schneider's mediumship started at an early age after his older brother Willi Schneider (1903-1971) had already become a medium.
Rudi was thoroughly tested by investigators such as Dr. Albert von
Schrenck-Notzing (1862-1929) in Munich, Dr. Eugene Osty (1874-1938)
in Paris, and Harry Price (1881-1948) in London, all of whom imposed
strict controls. During some of those investigations, instrumental re-
cordings were made of interference from an "invisible substance" that
broke infra-red beams projected around objects that were paranor-
mally moved. The interruption of the infra-red rays coincided with the

announcement from Olga (Rudi Schneider's control) that "she was going into the ray." In that way, instrumental verification was obtained about paranormal effects and movements of objects, similar to Crookes' instrumental verification of movements at the sittings with Home. Hundreds of records exist of Rudi Schneider's séances. The German-born British psychologist and psychical researcher Anita Gregory (1925-1984) made detailed analyses of four different phenomena that took place at Rudi's sittings (1968, 1985).

Séances with:	Indridi Indridason	Daniel Dunglas Home	Rudi Schneider	Rudi Schneider
	Minute Books	Crookes / Dunraven	Schrenck-Notzing	Sittings at his home
	N = 47	N = 48	N = 84	N = 173
	%	%	%	%
No phenomena	0	Many	25	7
Movement of objects	55	81	74	89
Visible materializations	10	58	37	52
Levitation of medium	26	13	4	22
Sitters touched	36	67	8	25

Table 2. The frequency of four different phenomena taking place at the séances of Indridi Indridason, Daniel Dunglas Home and Rudi Schneider.

In table 2 we compare the frequency of the four phenomena that Anita Gregory lists for Rudi Schneider and the same phenomena occurring with Indridi and Home. By the time Schrenck-Notzing investigated Rudi his abilities had started to fade. We therefore include the last column showing earlier sittings that took place at his home. Movements were most common with Rudi, visible materializations with Rudi and Home, levitations of the medium with Indridi, and experiences of touch with Home. These four phenomena were common to all these mediums. With Schneider, Anita Gregory does not mention the phenomenon of direct voice that was so prevalent with Indridi.

Einer Nielsen is the best known Scandinavian physical medium and his mediumship started when he was a young man as did Home's and

Rudi Schneider´s. With Einer Nielsen, human figures were formed from ectoplasm that extruded from his nose and mouth; movements and levitations of objects were also observed as well as levitations of his body. He was investigated by experienced researchers, such as Schrenck-Notzing in 1921 and very thoroughly by engineer Fritz Grunewald, Professor Christian Winther and medical doctor Knud H. Krabbe later that same year (Grunewald, 1922a, 1922b).[1]

Before the beginning of the séances Nielsen was fully undressed. Both before and after the séance, all bodily orifices including his rectum, were examined. He was then dressed in a tricot; his hands and head were also covered with semi-transparent material that was sewed to his tricot. Then Nielsen was placed in a closed, transparent box-like structure (cabinet). In spite of all these precautions, ectoplasmic forms were produced both inside and outside the cabinet. The conclusion by both teams was that the phenomena were genuine.

A University Committee in Oslo attempted to investigate Nielsen in 1922. They treated him harshly, observed no phenomena and concluded that previously observed phenomena were fraudulently produced (Universitetskomiteen i Kristiania, 1922). Parallel to this investigation there was a Norwegian Society for Psychical Research investigation that was also extemely critical (Norsk selskab for psykisk forskning, 1922). Here, as in the Grunewald investigation, Nielsen had to change clothes, all bodily orifices were examined, and nothing was found. In the first three séances ectoplasmic human-like forms appeared, but none in the fourth séance. In that last séance some smell of faeces was perceived, and Einer did not want his rectum examined, but later his anus was examined. When his tricot was examined after the last séance, a 12 mm wide and 6 to 8 mm long hole was found near where his headcover was sewed to his tricot. Traces of faeces were found on Einer´s hand and at his anus along with a 3 cm long thread. Now his rectum was examined and nothing found. This committee concluded that Einer Nielsen must have been able to free his hand from the tricot, take some material from his rectum, get it through the tiny hole, portray it as an ectoplasmic form and then swallow it. None of this was directly observed but assumed to have taken place and is therefore a highly dubious conclusion. On this assumption the committee

---

[1]   Fritz Grunewald was an engineer and psychic researcher in Berlin; Professor Christian Winther was in Copenhagen, as was neurology professor Dr. Knud H. Krabbe.

concluded that the phenomena were not genuine. The world press announced Einer Nielsen as a fraud.

Eric Dingwall (1890-1986) wrote in the *Journal of the Society for Psychical Research* (1922, pp. 327-328):

> ... it is difficult to accept the committee's findings as to fraud on part of the medium. There is really very little evidence to indicate that the medium acted as the committee allege.

Einer Nielsen was invited on three occasions to Iceland, first in 1924 when he held 22 séances of which we have detailed reports (Kvaran, 1924). In light of the Oslo investigations, extraordinary precautions were taken and Nielsen was thoroughly tested. The meetings were held at the home of Einar H. Kvaran, President of the Icelandic Society for Psychical Research. Einer Nielsen also stayed with Kvaran during his visit.

The conditions at the séances were as follows: One corner of the room where the sittings were held was converted into a cabinet with two curtains down to the floor and a slip in the middle so that the cabinet could be opened and made visible. The sitters sat on 12 chairs in one row in front of the cabinet. They held hands during the séance and the harmonium was placed some distance behind them. On it was a red lamp that could emit variable light depending on the wishes of the medium or his controls. The light was always bright enough for the sitters to see each other.

Nielsen was given several sittings to get used to the new environment in which various phenomena were observed, but there were also a few sittings with no phenomena. Then tighter controls were imposed. The investigating committee consisted of two physicians, one Supreme Court judge and two other persons. First the room was carefully examined, and then Einer was brought in and undressed until he was naked. His clothes were carefully examined piece by piece by each member of the committee, his nose and mouth were examined and he was brought into the cabinet where his rectum was inspected. Nothing suspicious was found. Then his clothes were given back to him except for the jacket and his tie. A more detailed description is available from the senior author and published in *Dansk Tidsskrift for Psykisk Forskning* (Haraldsson, 2010).[2] After this, other

---

[2]   The English version of the detailed description of the Icelandic sittings with Einer Nielsen is deposited in the Erlendur Haraldsson fonds at

sitters were invited into the séance room; those sitting close to the medium were also inspected.

After the séance started, a whitish figure appeared through the opening of the curtains. She was clearly visible with a headscarf and her skirt was wide and half length. She disappeared and then the lower part of the skirt became visible. She appeared again but her face was unclear. At one time the curtains were opened and the medium was seen in his chair with ectoplasm from his chest down to his knees, wide at his chest but becoming narrower further down. It was not like a flat piece of cloth or scarf but a thick, shining white mass. Then the curtain was closed again.

Later in the sitting the curtain was lifted at the wall and the sitters nearby saw the medium with ectoplasm from his chest up over his face and above his head. They found no indications of fraud, and there was no smell or trace of faeces in any of the Icelandic sittings. The report of the committee was signed by all its members.

Einer Nielsen also conducted telekinetic sittings where he sat in the middle of a circle with both of his hands held by sitters at his side. Objects on a table and on the organ were lifted and moved around, sometimes touching the sitters. Three times he levitated at such sittings so that those holding his hands had to stretch their hands as high up as they could.

In summary, the sitters made the following observations regarding the forms that appeared: The human forms were various sizes, tall and short; also the hands were of various sizes, including the hands of small children. Sometimes the lower part of a figure was seen but not the upper, and vice versa. The figures had veils of varying length and sizes. Some of the figures could be seen distinctly, others were nebulous and dark. On a few occasions, the medium was seen with a figure at its side and once with one on each side.

Direct voice phenomena, so common with Indridi, were not observed with Einer Nielsen or Rudi Schneider, nor were the lights of various forms and colors that were common with Indridi. In this way, these mediums differed significantly. In fact all four mediums, Indridi Indridason, Home, Schneider and Nielsen had their particular characteristics, one type of phenomena occurring with one of them and not or to a lesser extent with the others.

---

the University of Manitoba Archives & Special Collections, MSS 459 (accession A15-77).

What all of them had in common were inexplicable movements of objects around them, and most important for all of them was contact with those who had died. Spirit communication was central to the Spiritualist movement, in which these mediums played an important role in their native countries and internationally.

CHAPTER 25

CONTEMPORARY CRITICISM

We have provided an overview of the development of Indridi Indridason's mediumistic phenomena. Appendix A contains a summary of the sequence in which the phenomena occurred. It seems reasonable next to examine criticism of Indridi as it appeared in the contemporary popular press in Iceland.

Contemporary sources reveal that in Iceland Indridi became undoubtedly one of the most famous public figures of his time. Fierce controversy raged about him in the Reykjavik newspapers from 1905-1908 and some, especially *Logretta, Reykjavik* and *Thjodolfur*, seemed determined to have him charged with and convicted of fraud. For lack of evidence, however, no case was brought against him. Other publications, for example, *Fjallkonan* and *Isafold*, accepted the Experimental Society's viewpoint and supported Indridi.

The contemporary criticism published in the newspapers can be divided into four main categories:

1. Jokes, sarcasm and scorn about Indridi and some of the Society's members.
2. Political criticism of Einar Kvaran and Bjorn Jonsson, who were also actively engaged in national politics. They were accused of using Indridi to attract votes for their party (Thjodraedisflokkurinn). However, there is no evidence that Indridi made any difference whatsoever to the political fortune of that party or that they ever tried to use his mediumship to gain votes.

3. Theological criticism, mostly from fundamentalist sects, that the phenomena were evil, of diabolical origin.
4. Criticism of healing experiments. Indridi's healing ability was disputed by the newspapers that were against the Society. Other newspapers claimed that he had healed many people, but no detailed accounts were given, nor any names of people reportedly healed. We have rather detailed accounts of experiments to heal a certain Jon Jonsson, but the results appear to have been ambiguous. Healing was not a prominent feature of Indridi's mediumship and only practiced for a short period.

Apart from the healing experiments, no substantive contemporary criticism appears to have been directed at any particular phenomena or psychic occurrences. Accusations were however made regarding personalities that were supposed to have appeared at Indridi's séances, but who were still alive (*Logretta*, 1908; *Reykjavik*, 1908b). *Logretta* (1908, p. 207) published, for instance: "A man who came there [to Einar and Indridi] from here [sic], and who had heard mention of their conversation with the deceased spirit of Thordur, told them the story [probably that Thordur was alive]. They reacted as if somebody had poured cold water over them." Einar Kvaran responded to the accusations and reported that none of the gossip had been true (Kvaran, 1908, p. 278).

The criticism of Indridi was mostly general and non-specific. It came most often from those who did not attend any of his sittings and seems to have been predominantly conjectural. In reading through the contemporary newspapers, we note that those few who did actually attend sittings, and afterwards criticized Indridi's phenomena, complained about the séances taking place in darkness and reported that they had not been able to observe properly what was going on (*Reykjavik*, 1908a). The contemporary newspaper articles that made accusations were, in our opinion, short on substance and consequently of little value. For instance, Agust H. Bjarnason (1875-1952), later Professor of Philosophy and Psychology at the University of Iceland, wrote after attending a single lecture presented by Einar Kvaran about the phenomena (Bjarnason, 1906, p .82):

> What, furthermore, proved the truth to me that the medium was hysteric and epileptic or at least something in that direction, is what has been told about his mother: that she is or had been hysteric, especially at the time when she married. She had then frequently

fallen into a coma and stayed in that condition for a long period of time.

—AUTHORS' TRANSLATION FROM ICELANDIC.

Although the person who wrote this was a prominent academic, to the best of our knowledge, there is no evidence to support the claim that Indridi was either hysteric or epileptic. Einar Kvaran reported that, because of their fathers' involvement in the Experimental Society, his children and those of Haraldur Nielsson had not had any "peace" in the streets of Reykjavik, although later on public opinion turned in their favor (Kvaran, 1934). Sigurdur Haralz (personal communication, 1985) recalls that some people threw stones and snowballs at him as a child solely because of his father's involvement with the Experimental Society.

Einar Kvaran was accused by some of the newspapers of lying when reporting the phenomena; he was also accused of being Indridi's accomplice in fraud.

For instance, in the newspaper *Reykjavik* (1906b, p. 43) was written:

Nobody thinks that Mr. E.H. [Einar Kvaran] has lost his wit, so either this activity of his must be caused by credulity of an extreme sort, or he is an accomplice in this sorcery, in which case it is an unmitigated shame to present this to the believing public.

—AUTHORS' TRANSLATION FROM ICELANDIC.

Two years later, an article in *Reykjavik* (1908b, p. 197) continued:

Icelanders have now got charlatans, moreover, professional charlatans. These are the ghost-conjurors. *Einar Hjorleifsson* [Kvaran] brought this sorcery into the country, like so many other things. . . .

—AUTHORS' TRANSLATION FROM ICELANDIC.

Finally *Reykjavik* (1908b, pp. 205-206) summarized its previous criticism as follows and said the charlatans had:

1. Made spirits do surgical experiments on sick people;
2. Made deceased skalds [ancient Scandinavian poets] write poems and novels;

3. Organized a congregation in Reykjavik;
4. Built a "temple;" and that:
5. Their congregational fee was higher than in the Christian congregation;
6. Einar and Indridi had gone around the country to demonstrate their sorcery;
7. They had taken fees for the shows;
8. They had refused Stefan Stefansson, school director, admission to the shows;
9. They had everywhere refused to use light;
10. Indridi had once been seen to kick a chair that a spirit was supposed to have transported;
11. Bjorn Jonsson had on that occasion been hurt on his head;
12. The conjurors had said that a man was dead when he was alive.

Reykjavik related these 12 facts and added that Einar Hjorleifsson Kvaran and Indridi Indridason had deceived people at these shows.

.. *Reykjavik* will not stop until the imposture of *Einar and Indridi* has been demonstrated. They both *say that* their sorcery is supernatural, but they must both know that this is untrue, and receive nevertheless money from people for that. But this is imposture.

—AUTHORS' TRANSLATION FROM ICELANDIC.

The only item in the above criticism that is relevant to the question of the paranormality of the physical phenomena is that Indridi had on one occasion allegedly been seen to kick a chair that was supposed to have been moved by "spirits." Unfortunately no details are given, so this criticism cannot be properly assessed. Einar (Kvaran, 1908, p. 278) replied that the accusation was untrue and said that there was no ground for this gossip. Bjorn Jonsson added, at the end of the same article, that he had received a wound to his head when a chair on which he was sitting at his home had broken, causing him to fall and hit his head on the window frame.

No evidence was presented to accompany the accusation that Einar was Indridi's accomplice in producing the phenomena by fraud. A relevant point is that Indridi's phenomena were also reported to have occurred on many occasions when Einar was absent. The reason Einar Kvaran was singled out as an "impostor" may have been that he was the first to publish the Experimental Society's results with Indridi, and he kept on doing so in Icelandic newspapers for as long as Indridi acted as a medium. Furthermore, Einar was involved in Iceland's national politics and had political ideas that were in opposition to the newspapers that attacked him. We know of no source that accused Haraldur Nielsson or Gudmundur Hannesson of being Indridi's accomplices.

Further Comments and Criticism of Indridi's Mediumship

The loudest criticism of Indridi's mediumship came from religious groups and persons who never attended a séance. They accused Indridi and those around him of resurrecting old superstitions and of conjuring up the dead; they saw the devil behind the phenomena. No reply is needed to such accusations.

Brynjolfur Thorlaksson mentions in his memoirs that Indridi was a great imitator and that that was sometimes used to accuse him of conscious or unconscious ventriloquism. This might, however, explain voices of people Indridi had known but most of the communicators were personalities he had never met, which is obvious when we recall his young age. This could, at best, be a potential explanation for very few of the voices that were heard and recognized by sitters. On the other hand one can speculate that Indridi's ability to imitate and sing may have made it easier for the forces that acted upon him to stimulate the responses they desired.

Moreover, a considerable part of the talk at séances was direct voice, namely not coming from the medium's throat but from the space somewhere around him, sometimes some distance away, like a whisper in someone's ear while the medium was held in another part of the room. Sometimes two voices independent of the medium spoke with one another or at the same time. This cannot be explained by imitation. Gudmundur Hannesson (1924b, pp. 266-267) wrote that some persons reported hearing two voices speak at the same time:

> They declared that this had happened, and I think it inconceivable that anybody should by ventriloquist means be able speak in two voices at the same time. I never heard this and therefore was so bold as to doubt the story.

However, at least there happened one thing which greatly surprised me, and which decidedly seemed to clash with the theory of ventriloquism. It was a frequent occurrence to hear the voices sing, sometimes short and faintly, sometimes loudly and whole melodies. At least twice I heard two voices sing the same tune together as plainly and distinctly as one could wish. One was the sonorous voice of a woman, the other a trembling bass voice of a man. Both these voices came from the inner quarter where, as far as I know, nobody was then but the medium, and the distance between them (the voices) was at least eight to ten feet. This observation was too distinct to leave any possibility for doubt...

Since I have spoken of the singing I may mention that it was frequently the product of genuine art and gave the indubitable evidence of trained and skillful singers. A member of the Society, one of its best judges of music, told me that, in his view, the best proof of the genuineness of the phenomena was that nobody in the house could sing with such perfection as the voices sometimes evinced.

The movements and levitations of objects and of Indridi himself might be divided into two categories, the first being those occurring in the darkness of the séance room. Gudmundur was allowed to impose all the controls he wanted, apart from lighting where with permission he was usually allowed to light a light very briefly. He isolated the medium, and one or two persons who held the medium, from the sitters by fastening a tightly knit net across the hall with only one small opening which he guarded himself. In spite of this the movements continued. He placed phosphorescent spots on some objects, and they could then be seen flying around the room, often in irregular movements. The ever extremely cautious Gudmundur wrote (Hannesson, 1924b, pp. 260-261):

I continued to attend séances of the Society for a whole winter, and there was hardly one at which I did not try to detect fraud in one way or another. At almost every séance I noticed something which I considered suspicious, sometimes very suspicious, and at the next one I used to be especially vigilant on that particular point. But in spite of all, I was never able to ascertain any fraud. On the other hand the bulk of the phenomena were, as far as I could judge, quite genuine whatever their cause may have been. A great many things I had no means of investigating, and so can pass no judgment as to whether they were genuine or not.

There was particularly one species of these wonders which I did all I could to investigate, viz., the unaccountable movements of inanimate objects, apparently independent of any living being...

I am acquainted with various tricks used by jugglers for imitating the phenomena. The movements were often of such a nature that to do them fraudulently would have been exceedingly difficult, e.g., taking a zither, swinging it in the air at an enormous speed, at the same time playing a tune on it. This was however frequently done while I was holding the hands of both the medium and the watchman and there seemed no way for anybody to get inside the net. Sometimes the moving required such force that nothing could explain it unless there was an able-bodied man in the inner quarter working at his convenience. But against this explanation there were two objections: (1) that there seemed to be no way open into the place; and (2) that a light was often lit so suddenly that such an assistant would have had no time for escaping.

During the poltergeist period some of the phenomena occurred in full light and were witnessed by more than one witness. Such was, for example, the case when two persons who controlled Indridi saw that he had been lifted into mid-air above his bed and seemed about to be thrown out through a window. With considerable effort, Indridi's protectors managed to drag him down on to his bed. On this evening he was also dragged along the floor as if by invisible hands. The cause of these violent movements, and the throwing and breaking of objects, was assumed to be the disruptive spirit of "Jon" from the Westman Islands.

Einar Kvaran (1906) wrote that rumor spread through Reykjavik that Indridi used a particular type of lamp to produce the light phenomena. Einar provided a two-fold answer to this criticism. This lamp was not able to produce a variety of different colors and light of varying brightness. Secondly, Indridi lived at the Kvaran home at this time (the experimental house had not yet been built) and Einar and his wife knew what belongings Indridi had with him. Never did they have any suggestion that there were any lamps or other suspicious equipment in his possession.

With good reason perhaps, one tends to be particularly suspicious when famous or historical personages appear at séances. This, however, is not unique with Indridi and is well known in mediumship. Such communicators are part of F.W.H. Myers' "B" group (see chapter

17, Communicators and Controls). There were some of these controls with Indridi. The case of Grieg is one, although his appearance may be understandable given the likelihood that he had known some Icelanders from his several years' stay in Copenhagen. The fact that so much singing and music took place at Indridi's séances and the presence of the musician Brynjolfur Thorlaksson and the composer Sveinbjorn Sveinbjornsson might also explain Grieg's participation.

Much more remote are the appearances of Kjartan Olafsson and Gudrun Osvifursdottir which undeniably fall into Myers "B" group. They are leading figures in a famous saga written in the thirteenth century and are once or twice mentioned in the minutes as communicators. On several occasions the nationally famous religious poet Hallgrimur Petursson (1614-1674) appeared. He wrote a hymn that is still sung at almost every funeral in Iceland. Jorgen Jorgenson (1780-1841) can perhaps be included in this category. He was a Danish adventurer who, as a commander on a British warship, captured Iceland and declared it independent during the Napoleonic wars. The British Navy soon captured him and sentenced him to be transported to Australia for life. None of these persons revealed anything new or unexpected about their lives. Nothing like what we have in the remarkable case of Emil Jensen whose identity was discovered and "proven beyond a reasonable doubt."

In Indridi's mediumship the overwhelming majority of communicators fall into Myers "A" group, namely persons recently deceased.

CHAPTER 26

DR. GUDMUNDUR HANNESSON'S INVESTIGATIONS

In the winter of 1908-1909 the phenomena were mostly the same as those of the preceding winter, except that the light phenomena continued only as nebulous fog-like light. There are reports of direct voice phenomena (frequently loud singing), levitations and movements of objects, musical instruments being played, and touches as if by invisible hands. The Society made attempts to make precise measurements of how objects moved and were transported through the air. Other phenomena such as gusts of air and direct writing (as if by invisible hands) were also reported.

During this period, Dr. Gudmundur Hannesson asked the Society for permission to attend séances in order to investigate Indridi and his phenomena (Nielsson, 1922b, p. 462; 1924a, p. 235). Gudmundur was held in the highest regard in Iceland as a scientist. He was appointed Professor of Medicine at the University of Iceland in 1911, and he held that position until his death in 1946. He had conducted medical as well as anthropological research; he founded the Icelandic Scientific Society and he served two periods as President of the University of Iceland. He was also a member of the Reykjavik City Council. He was an Honorary Member of both the Icelandic and Danish Associations of Physicians. The University of Iceland awarded him an honorary doctorate after his retirement. Dr. Hannesson had a greater reputation as a scientist in Iceland than any of his contemporaries; he was known for his integrity and impartiality.

Dr. Hannesson's request was accepted and he chose as his assistant an ophthalmic surgeon, Bjorn Olafsson (Nielsson, 1922a, pp. 27-28). Gudmundur and Bjorn knew Haraldur Nielsson personally but they had not participated in any of Indridi's séances. Gudmundur seems to have been known for his disbelief and skepticism about the reports of the phenomena (Nielsson, 1922b, p. 462; 1924a, p. 235). Gudmundur's report was published as a serial in an Icelandic weekly newspaper (Hannesson, 1910-1911) and much later it appeared in the *Journal of the American Society for Psychical Research* (Hannesson, 1924b). The report has been reprinted twice in Icelandic periodicals (Hannesson, 1951; 1973).

Gudmundur's First Séance

Gudmundur Hannesson attended his first séance to get acquainted with the setting and phenomena. On that first occasion, he did not demand any experimental controls (Hannesson, 1951, pp. 27-31). The séance was held in the evening. When the large hall of the experimental house (having about 100 seats) had been filled, the door was locked. Closed shutters already covered the large windows of the hall. Indridi and his watchman seated themselves on two chairs in an empty area in front of the sitters, who sat in rows on benches. As already explained, the watchman was to control Indridi during the sitting by holding him. The following phenomena occurred:

> Indridi fell into a trance and spoke with a totally different voice: "Good evening. How are you?" Greetings were also heard from many different directions in the empty space around Indridi and his watchman, most of them close to Indridi, but some quite far away. Other voices were heard in the corners of the hall or close to the ceiling. All voices had unique characteristics; each spoke in its own way.

> A trumpet was apparently moved from a table, because through it a voice spoke close to Gudmundur's ear and then the voice was again heard high above the floor at different locations in the hall. Often sitters called to the watchman and asked about the medium while this was going on, but he always reported that Indridi was

sitting quite still in his chair and that he was firmly holding both of Indridi's hands.

A musical box was moved. It spun about at high speed in the air and played a melody. It sounded as if it was circling close to the twelve-foot-high ceiling and "possibly striking against it" (Hannesson, 1924b, p. 245).

However, the ceiling was so high that nobody could have reached it. Furthermore, the music box was heavy and there was complete silence in the hall while it was moving. No footsteps were heard on the wooden floor that would indicate a man walking about with it. At the same moment somebody asked about Indridi, and the watchman said he was sitting motionless but shivering and he was holding both of Indridi's arms. Then the music box landed with a thump on the table again. The big trumpet was pulled along the floor on the iron stand, and tumbled over. The "tin funnel," which was possibly a smaller trumpet, was then moved about on the floor in a noisy manner.

The table on which the music box stood moved and rocked to and fro along the floor until finally it was turned upside down. One of the benches with sitters on it was pulled and dragged along the floor. All loose objects in the room seemed to be more or less in motion.

Voices were heard, and knocks were audible on the walls. The knocks responded to sitters' questions. If someone asked for a resounding blow to be struck against the ceiling or some other place not easy to reach, it was at once heard coming from the location requested. Sitters also spoke to the independent voices, which instantly replied. Gudmundur commented on these conversations (Hannesson, 1924b, pp. 245-246):

Further, there are the voices speaking, many of which cannot be distinguished from those of living people. They reply unreservedly when spoken to; sometimes humorously, sometimes solemnly, just according to the individual inclination of each one. We may happen to converse with a humorist making fun of everything; or a deceased clergyman may raise his voice and say a pathetic prayer. It is, however, quite common that the voices of those appearing for the first time are hardly intelligible but gradually become plainer as time goes on.

These "dead" people are questioned about anything between heaven and earth, but little benefit is derived from their answers, and it is not unusual that they commit themselves to actual mis-statements about things known to persons who are present. They seldom have a clear recollection of their life here. Their answers vary greatly, but most of them are unlike what one would expect from the spirits of eminent personages.

At the end of the two- or three-hour long séance, Indridi's control woke him by shouting, using direct voice, quite close to his ear, "Wake up!" But Indridi tended to fall back to sleep. After three such calls he regained consciousness. Gudmundur described the situation as follows (*ibid.*, p. 246):

> The voice shouts once more and the medium jumps up in consternation. He is somewhat confused and asks if the members are present. When a light is lit he again starts and turns his face away from it. Apparently he is not fully awake yet; he staggers out of the hall hardly able to keep on his feet.

Experimental Controls at Gudmundur's Second Sitting

As described earlier, the experimental house had been built according to the Society's specifications (see Figure 1 on page 191). Gudmundur satisfied himself that there was neither a cellar below the floor nor space above the ceiling, the roof being flat. It would be easy to discover any interference with the wooden floor, as it was covered with linoleum, which would "soon betray any interference" (Hannesson, 1924b, p. 248). Gudmundur divided the hall into two parts by firmly nailing a net from the ceiling down to the floor and out to the walls on both sides. Thus the sitters' benches were separated by this net from where the medium and the watchman sat which was about one-third of the hall. Gudmundur describes the net as follows (*ibid.*, p. 248):

> It is made of strong yarn and the meshes are so small that it is quite impossible to get a hand through them. It is fastened on all sides with laths [strips of wood], which are threaded through the meshes and screwed firmly to the walls, the ceiling and the floor.

Shortly before the next séance began, Gudmundur checked that the laths were securely fastened and the knots of the mesh were firm and did not slide. In the middle of the net, down by the floor, a slit provided an opening to the inside (we are not told the size of the slit). Gudmundur continues (*ibid.*, pp. 248-249):

> We [Gudmundur and his assistant] examine the floor [inside the net]. It is covered with linoleum, which is apparently sound, with closely joined edges. Then the walls. They are ordinary unpainted panels. No suspicious joinings or movable parts are detected. The panel is nailed down in the ordinary manner. In one corner there is a cupboard in the wall containing a miscellany of small things. We examine it, lock the door and seal it. Finally there is the ceiling. It is of panels like the walls and nailed in the usual way. We examine the lectern, the chairs, the table, and the few other things that are in the place: every movable article is carefully searched for secret contrivances, but nothing of a suspicious nature is found. And no hidden cords are to be found.
>
> We now take the table and other movable articles which were so close to the medium that he might have reached them with his hands or feet. These we move eight to ten feet away. There are then left in the center only the two chairs on which the medium and the watchman are to sit.

In the Icelandic report about this séance, a more detailed description is given, mentioning further precautions, such as the fact that: Gudmundur examined all crevices in the walls, the floor and elsewhere for hidden threads, and scraped with iron into the crevices when they could not see clearly into them (Hannesson, 1951, p. 35). No strings were found. After Indridi and his watchman were seated behind the net, the slit in the net was carefully threaded together with string, which was tied with a knot and the ends sealed with a seal that Hannesson kept in his pocket.

The second séance that Gudmundur attended was similar to the first one, that is, the same number of people attended, the large hall again was full to capacity, and similar phenomena occurred. Haraldur Nielsson, who acted as watchman to control the medium, was repeatedly asked about Indridi's position, especially when something was taking place. He always stated that he was holding one or both of Indridi's hands and that Indridi was sitting still. Once or twice a match was lit, and sitters could then see the medium sitting in the same position as the watchman had described.

One incident is of particular interest here. Gudmundur reports (Hannesson, 1924b, p. 250):

Suddenly we are startled by hearing the music box (which was placed in the empty [enclosed] area but out of reach of Indridi) play a tune and circle around in the air at a great speed.

We at once ask the watchman (Haraldur Nielsson) what the medium is doing. He says that the medium is sitting motionless in the chair and that he is holding both his hands.

If the watchman were not a man of unquestionable integrity we should have no hesitation in calling him a liar. . . .

It [the music box] now falls on the table with a great thump. The old familiar voice roars through the trumpet that he has not been at a loss to move the music box, though it was further away from the medium than usual. He is proud of it and asks us what we think of his performance.

Then began "the same game as at the previous séance: every movable thing goes mad and tumbles about. It is anything but quieter [i.e., it is even noisier] than it was on the former occasion" (Hannesson, 1924b, p. 250).

An examination of the seals, as soon as a lamp was lit at the end of the séance, revealed that they were intact. Gudmundur and his assistant went into the enclosed space and carefully examined everything, to see if they could spot anything that could possibly give them a clue as to the source of the movements, but found nothing.

CHAPTER 27

HANNESSON IMPOSES STRICTER CONTROLS

A t the third séance Gudmundur Hannesson imposed stricter controls. Again the hall and every item in it was carefully searched from floor to ceiling (Hannesson, 1924b, p. 252):

No effort is now spared in examining everything as minutely as possible. The hall is searched from floor to ceiling, and also every article that is in it. Nothing seems too trivial to be suspected that it may in some way serve the purpose of the impostors.

This is no joke, either. It is a life-and-death struggle for sound reason and one's own conviction against the most execrable form of superstition and idiocy. No, certainly, nothing must be allowed to escape.

We undress the medium and examine his clothes. The watchman invites us to examine him. Also the door is locked and sealed and also the cupboard in the wall. The slit in the net is not fastened this time. We are sitting close in front of it, and can watch it.

The Icelandic version of his report provides a few additional details about precautions taken, that the whole hall was carefully investigated, including all the benches, tables, etc. (Hannesson, 1951, p. 39). Furthermore, Gudmundur reports that the doors of the hall were locked and sealed, namely both doors of the hall: one providing entrance to the materialization room and the other leading to the lobby. Only five persons were allowed to attend this séance. Indridi Indridason and his watchman sat inside the net on two chairs, but Gudmundur and his assistant sat outside, with Einar Kvaran seated between them. Neither singing nor music was allowed, so that possible footsteps, opening of shutters and other movements could be heard more easily.

The following occurred. Indridi's control personality remarked that this might be an unusually noisy sitting, since some new and uninvited "visitors" ("spirits") had arrived. Independent voices were then heard swearing.

Objects were thrown to and fro with great force. The two researchers lit a match and saw the watchman, Haraldur Nielsson, and Indridi in the same position as the watchman had reported when things were thrown. They were sitting, and Haraldur was holding both of Indridi's hands. The chair was roughly snatched from under Indridi and thrown into a corner: it sounded as if it had broken. Haraldur got up to support Indridi, who appeared to be very weak. Haraldur's chair was immediately thrown away.

Gudmundur reports (Hannesson, 1924b, p. 253):

> The watchman asks for the chairs to be brought back to him, so that he need not leave hold of the medium. I offer to go in and fetch the chairs, and a match is lit while I slip through the [slit in the] net. I can see the two men standing in the center, and every article inside the net. The chair is lying out in a corner. I make for it, and in spite of the dark I find it at once. The very moment that I turn round to take the *chair I am struck a heavy blow in the back* [Gudmundur's emphasis], as if it were with a closed fist. Yet a few seconds previously there was nothing to be seen in that corner. I forthwith take the chair to the men and find them standing exactly as before.

When asked, the watchman said that they had stood there all the time without moving. Then Gudmundur fetched the other chair and left the enclosed space through the opening in the net. Gudmundur continues (ibid., p. 253):

> Some moments later the watchman shouts, saying that things are getting serious, for the medium is now drawn up into the air with his feet turned towards the ceiling and his head downwards; and that he

is pulling at both his (the medium's) shoulders. We hear a good deal of struggling going on, the combatants shifting backwards and forwards about the floor. The watchman says that the medium is pulled with such force that he is put to the limit of his strength to keep hold of him.

After a while the pull is slackened, the medium sinks slowly down and the watchman manages to put him on the chair.

Then what seemed to be the independent voices of the "uninvited visitors" said that they were going away to get more power. When the uninvited visitors "returned," the chairs on which Indridi and the watchman were seated were repeatedly snatched away and finally broken to pieces. Gudmundur continues (*ibid.*, p. 254):

Suddenly the commotion starts afresh and the voices speak again. The chairs under the medium and the watchman are time after time snatched away and finally broken into pieces. The medium is pulled up into the air with so much force that the watchman, as he says, is repeatedly almost lifted off the ground. All this is accompanied by so much scuffling and struggling that apparently it is going to be unavoidable to go to the aid of the watchman, who is exerting himself not to let the medium go—up into the air!

The scuffle is now carried towards the lectern. Suddenly the watchman shouts that things have taken a dangerous turn, for the medium's legs have been quickly pulled down into the lectern while the small of his back is resting on the edge. He fears that the medium will not be able to stand this and that it will result in disaster, for while he is pulling at his shoulders with all his strength "the others" are pulling at his legs.

We are about to go inside to give assistance, when we hear some still rougher shuffling and the watchman says that everything is again all right. He has, he explains, put one foot against the lectern and in that way been able to pull the medium out and get him on the floor. The tumult now ceases.

Independent voices were frequently heard speaking, using rude language and threatening the medium. At this point (according to the voices), the "uninvited visitors" went away again to fetch more power. The watchman said he had clasped his arms around Indridi's waist and pinned his arms down. Additionally, he said, he was squeezing both Indridi's knees tightly between his own. Gudmundur lit a match and saw them on the lectern step, in the position described.

The uninvited visitors "returned" and the pulpit was pulled once or twice so that it sounded as if everything was breaking.

A terrific crash was heard and a heavy thump. The watchman and Indridi had been thrown into the air and fallen on the floor. The whole lectern had been torn loose. It had been built at the same time as the house and firmly nailed to the end wall. The upper part of the step (to the lectern) was equally firmly nailed to the lectern, but not quite so securely fastened to the floor. Haraldur, the watchman, reported on this incident (Nielsson, 1922b, p. 463):

> After a terrible struggle with two vulgar entities, while I kept my arms around the shoulders of the medium, pressing his legs between my knees, a pulpit situated near the wall inside the net and solidly fastened by nails to the floor had its panels all of a sudden jerked upwards from the floor and flung outwards to the net. It will be observed that this involved wrenching the woodwork out of the floor as well as from the wall, the pulpit being firmly fixed to both. After this I, myself, while continuing to hold the medium was thrown with him up into the air, so that we crashed to the floor violently, I, with the result of swollen hands, he, with a little perceptible sore caused by a nail upon which he fell.

Gudmundur found something bulging through the net near the bottom, and noticed it was the corner of the lectern. He grasped hold of it with his hands and challenged the "spook" to pull it away. "Eat hell," replied a voice, and the lectern was dragged, with considerable force, a little way along the floor.

Gudmundur reports (Hannesson, 1924b, p. 255):

> I cannot refrain from retorting in some uncomplimentary term. By way of reply I get some broken glass, and other rubbish that was lying on the floor, thrown into my face. This was thrown from the empty [enclosed] quarter and from a different direction [Gudmundur's emphasis] entirely to that of the medium and the watchman, who were lying on the floor close to my feet.

Who in the world was it that threw these things?

The watchman, lying on the floor, took hold of one of the table legs with one hand and held the other tightly around Indridi. The table suddenly levitated, and the leg was wrenched out of the watchman's hand. The table crashed noisily upside down on the floor close by them. After that the disturbances stopped.

When the lights had been turned on, the sitters saw the wreckage of the lectern lying broken on the floor, and an unpainted panel where it had previously stood. Pieces of broken chairs, glass from a water-bottle, which had been on a shelf above the lectern, and other items were strewn over the floor. Gudmundur reports (*ibid.*, p. 256):

> We suggest that everything be photographed in its present condition and so leave everything untouched. But we take the opportunity of examining the lectern and the floor underneath it, for these seemed the likeliest place for concealment of secret devices. Unfortunately we gain nothing by this, except the certainty that nothing was, nor could have been, hidden there. We also examine the nailing, which seems to have been quite secure. ...

> ... We rehearse the phenomena in every detail, and recognize that there is no possibility of explaining the lifting of the medium by supposed cords from the ceiling.

On the one hand, the primary weakness of this report can be said to be the darkness and that Gudmundur did not actually witness the levitations himself. But on the other hand, Haraldur had an impeccable reputation as a professor at the University of Iceland at the time, as well as being a highly respected minister of the church. Haraldur Nielsson was, and still is, considered to be one of the greatest theologians and preachers that Iceland has had. It seems extremely unlikely that he was reporting something other than what he was witnessing. Gudmundur Hannesson ends his report on Indridi's phenomena by stating (*ibid.*, p. 272):

> But finally I want to mention that, in spite of all observations, I never discovered any dishonesty on the part of the watchman [Haraldur Nielsson], who as a rule was in charge of the medium and to whom I have repeatedly referred to above. On the contrary, as far as I was able to judge, his observations were very keen and accurate. On a single occasion only I found a slight and excusable misunderstanding due

to the darkness of the room. This man has had better opportunities than any other to observe the phenomena. To be constantly deceived he would therefore have had to be more than blind. His verdict of the phenomena is that there can be no doubt whatever of their actuality [authenticity], and he is a trustworthy man, highly respected by everybody.

Levitation of a human body has sometimes been observed at séances of various celebrated mediums, but reports of such phenomena have often been hotly debated. The historic levitations of D.D. Home have been frequently quoted and referred to in the literature of psychical research. The Danish Einer Nielsen was also observed to levitate as we have already discussed. Some of the most astounding cases of levitation of which there are records, however, are those of St. Joseph of Copertino (1603-1663). His levitations, and flights over some distance, were reported on nearly one hundred separate occasions under a variety of conditions and in many different surroundings (see especially Dingwall, 1947; Thurston, 1952, pp. 15-18). Indridi's levitations must be considered an important addition to these reports for they were witnessed by many observers, taking place both during séances and spontaneously, as is described in this book.

CHAPTER 28

TIGHTLY CONTROLLED SÉANCE AT HANNESSON'S HOME

We discovered with Gudmundur Hannesson's descendants unpublished handwritten notes describing some séances (Hannesson, 1908-1909, pp. 1-12). The most remarkable of these occurred on 12 December 1908. Present were Indridi Indridason, Einar Kvaran, Bjorn Olafsson, Gudmundur, Haraldur Nielsson and Karolina Isleifsdottir (1871-1927), who was Gudmundur's wife and had stated her disbelief in the happenings. Description of the phenomena was recorded by hand in darkness and the draft rewritten the next morning. This is evidently a more detailed account of the séance Hannesson described in his article in *Nordurland* (1910-1911) and in the Journal of the *American Society for Psychical Research* (1924b, pp. 258-260), neither of which mention some important experimental precautions he took.

This séance was held in Gudmundur Hannesson's recently-built house in order to control for possible fraud by accomplices and equipment that might possibly be hidden in the experimental house though after having examined the hall thoroughly Gudmundur reported that he had been convinced that it contained no secret door or contrivances (Hannesson, 1924b, p. 258). Indridi had never visited this home, states Gudmundur. The room was chosen by Gudmundur only thirty minutes before the séance started. Prior to the sitting, Gudmundur and his wife, who lived alone in the house, moved every loose object into one corner of the room and made sure that it was out of reach. The curtains were removed and the windows covered with blankets.

When the sitters arrived, Indridi undressed in bright light in the presence of Gudmundur and put on clothes provided by Gudmundur. The only clothes he got back after examination were socks, which had been turned inside out, a neck cloth made of silk, and suspenders. Indridi's hair was examined. The watchman, Haraldur Nielsson, was also examined (we are not told how). Doors were locked and sealed. "All round Indridi's body was sewn strong string" which was fastened "securely to the jacket" he was wearing. The front of the jacket was sewn together. The watchman was to "hold the string" (probably the string which was left over from the string around the medium). If the string was not loosened, and not pulled out further than his knee could stretch, then Indridi could not reach anything except his own and the watchman's chair.

Phosphorescent tape[1] was put on Haraldur's shoulder. To make it easier to follow any movements by the medium, Indridi was seated in a wicker chair which creaked as soon as he moved. A red "photographic lantern" was lit, other lights being turned off, and the séance began at 8:45 p.m.

The following took place (Hannesson, unpublished notes, 1908-1909, pp. 1-6):

> ... Very good silence at beginning of séance. Konrad [Indridi's primary control personality] greeted us and was satisfied with the environment. [The personality] Jon ordered that the red light should be turned off (spoken independent of Indridi) [as direct voice], but not until after a matchbox was thrown.

> Matchbox thrown. At 8:57 a *matchbox thrown* on the table to us. H.N. [Haraldur Nielsson] thought it had been in his pocket, but did not

---

[1] Gudmundur had obtained from abroad some phosphorescent tape which lit up in the dark. To the best of his knowledge, nobody in Iceland had such tape at the time. The phosphorescent tape was then usually placed on the zither and other objects to observe their movements in the darkness. Sometimes the tape was put on Indridi and the watchman to see if they moved.

notice it being removed. After this no light and therefore not possible to see what time it was.

A hand grabbed H. [Haraldur]. According to what he said, [the hand grabbed him] from the right side (medium on the other side). He saw an *arm go past* the window where a little light shone through a slit in the blankets.

H.N.'s nose touched. — H.N.'s nose touched by an arm. Only one of medium's hands held at that moment; the other one was said to be resting motionless on the back of a chair.
— Unclear knocks in the north side of the living room, quite far away from medium.
— Down by the floor a voice says "Shut up" [in Icelandic]. Medium's chair levitates a bit at the same time (H.N.).
— The string [probably the one Nielsson held on to] pulled but controller [Haraldur] says that medium had not moved at all.
— Shortly afterwards H.N. is struck (from the right side?).
— H.N.'s beard is pulled twice; the back of [Haraldur's] hand is pulled once without him noticing the medium do it. A hand or fingers are felt on the middle of the string.
— H.N. understands an unclear sentence [in English] as "hold mouth." The voice independent of the medium. H.N. is corrected by the same voice [in Icelandic]: "What a damned fool not to say "'hold your tongue" [in English].
— H.N. felt his right cheek being touched while he held both hands of the medium.
— Medium's neck cloth is thrown on the table to us. [It] was around medium's neck.
— A hand is noticed on H.N.'s forehead. One of medium's hands controlled.
— H.N. feels a foot touch his shin below the knee. He is quite sure of medium at that moment.
— Medium levitates. [Such that] his hips [were] at the same height as H.N.'s shoulders [who was] sitting. The knee [probably Haraldur's] pushed up and hits the bottom of Indridi.
— Clear knocks on the north side of the living room further away from medium, approximately over the buffet. Moved horizontally closer and closer.

— A weak female voice says, "I am talking to my brother—
Gudmundur my brother—I have very little power." The voice
clearly independent of the medium. A conversation by means
of knocks on the north wall attempted, but did not go smoothly.
However, [the knocks] answered clearly a few times and the
knocks easily heard some distance from the medium.

— Same voice says faintly, "Bye" [in Icelandic].

— The ghost-voice that has been interrupting previous sittings says
[in Icelandic], "Keep your mouth shut, cow!"
Now the phosphorescent star is no longer seen. As long as it was
illuminated it was clear that H.N. was sitting still.

— A piece of bread thrown to me. Unknown from where.

— Whistling close to the ceiling.

— A Norwegian man (the doctor) speaks very clearly independent
of the medium.

— Twice H.N. was hit by a strong wind, such that it was heard. He
asserts that it is not the medium.

Foregoing is based upon my notes in the darkness. Much conversation
not written down. At this point the medium became restless and was
felt to levitate [probably by Haraldur]. The chairs of H. and the medium
fall over. After permission [probably from the controls] I (G.H.) move
my chair to the other side of the medium, and pick up the [other two]
chairs. The medium is then blocked in the corner of the living room
between me and H.N.

Neither of them moved away. The medium's chair levitates a few times,
but not with sufficient force that it could not be held down with one
hand. The chair felt as if it kind of sprawled or was alive when it was
held. The medium was raised up and H.N. thought that he was being
pulled up by his head. He did not levitate, though, from the floor. I
found nothing on the head when I felt around it.

I heard many times amazingly clear speech independent of the
medium, very close to me, mostly swear-words and curses of the
disruptive visitors. Most of the time the voices came from the corner
behind the medium or from the north side of him. 2 x [twice] somebody
screamed suddenly and quite loudly about a palm's distance from
my head such that I was startled and punched automatically in that
direction, but didn't feel my fist come across anything.

— Once [air] was blown very clearly in my face and, according to what I thought, quite far away from medium's head (ca. 1 alin) [two feet; 62.7 cm.] and from a different direction. *Meanwhile the medium was talking* (Sigmundur) [a control personality], and I heard the controller [Haraldur] on the other side.

Apart from that nothing in particular happened. Afterwards, when the house and the string around [the] medium were examined, nothing suspicious [was] found. The sewing was not disturbed. This written on the morning 13/12 [13 December 1908] based upon notes.
Gudm. Hannes.

Damage or a scratch [noticed on the wall] from medium's chair in the corner indicates that the chair has levitated at least 35 cm.

The female voice mentioned "proof of identity."

The Norwegian doctor was talking about there being a "god passiv stemming" [in Norwegian, meaning "good passive atmosphere"].

Once something was said unclearly; it seemed to be in English. H.N. said he thought it was "hold your mouth." At the same instant the voice of a disruptive man said, quite far away: "Damned fool not to know that one says, 'hold your tongue'!"

—AUTHORS' TRANSLATION FROM ICELANDIC.

In his paper, Gudmundur reported the incident when his face was blown upon as follows (Hannesson, 1924b, p. 259):

When I had been sitting with the medium for a few minutes I was blown in the face with considerable force, the sound being clearly audible all over the room. *At the same time the medium was speaking uninterruptedly* [Gudmundur's emphasis]. He could therefore not have done this with his mouth, and I had no suspicion that either he or the watchman had any instruments for blowing. Besides, his face was turned away from me and his hands were held. *The blowing moreover came from the opposite direction to that in which the watchman was sitting* [Gudmundur's emphasis]. The rest of those present — the two unbelievers and the President [Einar Kvaran] sitting between them—were a good distance off at the other end of the room. It therefore seemed impossible to account for this blowing.

A moment later one of the invisibles uttered some abusive words close to my face, as it seemed to me. I immediately struck out with my closed fist, intending to give him a sound box on the ear, but as usual there was nothing but the air.

CHAPTER 29

HANNESSON'S LAST TWO SITTINGS WITH INDRIDI

We have reports of two séances that Gudmundur Hannesson published in *Morgunn* (1924a); both describe well his precise method of observation. We shall describe the séance that took place on 8 June 1909. Shortly before the séance started, Gudmundur examined the net to make sure it was secure and undamaged. The slit was threaded together and Bjorn Kristjansson (1858-1939) and Gisli Petursson sealed the ends of the string together. Inside the net, with Indridi Indridason, sat both Skafti Brynjolfsson and Haraldur Nielsson to control the medium, but also Gisli and Gudmundur, who were there to take notes of the directions of the movement of several pieces of phosphorescent tape, if it moved. Things were arranged as shown in Figure 2 (page 192). One trumpet was placed inside the pulpit (door X); also placed there was an open envelope, on which was glued phosphorescent tape. On the large table lay the zither (to which about three inches of phosphorescent tape had been fastened), and one trumpet. On the small table (number 8) lay a few sheets of paper and a pencil. Gudmundur and Gisli checked to see if anything had been written on the sheets and they marked the two top sheets by tearing off and retaining a corner. The enclosed space inside the net was searched and examined by Gudmundur and Gisli. Nothing new or suspicious was discovered.

The following phenomena were described by Gudmundur (Hannesson, 1924a, pp. 218-222):

1. As sitters were singing at the beginning of the séance, Gudmundur heard a female voice accompanying them after Indridi had fallen into trance. The voice seemed to originate from inside the enclosed area.

2. The zither levitated many times. It was seen flying at different speeds in various directions (indicated by the phosphorescent tape). There is no doubt that some of the movements were so far away from Indridi that he could not have reached them.

3. The strings of the zither were touched and the instrument played a little several times, both while it was in the air and when it was on the table. Once the zither lightly touched Skafti Brynjolfsson's forehead. Simultaneously, Haraldur Nielsson was holding Indridi's right arm. Skafti thought it impossible for Indridi to have been able to reach that far with his left arm.

4. The phosphorescent tape was apparently taken off the zither and moved around in the air. To the left, the farthest it reached was about six feet from Indridi (Bjorn Kristjansson sat on the third bench on the right-hand side of the hall, close to the aisle in the middle. He saw the phosphorescent spot come as far as his right side, or further). To the right, it did not reach further than in front of Skafti, his wife agreeing on this point. In a forward direction, it reached the net and then fell down from about six feet high and was taken up again. Then it went close to the wall about one foot above the pulpit, close over the heads of Skafti and Haraldur. While these transportations were taking place, one of Indridi's arms was firmly held by Haraldur, and sometimes both arms were held. His feet were not controlled.

5. Gudmundur reports on the phosphorescent tape (Hannesson, 1924a, pp. 218-220):

While the phosphorescent tape was being moved close to the net, *a dark spot was seen* ([by] Einar Hjorleifsson [Kvaran], Groa Brynjolfsson) *in the middle of the tape*, as if it was being held by two fingers. Once it [the phosphorescent tape] stayed in the air, quite close in front of the face of H.N. [Haraldur Nielsson] and was then either bent or stretched. H.N. saw *two flesh-colored fingers* inside the curve [of the tape]. Simultaneously, he was holding *both of* the medium's *hands.*[1] When the tape was being moved it often seemed as if *something opaque was covering it* and obstructing the view of it temporarily from alternating sides. The tape was finally thrown over to G.P. [Gisli Petursson], landing quite close to his feet.

H.N. was definitely holding both of the medium's hands, and could feel one of his knees, while the tape was being bent and stretched in the air. One of the medium's hands then clapped on H.N.'s hand, such that it was heard all around the room.

H.N. reported that he had seen two pinkish, flesh-colored fingers on the tape inside the curve [of the tape] when the tape was swinging in the air close to him, slightly above his eyes. At that moment he was holding both the medium's hands.

Skafti said he had seen a dark spot on the tape, his wife reporting the same, but did not notice any fingers.

—AUTHORS' TRANSLATION FROM ICELANDIC

6. The end of the large table furthest away from Indridi tilted and moved, in small jerks, towards the net and then to the right, closer to Gudmundur, and in the end it rolled over on its side. Skafti held firmly onto the end furthest away from Indridi, but it tilted nonetheless. Indridi was sitting at the other end of the table and Haraldur was holding his right arm.

7. The big trumpet and the iron leg followed the table around from the left-hand (east) side of the hall inside the net to the west side of the hall and ended on the east side of the table.

8. The little table was turned upside down, probably by the large table and the trumpet.

9. Shortly before the large table moved, a crack was heard in the pulpit as if something was pulling at it very forcefully.

10. Indridi's chair was thrown across the floor in the direction of Gisli Petursson.

---

[1] Sk.Br. [Skafti Brynjolfsson] does not know for sure about the medium's hands when the tape was being bent and stretched in the air. [He] saw very distinctly a dark spot on it, as if someone was holding it.

Gudmundur (Hannesson, 1924a, p. 220) also reports on phenomena that occurred after the séance had ended and most of the sitters had left:

1. The shelf (nailed down firmly) was torn off the pulpit with a loud cracking noise. Thrown onto the floor. Both medium's hands were held while this happened (H.N. only, or rather Sk.Br. and H.N.[2]).

2. The open envelope suddenly appeared out of the pulpit, levitated a bit higher in the air, then moved to the net and swung in an arc west to the wall. Skafti saw the envelope when it appeared in front of him to his left. It seemed to him that it was by the net. Then it moved up the net and swung in an arc towards the window. The glue was sticky at the end of the séance. Skafti and Haraldur asserted that Indridi had had no opportunity to go inside the pulpit and remove it.

3. The net began to shake violently close to the harmonium; this was repeated many times. Indridi was standing between Haraldur's knees and both his hands were being held while this occurred. Gudmundur could feel the harmonium shaking, and it seemed to him that that motion was causing the net to shake. This was repeated many times. Meanwhile only normal shivering was felt on Indridi's body; there were no strong movements (*ibid.*, p. 221).

4. Various things from inside the wall cupboard were moved onto the floor. The medium stated that the things had been apported through solid matter. Skafti Brynjolfsson, who sat next to the cupboard, had not noticed the door opening or closing. This door was stiff and it could easily be heard if it was opened. No sitter heard it open or close.

Gudmundur Hannesson wrote this report on the basis of a draft written during the séance and in accordance with the statements of Skafti Brynjolfsson, Haraldur Nielsson and Bjorn Kristjansson, each of them being interviewed individually the next morning. They had had no chance to confer with each other after the séance. This account was attested to by Skafti and his wife Groa Brynjolfsson.

---

[2] When the shelf of the pulpit was thrown: the medium was held, but it is not clear whether both [watchmen] were holding or only H.N. Skafti Brynjolfsson asserted that the medium could not have reached the pulpit with his arms.

Gudmundur Hannesson's Last Sitting

Gudmundur Hannesson attended numerous sittings with Indridi during the winter of 1908-1909. The last sitting for which we have an account reported by Hannesson was held on 11 June 1909 (Hannesson, 1924a). Preparations were the same as at the sitting on 8 June. Gudmundur examined the net and the whole hall in good light, and all the furniture inside the net, but did not notice anything suspicious. The doors into the hall and of the wall cupboard were locked and sealed.

Gisli Petursson sat in Skafti Brynjolfsson's seat, as the second watchman, and Skafti sat in Gisli's seat on the bench at the west side of the hall. Einar Kvaran sat on a chair which had been placed upon a large table in front of the net in the middle of the hall, to observe how high the objects (with the phosphorescent tape) might move. Ari Jonsson sat on the front bench, one or two seats from the east wall, to observe how far east the objects moved. Bjorn Kristjansson sat on the second bench, in the second seat from the aisle in the middle, to see how far west the objects moved; Skafti was to observe how far south, and Gudmundur how far north toward the net.

The séance took place in darkness. Let us quote Gudmundur on the measurements of the zither movements (Hannesson, 1924a, pp. 223-224):

> The zither with the phosphorescent tape moved [Gudmundur's emphasis] repeatedly in different directions and by various curved, randomly twisting and direct trajectories in all different directions within the enclosed space. Sometimes slowly, sometimes at an incredible speed. It reached "much" higher [probably quoting Einar Kvaran] than E.H.'s eye-level about 3 1/3 alin[3] [about 6 feet, 8 inches], probably close to the ceiling, to the left side of Ari J. (to the east side, nearly all the way to the wall panel); to the right it reached further than B.Kr. [Bjorn Kristjansson] (further west than the pulpit). On one occasion the light-tape [the phosphorescent tape on the zither] moved to the left of G.H. (nearly all the way to the net), [and] on a second occasion "a bit" [probably quoting Skafti Brynjolfsson] to S.Br.'s right side.

---

[3] The Danish/Icelandic unit of linear measurement known as an "alin" is the equivalent of 63 cm or 24.8 inches, so slightly more than two feet.

The zither moved, therefore, to the net, all the way to the east wall, [although] not all the way to the bulk-head (probably 1 to 1 1/2 alin [probably 2 to 3 feet] short of it), somewhat beyond the pulpit in a western direction and close to the ceiling.

While the zither was moving, the medium's right hand was being held continuously, most often by both G.P. [Gisli Petursson] and H.N. [Haraldur Nielsson]. The medium never stood up. Sometimes both his hands were held, while the zither was in the air (by both G.P. and H.N.).

The zither was played a little, both while it was quite high in the air (ca. 3 alin [ca. 6ft.]) and also while it was resting on the floor.

That the zither moved could be observed, because:

It disappeared from the table.

It was played and the sound was heard to come from where the phosphorescent tape was seen.

Once it came from G.P.'s right side (the side away from the medium) and touched his mouth, and on a second occasion it touched his arm.

—Authors' translation from Icelandic.

Various other phenomena took place during this séance, including interesting movements of a table *(ibid.,* p. 224)**:**

The large table moved out onto the floor and then, apparently, onto the pulpit. It was as if the table was struck harshly against it [the pulpit] more than once.

… While the table was moving, both the medium's hands were being held by both G.P. and H.N. Furthermore, G.P. kept both his [Indridi's] knees between his own knees, and the medium's head rested on G.P.'s forehead.

… Once while the table was moving, it was as if somebody pulled at the pulpit with quite a force, and *it was shaken* so much that it cracked.

—Authors' translation from Icelandic.

Towards the end of this séance, while some knocks were heard, Gudmundur sent one of his assistants outside the experimental house to see if there was anybody outside producing them. Nobody was seen. The seal of the net was intact after the séance. Gudmundur wrote this report with the help of a draft written during the séance while the phenomena were occurring, and to some extent from memory, on 12 and 13 June 1909. It was attested to and signed by Mr. Skafti Brynjolfsson and his wife, Mrs. Groa Brynjolfsson.

So it went, on and on, at the séances of the Experimental Society. Gudmundur Hannesson's descriptions resemble those of William Crookes in that the emphasis is clearly on the physical phenomena and rather cryptic in style. On the other hand, the minute books that were written mostly by Haraldur Nielsson resemble more closely the reports of the Earl of Dunraven. They described more of the messages, what was said, and what was of potential relevance to the question of life after death and the origin of the communicators. These men had quite different approaches.

"The Norwegian doctor" was recognized as Daniel Cornelius Danielssen (1815-1894) who made pioneering discoveries in the treatment of leprosy. He was prominent in his time and a member of the Royal Swedish Academy of the Sciences.

Konrad Gislason (1808-1891) was one of the main controls and communicator at Indridi´s séances. Konrad was Professor of Icelandic and Nordic Studies at the University of Copenhagen and a prominent scholar.

The Danish medium Einer Nielsen levitating during a séance while sitters
hold both of his hands.

INDRIÐI MIÐILL

ENDURMINNINGAR
BRYNJÓLFS ÞORLÁKSSONAR SÖNGKENNARA

ÞÓRBERGUR ÞÓRÐARSON
FÆRÐI Í LETUR

Víkingsútgáfan

UNUHÚSI GARÐASTRÆTI 15—17 — REYKJAVÍK 1942

The title page of Thordarson's book *Indridi Midill* (Indridi, the medium) which describes Brynjolfur Thorlaksson's vivid reminiscences of Indridi.

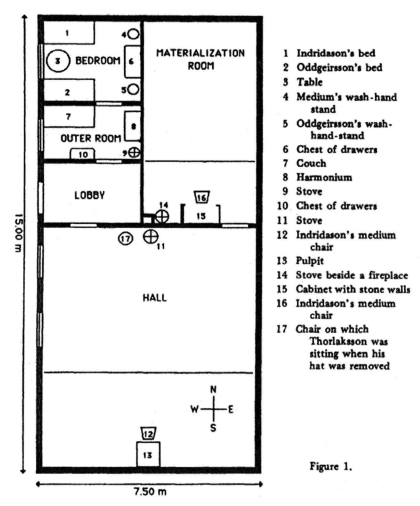

1 Indridason's bed
2 Oddgeirsson's bed
3 Table
4 Medium's wash-hand
    stand
5 Oddgeirsson's wash-
    hand-stand
6 Chest of drawers
7 Couch
8 Harmonium
9 Stove
10 Chest of drawers
11 Stove
12 Indridason's medium
    chair
13 Pulpit
14 Stove beside a fireplace
15 Cabinet with stone walls
16 Indridason's medium
    chair
17 Chair on which
    Thorlaksson was
    sitting when his
    hat was removed

Figure 1.

A plan of the Experimental House (adapted from Nielsson, 1924b, p. 167).
Thordarson also made a sketch of the house, which resembles Nielsson's in
every detail. We have added No. 17 to the picture, as well as a few details to
other items from Thordarson's sketch, which was made based upon a drawing
from the Building Office of Reykjavik and the accounts of Thorlaksson and the
carpenter Jon Gudmundsson (Thordarson, 1942, p. viii, 38.)

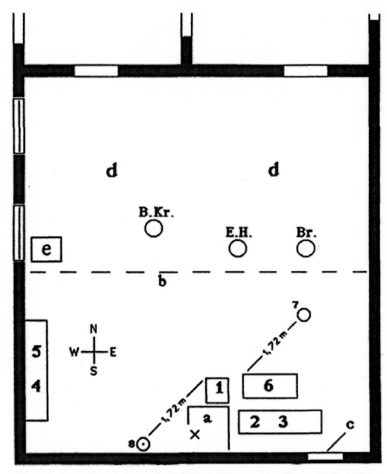

Figure 2. *Location of objects and sitters at Hannesson's séance with Indridason on 8th June 1909 (adapted from Hannesson, 1924 a, p. 226).*

a	the pulpit (immovable, since it had been nailed to the wall)	1 Indridason's chair
		2 Nielsson's chair
b	the net	3 Brynjolfsson's seat
c	the cupboard (closed, but not locked)	4 Petursson's seat
d	audience space	5 Hannesson's seat
e	harmonium	6 the big table

Br. Mrs. Brynjolfsson's seat

E.H. Kvaran's seat

B.Kr. Kristjansson's seat

7 the large trumpet on a lattice
8 the small table, on which writing implements had been placed

Location of objects and sitters at Hannesson's séance with Indridason on 8 June 1909 in the large hall of the Experimental House.

The two minute books of the Experimental Society that reveal interesting details about Indridi´s mediumship.

Brynjolfur Thorlaksson (1867–1950) was organist at the Reykjavik Cathedral. He attended numerous séances and his vivid reminiscences were recorded by Thorbergur Thordarson.

The Icelandic composer Svein-bjorn Sveinbjornsson (1847–1926). The minutes of the Experimental Society describe interesting communications between Sveinbjornsson and fellow composer Edvard Grieg.

Gudmundur Hannesson (1866-1946) – a true skeptic – conducted a thorough investigation of Indridi's mediumship during 1908-1909 and imposed strict controls. He was a prominent scientist, Professor of Medicine, and twice President of the University of Iceland.

CHAPTER 30

HANNESSON'S CONCLUSIONS

Gudmundur Hannesson made a particular effort to investigate the unaccountable movements of objects that were frequently observed. Since none existed anywhere in Iceland, he ordered from abroad some phosphorescent tape which glowed well in the dark. He placed the tape on a zither, among other objects, to be able to observe how it moved (Hannesson, 1924b, p. 262):

> It was a shock to me to see the zither start. The movement was entirely different from what I had anticipated, and most resembled the play of children throwing [directing] a ray of the sun about a room with a mirror. The phosphorescent spot shifted from one corner of the room to another with lightning speed, but in between remained almost stationary; now floating with varied speed in different directions, sometimes in straight lines, sometimes curved lines, sometimes spiral lines; now flashing again in all directions in lines several yards long, as far as one could judge in the dark. This was repeated several times over a period of a few minutes. Finally the zither fell on the table again, and the phosphorescent spot was seen in the same place as before.

Gudmundur was acquainted with various tricks used by conjurors for imitating the phenomena. He took certain precautions to be sure that neither Indridi nor the watchman were sitting close enough to the objects to be able to move them (*ibid.*, p. 261):

One had simply to make sure that neither the medium nor the watchman, nor an accomplice inside or outside the house, should be able to move the things. The first condition I tried to obtain by sitting with the medium and the watchman, and the last by examining the room and preventing the access of others.

At least twenty times when Gudmundur sat alone with the watchman and Indridi Indridason inside the net during séances, he himself managed to ensure that they could not have caused the movements of the objects. He kept a close guard over them (holding their hands and legs) while various things were in movement. On this point Gudmundur concluded (*ibid.*, p. 261):

> Over and over again I made sure that *neither of them* [Gudmundur's emphasis] was moving the things, either directly or indirectly. On this point I have no doubt whatever.

Gudmundur examined the hall, Indridi and the watchman. He stated that there was hardly any possibility for anyone to move the objects in the way that they had been observed to move (*ibid.*, p. 261):

> Often I could see no conceivable possibility that anybody, inside or outside the house, was moving the things. . . . The movements were often of such a nature that doing them fraudulently would have been exceedingly difficult, e.g., taking a zither, swinging it in the air at enormous speed and at the same time playing a tune on it. This was, however, frequently done while I was holding the hands of both the medium and the watchman, and there seemed no way for anybody to get inside the net.

Sometimes such strength was needed to perform the movements that nothing could explain them except possibly that "an able-bodied man" had been able to move freely inside the area enclosed by the net (Hannesson, 1924b, p. 261). There are two arguments against this.

1. No entrance seemed open into the enclosed space, and
2. Often light was produced at such short notice that an accomplice would have had no opportunity to get away.

Once a light was suddenly lit whilst disturbances were going on and Gudmundur thought he saw the trumpet move forward two or three inches. After this meeting, a woman who had sat closer to the trumpet asserted that in the light she had clearly seen it move. This was the only occasion on which Gudmundur saw a trumpet move in full light.

Gudmundur finally stated (Hannesson, 1924b, p. 261):

> After prolonged observation I saw no way round the inference that the things move often, if not always, in an altogether unaccountable manner, without anybody either directly or indirectly causing their movements by ordinary means. But although I cannot get away from this conclusion, I am utterly unable to bring myself to believe in it altogether. It is not easy for unbelieving people to accept the theory that inanimate things move about without any natural causes.

> Naturally, like many others, I felt that much was wanting when light was absent. Everybody would prefer to see the movements.

The zither moved much further away than one could possibly reach with a hand or a foot, reported Gudmundur (*ibid.*, p. 262), and much faster than it was possible to run with it around the floor. Also, the trajectories were too complicated (varying and irregular) to be imitated by some swing or string mechanism. Besides, no string or pole was ever found in the area that could have been used for such purpose. Gudmundur wrote (*ibid.*, pp. 262-263):

> Then it occurred to me that possibly this might have been done by fastening the zither to the end of a strong pole and then swinging it. The pole would, however, have had to be both long and strong, and the zither firmly tied to it. I was unable to see how such a pole could have been available. Where could it have come from all of a sudden, and what might have become of it?

> There was still another piece of evidence against this: while the instrument was shifting about, its strings were played upon several times.

Gudmundur asked himself, what if a reflection like that of the phosphorescent spot had been projected into the room with a mirror? He tried this in darkness, but the light from the phosphorescent spot was much too faint.

And what if the phosphorescent reflection was perhaps produced by some other flash mechanism by the medium himself? Gudmundur felt certain that nobody in Reykjavik had this particular phosphorescent color, and he reports (1924b, p. 263): "I have since ascertained many times over that I was right in assuming it was the zither with my phosphorescent tape which was actually flashing about the room."

Gudmundur considered two further explanations: First, Indridi did not sit still, but stood up and held the instrument. Secondly, in that manner it would have been closer to the eye than it appeared. Gudmundur excluded the former explanation through repeated sittings with Indridi and the watchman inside the net, and keeping close guard over them and feeling the hands of both of them while the zither was flying in the air. He examined the latter explanation by making a contemporaneous comparison of the various directions involved. These observations showed that the zither moved at least eight to ten feet away from Indridi. Additionally, the watchman held Indridi's hands and asserted that Indridi had not moved. This argues against the explanation that the zither had been closer to the eye than it seemed to be and that its movements had really been much less. Gudmundur thus concluded (*ibid.*, p. 263):

> My experiments with phosphorescent color thus led to the same conclusion as my former observations in the dark: *the things actually moved by some incomprehensible means* [Gudmundur's emphasis], and even in such a manner that often I could not see how anybody should have been able to produce such movements, however willing to do so.

The unaccountable movements of objects was as great a mystery for Gudmundur Hannesson as it was for William Crookes. The movements seemed to defy the law of gravity, or rather, some unknown force made the objects move. Crookes called it the "psychic force." Gudmundur did not give this force a name. Indridi and his controls had their explanation; the spirits of the departed moved the objects.

One important question arose (Hannesson, 1951, pp. 151-153): why had no one produced a light during the greatest movements? Gudmundur was allowed by the Society to carry out investigations of the phenomena on the condition that the Society approved his procedures. The Society followed orders from Indridi's controls in not having light during séances. Gudmundur once unintentionally switched on an electric torch without asking for permission. He heard one of the "ghosts" shout in front of his face: "You damned scoundrel!" (Hannesson, 1924b, p. 265; 1951, p. 153). At the same time the torch flashed and lit up the whole inner area. Gudmundur saw Indridi hanging limp in his chair in the same position as the watchman had stated, and everybody sitting still in their own seats.

Often a light was turned on with such very short notice that it would have been nearly impossible for an accomplice who had been inside the enclosed space to escape in so short a time, which was a matter of just a few seconds. A sitter asked, "May we have a light?" and the control instantly replied, "Yes." At the same moment an electric lamp or a match was lit. Gudmundur (1924b, p. 265) commented: "This especially precluded that a man who might have been in the inner quarter could escape, but I was on the whole more suspicious of such an assistant than of the medium himself." Our sources do not mention, however, whether a request for light was ever refused.

Was Indridi a Ventriloquist?

Gudmundur suspected at the beginning of his investigations that Indridi was a ventriloquist (Hannesson, 1951, pp. 154-156). Frequently he heard the voices sing, sometimes briefly and faintly, sometimes loudly singing a whole melody. He thought that often two voices were separated by such a short interval that it was difficult to say whether or not the second one overlapped with the first. Gudmundur reported one such incident that occurred at the beginning of a séance (Hannesson, 1924a, p. 223):

> While the playing went on, in order to allow the medium to fall into deeper sleep, *a clear female voice* started singing inside the net. But then *a clear male voice* took over. For a moment, both S.Br. and G.H. [Skafti Brynjolfsson and Gudmundur Hannesson] thought they heard these voices **sing** *simultaneously.* They [the voices] were both heard very close to me [Gudmundur].
>
> —AUTHORS' TRANSLATION FROM ÍCELANDIC.

Both Gudmundur and Skafti were inside the net with Haraldur and Indridi when this occurred.

At least twice it happened that Gudmundur heard two voices sing, as clearly and distinctly as one could wish, the same song at the same time. There was no possibility for doubt, according to Gudmundur, since this observation was too distinct (Hannesson, 1924b, p. 267). One voice was a high, sharp, female voice, but the other the deep, quavering, bass voice of a man. They both came from the enclosed area, which was empty except for Indridi (and presumably the watchman), and there appeared to be at least eight to ten feet between the locations of the voices.

It seems unlikely that two of the sitters could have been capable of highly professional ventriloquism. The voices also demonstrated talented vocal ability, practice and artistic bravura (Hannesson, 1951, p. 155), but Gudmundur adds, "I am no authority on the subject of music, so I shall judge as little as possible this singing at séances" (Hannesson, 1924b, p. 267). Indridi had never learned to sing, although he sang in the Reykjavik Cathedral choir. A friend of Gudmundur reported to him the following incident (Hannesson, 1924b, p. 267):

A friend of mine was once invited to a séance of the Society, previous to my going there. He was a good singer, but a humorist and jester. Before he went, he told me where he was going, and that he had a trick up his sleeve for the ghosts. He seemed to look upon the manifestations as rather a joking matter. When he came back he was amazed at the ghosts and their performances, and said that this was not altogether natural. "I had heard," he said, "that Mr. N.N. [probably a deceased person] was appearing there and singing, and I knew that he used to be an excellent duet singer. I thought I should soon find out if there was here the question of a trained singer or not, but for further certainty I was going to offer to sing with him a duet. He appeared, and I did as I had intended. He agreed and consented to my taking the lower voice while he was to take the higher. I purposely began too high so as to make him break, but I failed miserably in my reckonings. He sang the higher voice with such power that the whole house resounded and I was absolutely amazed." My friend thought it very improbable that there was in the whole town a singer who could do what this "voice" had done.

Final Remarks about Gudmundur Hannesson

Many interesting phenomena are described in Hannesson's hand-written notes, such as various and apparently different materialized hands being observed, violent loud knocks being heard all over the hall (on walls and ceiling) in response to questions, attempts to obtain on "camphor-black" fingerprints from the materialized fingers (although such attempts are not reported to have been successful), materialized hands pulling Gudmundur's hands, direct writing, the door to an empty room being locked from the inside, and male and female voices being heard speaking Danish and Norwegian away from the medium. However, the twelve pages of Gudmundur's notes that we have do not usually describe in detail the circumstances of the occurrences, and in many places they are very sketchy.

Gudmundur reported, for instance, a sitting on 1 February 1909 (Hannesson, unpublished notes, 1908-1909, p. 7):

> I [am] a watchman. H.N. [Haraldur] and I.I. [Indridi] both bending [?] while a music box and other objects transported [around]. The [music] box was wound up. A song, which was played on the harmonium, was accompanied on the bells [sic] inside the music box. Transportation of the objects could not have been caused by any of the three of us.

> Ol. Dav. [probably one of Indridi's control personalities or communicators] spoke very close to me, but unclear from where. [The voice was] heard as if [originating] in a small trumpet, which stood on the table next to me. While I listened closely to the trumpet, or the area above the trumpet, a mumbling was heard once in a while in the trumpet, as if somebody was saying, "Can you hear?" [This was] also heard even though the trumpet was held to the ear, in the air, or far away from the table in various directions.

> —AUTHORS' TRANSLATION FROM ICELANDIC.

On 8 February 1909, Gudmundur (unpublished notes, 1908-1909, p. 9) reported:

> Felicita [one of the controls] sang beautifully with a natural female voice, not at all as if it was being faked. Sigmundur [one of the controls] whistled songs skillfully and ["he"] was accompanied by

his brothers (many voices). The voices outside [the spirit voices] spoke very clearly.

A gust of wind 3 x [three times] -- very strong all over the bench (2nd bench) and [it] was also felt clearly on the benches behind. . . .

I saw once a very clear *light fog* [Gudmundur's emphasis], which covered a large part of the south wall. [I saw it] again [but then it was] unclear and smaller. *There is no doubt about this* [probably referring to the "light fog"]. H.N. did not notice it but everybody else did, I think.

—AUTHORS' TRANSLATION FROM ICELANDIC.

Gudmundur reports that often a strong gusty wind was blowing in the experimental hall during séances when the controls said they were trying to make themselves visible (Hannesson, 1951, p. 163). This happened even in a closed, windowless room, and the wind sometimes extended many meters and blew with such force that papers fluttered in an open notebook which was lying on Gudmundur's knees. According to Gudmundur (*ibid.*, p. 163), "No other sound was heard with this gusty wind that could explain where it originated from."

During séances of the smaller inner circle of experimenters the air in the small hall often became very hot. There were no doors or windows open, but on many occasions sitters still felt a cold breeze (Thordarson, 1942, p. 111). Once they sensed a very strong smell of seaweed when Indridi was in trance. The controls explained this by saying that the entire crew of a ship had just drowned and were in the hall at that moment. According to Haraldur Nielsson (1919b, p. 350; 1922a, p. 23), wonderful, delicious odors or fragrances often filled the whole hall and wafted over the sitters in waves.

Gudmundur Hannesson (1924b, p. 260) remarked, after numerous attempts to prevent trickery during the sittings:

I continued to attend the séances of the Society for a whole winter, and there was hardly one at which I did not try to detect fraud in one way or other. At almost every séance I noticed something which I considered suspicious, sometimes very suspicious, and at the next one I would be especially vigilant on that particular point. But in spite of all [precautions], I was never able to ascertain any fraud. On the contrary, the bulk of the phenomena were, as far as I could judge, quite genuine, whatever their cause may have been. A great many things I had no means of investigating, and so can pass no judgment as to whether they were genuine or not.

Haraldur Nielsson (1924a, p. 29) writes that after this winter Gudmundur had declared that he was convinced of the genuineness of the phenomena. And when Haraldur was leaving for the first International Congress for Psychical Research at Copenhagen in 1921, Gudmundur told him: "You may state as my firm conviction, that the phenomena are unquestionable realities" (Nielsson, 1922b, p. 464).

CHAPTER 31

LATE OBSERVATIONS OF LEVITATIONS AND DIRECT VOICE PHENOMENA

Phosphorescent tape was sometimes placed on Indridi Indrida-son to see if he sat still. Haraldur Nielsson (1922a, p. 27) says that during the winter of 1908-1909 the phosphorescent tape was also sometimes put on his own shoulders when he was the watchman. One evening when the tape was put on the zither to observe how fast and far it flew inside the net, the tape dropped off the zither and fell on the floor. Haraldur reports (*ibid.*, p. 27):

> After a short while the tape flew into the air and both the medical doctor [Gudmundur Hannesson] who sat next to me to control the medium, and I, could see three fingers with the natural color of skin, hold it in the air and bring it to us.
>
> —Authors' translation from Icelandic.

Many of the objects that moved and levitated around the hall were borrowed from various people, for instance, the zither was owned by

205

Brynjolfur Thorlaksson, which minimizes the possibility that Indridi had put some device in it when he was alone.

During this time, we have an account of an object changing its position from one place to another without movement of the object being seen. Brynjolfur relates one such incident that involved Sigmundur and occurred outside regular séances (Thordarson, 1942, pp. 62-65). One autumn evening Brynjolfur and Indridi went for a refreshing walk and then to the experimental house. As they entered the lobby they heard a greeting from one of the controls, Sigmundur, from inside the hall where the séances usually took place, although the door to the hall was closed. Brynjolfur replied from the lobby:

"Greetings Sigmundur. It would be fun to chat with you." Then they opened the hall and entered. Outside was a clear sky, almost a full moon in the western sky, so there was good light in the hall. Brynjolfur relates (ibid., 1942, pp. 63-64):

I tell Indridi as we entered: "Sit there at the window."

Indridi does this, and sits down at the wall, south of the southernmost window. I take a seat at the eastern side of the door to the hall. Opposite me at the southern end of the hall was a pulpit with a desk at the top. When I have sat down, I say to Sigmundur:

"Can you take my hat off Sigmundur, and place it on the desk of the pulpit where I can see it?"

As I utter the last word, my hat is snatched off my head, and at the same moment I see it upside down on the pulpit. Then Sigmundur laughed. This was a soft grey brown hat. I did not see the hat fly to the pulpit. It was on the pulpit at the same moment it disappeared from my head

Brynjolfur then said to Sigmundur, "Can you place it back on my head?" At the same moment, the hat was back on my head" (ibid., pp. 64-65). Brynjolfur asked Sigmundur to do this once more. He did, and the hat was moved back and forth.

According to Brynjolfur, the hat was not seen being transported across the hall. It had been placed on the pulpit at the same moment that it disappeared off his head.

Bright moonlight from an almost full moon flooded the hall and there were no clouds (the shutters of the windows must have been open).

While this was taking place, Indridi sat motionless by the wall on the south side of the southern window at Brynjolfur's request. Brynjolfur sat by the wall on the east side of the door leading to the lobby. The pulpit was at the southern end of the hall opposite Brynjolfur, with a desk on top of it (see Figure 1 (page 191) for directions and positions).

A similar incident is reported in the second minute book on 17 September 1907: "While the medium is held down by H.N. and all his movements are controlled, notes are played several times on the musical instrument by an invisible force, and the lid of the instrument is thrown down on the hand of Br.Th. [Brynjolfur Thorlaksson]." Then a hat incident begins: "Simultaneously the hats of Gudmundur Jakobsson and H.N. were thrown straight up in the air and disappeared for a while. Later, the hat of Gudmundur Jakobsson is placed back on his head and shortly after that the hat of H.N. is placed on top of the hat of Gudmundur Jakobsson already on his head." Here there is a fundamental difference, the hats are not removed by request.

Direct Writing

During the winter of 1908-1909, direct writing was obtained at a séance when two assistants were present along with Gudmundur Hannesson and Haraldur Nielsson. Haraldur does not mention whether they guarded the slit in the net or whether it was sealed. He reports (Nielsson, 1919b, p. 350):

> Another time I had three assistants inside the net, two of them doctors and one a prominent Unitarian amongst the Icelanders in America. One of the doctors and I held both the medium's hands and both his knees, and we controlled each other's hands and knees at the same time. The two others observed the phenomena from some little distance. All the movable objects, such as a heavy table, the trumpets, a big musical box, etc., were carried about, some by luminous hands. On this night we also obtained direct writing while the medium was held in the manner described above. All the persons in the room could hear the pencil moving, and the great doubter of the party [Gudmundur], who was watching on the side of the medium on which the writing occurred, heard a fine female voice saying: "Though it is dark I can see after all." The paper then came floating down on us where we were sitting bent over the medium.

Haraldur provides us with more details of this particular instance in another paper (Nielsson, 1924b, pp. 462-463), such as "... the skeptical doctor [Gudmundur] taking care of the table, upon which he had put some paper and a lead pencil, which was at such a distance from the medium's left side [so] that he would not by any means be able to reach it, even if his hands had been free." The light was turned on and Gudmundur read what had been written on the paper. It was a short but friendly letter written by a discarnate lady among the group of controls. Haraldur is reported to have kept the letter and was going to have it photographed; the photograph is not known to exist today.

Brynjolfur Thorlaksson describes a case of direct writing which occurred when he visited Indridi in his living quarters in the experimental house (Thordarson, 1942, pp. 82-85). Only Thorlaksson and Indridi (not in trance) were present. Brynjolfur then tore a page from his pocket book and placed it on the table in Indridi's bedroom. There was no light on in the room, but an oil lamp was burning in the adjacent room where Indridi and Brynjolfur were with the door open between the rooms. Then both of them listened. After two minutes they heard "clear sounds, as if the pencil had fallen on the table and as if it had come down with one end first." Brynjolfur went in and saw the pencil not on the paper as he had left it but beside it. He took the paper and the pencil out into the light. On the paper was written "Singa sola mina vina." This was interpreted to be a combination of broken Norwegian/Danish/Icelandic which might mean, "Sing alone my friend," or "I sing alone for my friends." The handwriting was large and beautiful with upright (not leaning) letters. The senior author found in Bushnell's biography an example of Madame Malibran's handwriting; it appears large but not straight. Brynjolfur repeated this procedure and again direct writing was obtained. They "felt sure" that on the first sheet they had obtained the handwriting of a personality called "Malibran," a communicator purported to be a French female singer, as Indridi had asked her "in his mind" to write something on the paper.

The second sheet was signed "Edvard Grieg" (the famous Norwegian composer). Brynjolfur managed to find an example of Grieg's signature: it appeared to be "completely" the same as the one on the paper from his diary. According to Brynjolfur (*ibid.*, p. 83), Indridi had sat motionless in a chair in the outer room and never entered the bedroom while this was taking place.

Levitations during the winter of 1908-1909

Powerful levitation of objects was not unusual. During a public séance in the experimental house, the harmonium started moving away from Brynjolfur Thorlaksson while he was playing it (Thordarson, 1942, pp. 57-58). He said he had pushed his left foot against the floor but kept his right foot on one pedal of the harmonium and "followed it" in that fashion "jumping" along the floor. As this was happening Brynjolfur simultaneously told the sitters what was going on. Suddenly the harmonium was snatched away from him. Light was immediately turned on and the sitters saw that the harmonium had been moved onto a table on the east side of the hall. The harmonium was quite large and firmly built, its height being about that of a man's hip and its feet standing on small wheels. The levitation was done so skillfully that no sound was heard when it landed on the table. Two men had great trouble bringing it down off the table onto the floor and caused a lot of noise while doing so.

Kristjan Linnet was sitting close to the end of the harmonium when this happened and he confirmed Brynjolfur's account (Thordarson, 1942, p. 48). Linnet estimated the harmonium to weigh around 150 pounds (75 kilograms). Einar Kvaran (1910, p. 49) also describes this phenomenon, stating that the table had been a few meters from Brynjolfur.

Let us review one powerful levitation of Indridi after a séance in January 1909 (probably taking place in darkness). Haraldur reports (Nielsson, 1924b, p. 454):

> This time (18 January 1909), I and two others remained alone with the medium at the end of the sitting. The operators seemed to have difficulty in waking him . . . in a kind of semi-trance, he said: "Where are you going to take me?" A little later we three heard his voice coming from close to the ceiling and made some remarks about it. Then one of the control's assistants was heard to say, loud and directly from the ceiling: "Don't be afraid." Next all three of us clearly heard the medium being drawn along the ceiling of the room, the height of the room being twelve feet, and made to knock his fingers on it. After a while he was taken down and we were asked for light. He was then lying prostrate on the table, still in trance.

According to available sources, levitations of persons other than Indridi occurred rarely. Brynjolfur Thorlaksson says he once challenged the personality called "Jon" to levitate him during a séance in darkness (Thordarson, 1942, pp. 54-56; see also Kvaran, 1910, p. 49):

> ... Once, as so often, I was sitting by the harmonium after I had finished playing. Then I said to Jon from the Westman Islands: "It is not more than one man's job for you, Jon, to lift me up."
>
> Immediately —just as I finished the last word—I felt as if something covered me completely but did not grasp me in any particular part of the body. At the same moment I crashed down onto the floor, my hands and feet behind the harmonium. This happened at such lightning speed that I had no time to realize the route. I had no awareness until I fell down on the floor. It was a complete mystery to me whether I was thrown over the harmonium, shoved past it, or pushed through it. I was not conscious of anything until I fell down rather heavily on the floor.

—AUTHORS' TRANSLATION FROM ICELANDIC.

This occurred in the experimental house during a séance in darkness. The lights were turned on when the sitters heard Brynjolfur fall down on the floor, and they saw him crawling on his hands and knees behind the harmonium.

More about Direct Voice Phenomena

We have accounts from various sitters reporting direct voice phenomena, even two voices being heard simultaneously in Indridi's presence. We have already described how Thorlaksson heard that once two personalities sang "together" at a distance from Indridi, "Ak, vad vårt liv är eländigt" ("Oh, how miserable our life is;" a song in Swedish) (Thordarson, 1942, p. 87). Thorkell Thorlaksson and Kristjan Linnet were at this séance and remembered this particular song when interviewed by Thordarson.

Einar Kvaran (1910, p. 48) states that voices had often spoken and sang independent of Indridi. The voices even sang the same melody together "at the same time," one being a powerful baritone voice but the other a beautiful female voice. "The French woman" often sang during séances, either through Indridi or using direct voice (Thordarson, 1942, p. 72). She always sang in French, but while singing her "language" was unclear. On the other hand, her "ability to enunciate was amazingly clear when speaking words" and some French-speaking members of the Society communicated with her in French (*ibid.*, p. 72), but no further details are given. Nielsson (1919b, p. 350) reports on the direct voice phenomena:

> I have often heard two voices speaking or singing loudly, while I was sitting alone with the medium inside the net... holding both his hands and talking with the control.

> Sometimes the control spoke through the medium while the voices were singing, but more often he was silent while the singing was going on but started speaking the moment it ceased.

The voices very often sang beautifully, especially three of them, writes Haraldur Nielsson. He continues, "we could sometimes hear two voices singing simultaneously: the soprano voice of a lady and the bass voice of a man" (Nielsson, 1922b, p. 459). Nielsson (1922a, p. 17; 1924a, p. 234) further reports that at a séance one evening 26 different personalities, each with its own personal characteristics, had spoken through or at a distance from Indridi, who was in a very deep trance.

We have an account from Nielsson of direct voice phenomena occurring in full light in 1909 (Nielsson, 1925, p. 108):

> It was an afternoon in 1909. I was sitting with the medium on a sofa in my own drawing room. We were deep in conversation about some irrelevant matter when, all of a sudden, we heard the voice of "Jon" coming as if from just below the ceiling. That was the only time I ever heard him speak in full daylight.

Furthermore, one night in 1909, Nielsson slept in Indridi's bedroom to observe him while asleep (Nielsson, 1930, pp. 193-194). Before they went to sleep they chatted a little with two of Indridi's controls and Jon. Indridi was not in a trance during the conversation. They sat in Indridi's room, a light burned in the outer room and the door was open between the rooms. Before they went to sleep Jon promised he would wake them at a certain time next morning. At that precise moment the following morning, Nielsson woke up hearing Jon's voice shout, "Aren't you going to wake up?"

Brynjolfur sat at his home with Indridi once in broad daylight (Thordarson, 1942, p. 88). While playing a song by Chopin, he heard the French lady quietly crooning the song with him away from Indridi, who was sitting at the left side of the harmonium. Then he noticed that Indridi had gone into trance. Then Brynjolfur heard voices singing together, both male and female voices, also upper and lower voices. They all sang the same tune as Brynjolfur was playing. He could not hear the words but he heard the voices clearly. The song was like a "sweet sound" or an echo. Brynjolfur thought he heard the song coming from behind him, especially from his right side where Indridi was not sitting. He felt as if the singing came from far away, yet it seemed quite close to him.

Sigurdur Haralz (personal communication, 1985) still remembered clearly two occasions when many direct voice phenomena were heard around Indridi. Indridi was at a farm in the country. He was paying a visit to his fiancée, Jona Gudnadottir. Sigurdur was spending the summer at this farm, his father Haraldur Nielsson being the brother of the landlady Gudny Nielsdottir. Jona Gudnadottir, Indridi's fiancée, was Gudny Nielsdottir's daughter and therefore Haraldur Nielsson's niece.[1] On the first occasion, Indridi was alone in the room where he was to sleep. Sigurdur described it as follows:

> Indridi was to sleep in the living room. . . He was alone in there, the only person. We knew he was alone. Then many voices started talking. The people of the farm were in the kitchen when they heard Indridi in the living room. . . The voices spoke as grown-ups. Direct voice phenomena were heard around Indridi in the room where he slept. He was alone in there. This happened probably in the evening before he went to sleep. . . These voices bid him goodnight. They joked with Indridi and answered each other. We heard the words. The door between us and him was closed.

The second incident occurred in broad daylight, according to Sigurdur.

---

[1] Sigurdur Haralz was born in 1901 as Haraldur Nielsson's oldest son. He is one of two persons that we were able to find who had met Indridi Indridason. Sigurdur was only a child at this time, but his memory seemed quite good in spite of his age when the authors interviewed him on 16 January 1985. Sigurdur's younger brother, Jonas Haralz (1919-2012), who was one of the directors of the National Bank of Iceland, emphasized to us his older brother's excellent memory. The other person, Kristjan Albertsson (1897-1989) did not know Indridi personally as Sigurdur did, but remembered clearly Indridi's involvement in a public political meeting in Reykjavik.

The morning after his arrival, Indridi was standing on the lawn in front of the farmhouse, "probably to get some fresh air" after the night. Three people were present besides Sigurdur: Gudny Nielsdottir, Thorsteinn Bjarnason, a worker on the farm, and Gudni Jonsson, the husband of Gudny (although it is not completely clear whether Gudny was present). Suddenly, there on the lawn all around Indridi were voices that started to speak to him. The voices bid Indridi good morning and asked how he was. Some of the voices were joking with Indridi, teasing him jokingly but happily, and other voices seemed to be answering each other. Most of the voices spoke immediately one after the other, each with different characteristics. Some voices spoke simultaneously. Sigurdur did not hear any female voices; most of them were Indridi´s "closest controls." Their speaking lasted only a few minutes. No ventriloquist could have produced these voices, said Sigurdur (Sigurdur Haralz, 1985).

CHAPTER 32

THE LIFE BEYOND

W hat do the entities that appeared at Indridi Indridason's séances say about life in their realm of existence and their contact with the living? In the two minute books we find only occasional mention of those topics.

Here is one instance related to the Jensen case: On 4 January 1906 Jensen is asked if he had been in Copenhagen again. "No," he replied, "I have not been there for two weeks. I have been in the great hall that we use in heaven."

Indridi Gislason, a communicator who claimed to be the medium's paternal grandfather, said (minute book, 5 December 1906):

> I remember vaguely who the being was I met first after I died. I have often become aware of my guardian angel, he was rather coarse at first... I have often changed guardian angels. As our feeling of well-being increases, the better the guardian angel we get...you should all know that a guardian angel follows you all the time for good or evil; he can become devilish if you become so evil... We hear and see each other... Everyone has his own language, but still we understand each other... There is always peace here. I cannot deny that we think of those we knew on earth. Those who wish can guide those who are living on earth. I did, and went first to the one I loved most, my grandson.

For us every distance is equally short and long. It takes us more time to go across this hall than to go back to where we live. To get here, we must know about the place (think about it). It is the mind, but not solid flesh or blood that we must activate. The mind should be able to go to other planets... I have never made such a journey. We have met beings from other planets, but we are not trying to find out where those come from who are saved. I cannot state if the guardian spirits had [previously] been men, I rather think not. We go most to the country where we lived, except to furnish proofs for the unenlightened. Then we let the medium speak in foreign tongues.

—AUTHORS' TRANSLATION FROM ICELANDIC.

Mrs. Oddny Smith communicated on 11 September 1907 that "she at first believed that she had become well again but had not gone over to the other side [died]."

Konrad Gislason stated on 11 December: "Most people have difficulties following what happens on earth immediately after they die."

In the period when Gudmundur Hannesson attended the séances there seems to have been more descriptions of life in the realm of those who have died. He summarized them as follows:

Probably many are curious to know what these deceased people — as they claimed to be — said about their existence in the other world. I cannot see that it is to any purpose to go minutely into that matter as long as there is no certainty that their statements are to be depended upon. In most respects they described their existence in a manner that would seem to be quite acceptable to Christian people. They lived, retained their personality, and their happiness was according to their deserts and differed a great deal in each individual case. They said their memories of life here, their love for their friends and relatives, etc., survived. On the other hand, there was much that clashed with the teaching of the church.

Death... means little change, very similar — if not exactly — like going from one room into another. There was neither heaven nor hell... nor did men change into devils or angels... each one would simply reap as he had sown. Perfection had to evolve slowly from within, through experience.

(HANNESSON, 1924B, P. 268)

What is said about the life beyond in the surviving records of Indridi Indridason's mediumship does not reveal much and is lacking in detail and thoroughness. There is also the question of how much these descriptions are colored by the views of the medium and perhaps also the sitters.

CHAPTER 33

UNTIMELY DEATH

During a visit to his parents in the northwest of the country, Indridi Indridason and his fiancée fell sick with typhoid fever in the summer of 1909. Though his fiancée died, Indridi survived but never fully recovered (Nielsson 1922a, p. 30). No further sittings took place. Later it was found that he had contracted tuberculosis. He was admitted to the Vifilsstadir tuberculosis sanatorium where he died on 31 August 1912, aged only 28 years old.

Einar H. Kvaran wrote a tribute to Indridi that was published in the newspaper *Isafold* on 25 September 1912. A shortened version follows, translated by the authors:

> For years he was one of the most talked about men in this country. And, in his field he was without doubt one of the world's most significant mediums. It would be amazing if he would not be remembered now that he has passed away.

> He was cheerful among friends. His happiness was full of joy. His intellect was sharp, his understanding of people and affairs very clear, yet his knowledge from books left a lot to be desired. His use of words was clever and witty... His artistic insight was so astute that he was never rude in his playful attitude when he let his light shine and enjoyed himself.

He was magnanimous in nature, if not extremely so. I am not certain if I ever got to know a man who found it more difficult to give in when he felt somebody did him wrong... This was probably in his nature. When he was in that kind of the mood he could at times be difficult when dealing with people, especially when additionally he had had a problem with alcohol. It had taken a hold of him in his youth. He never managed to overcome the problem except from time to time when he tried hard not to drink and other people helped him to stop.

Along with great temper, unusual sweetness and flexibility had been bestowed upon him. When his mood was in balance, he expressed almost motherly love and a gentle, caring thoughtfulness. For this reason, everybody who got to know him well enough became fond of him despite whatever differences they might have otherwise.

The qualities just mentioned suffice for memories of Indridi to remain indelible forever, particularly for those who knew him best. When we add to those qualities the particular talent that Indridi possessed in such abundance, the talent of mediumship, then there is no wonder that we, who associated most with him after his talent emerged, will never forget him.

I shall not describe further the varied mysterious phenomena that occurred in the presence of Indridi Indridason... I have done that elsewhere. Now when we remember his passing, it must be stated that I, and many others who had the best opportunity to observe these phenomena, *know* for certain that they occurred and that there is no deception or illusion regarding the genuineness of the phenomena, neither any trickery on Indridi´s behalf nor any hallucinations in those of us who were with him. On that subject there is no doubt in my mind, and there can never be while I am of a sound mind. And that certainty has in various ways completely altered my view of existence... I know that no truthful and sane man, that would have had the same opportunity as me to investigate what happened with Indridi, could say anything other than that all doubt had vanished.

It is quite another matter to explain from whence these phenomena derived... I well know that the certainty about the origin of these phenomena is still not based on unshakeable proof except perhaps for a few people, yet it is certain that they really did happen. Whatever can be said for or against the origin, the fact remains that Indridi Indridason had no doubt on the subject. He harboured no other thought than that he had had connections with departed people, that he had seen them, heard them and talked to them and enjoyed from them various assistance and continuous love and affection for several years. He held that belief until the day he died.

I had a talk with him some 24 hours before he died. He was fully conscious, but extremely weak… His voice had become so weak that I had to pay great attention to hear what he was saying as I sat by his bedside. I felt it unthinkable that he would not be aware of his deteriorating condition….

I asked him if he was ever aware of his friends from the beyond. "Yes, often," he replied. "Every time I get drowsy I become aware of them." "Are you never aware of them, when you are fully awake?" I asked. "Yes, I see them also when wide awake, particularly when it is getting dark."

This was Indridi's last statement when facing his death. We talked about this a little more. His *certainty* of *them* was as profound as his certainty of *me*.

No man can fathom, except perhaps those who knew Indridi best, what suffering he had to tolerate at times for his conviction. To have the temper that had been bestowed upon him by nature, to be a victim of such humiliation and blame, and not to be able to do anything about it, would be hard to bear for anybody. The injustice of these humiliations became quite unbearable for him at times. He knew well that much about him could be criticized. But he also knew that in this matter he was innocent. The light-hearted spirit of youth had in a big way ruled his earlier life. Now he was for the first time in his life in possession of something, which to him was holy. He had experienced the unquestionable joy of gaining as loving friends people who had crossed over the ocean of death… All of this was degraded as lies and trickery. For this he was stigmatized as a villain and a criminal….

Indridi Indridason's Funeral

Indridi Indridason was buried on 9 September 1912. The sermon was delivered by Rev. Haraldur Nielsson. He speaks in his sermon about Indridi's battle with a prolonged illness that took him away from his wife of only one year and his young child. Following are excerpts from his sermon (Nielsson, 1912):

> But when we look at the other side of his life, it is in many ways much brighter. First we remember his day-to-day cheerfulness. He was particularly cheerful and joyous, and for that reason it was so pleasant to be with him. He was a gifted man in body and mind, intelligent with an exceptional taste for beauty and art; something rare to find in a man of his minimal education. All who came to know him must have noticed this. For this reason there was so much joy around him wherever he went. These qualities made him popular with all who came to know him. Not as obvious as his joyfulness, Indridi also showed much kindness and lovingness to those who worked with him on a daily basis.

> I feel convinced that Indridi could have enjoyed his great gifts much more than was the case. It is not surprising that these gifts were accompanied by some imperfections. Those possessing the greatest gifts often have to deal with frailty and weakness.

> Twenty-eight years is not a long life and his day-to-day life was not that eventful that one would expect him to leave much behind. But he did, I believe. Through his rare gift he left behind much that influenced our society. This gift will go into our history and preserve his name for posterity if I am not greatly mistaken. In our times new knowledge is coming forth about our psychic nature, and that knowledge is only obtained by examining those that have the kind of gift that Indridi possessed. Although such men evoke much attention in many countries and scholars argue about how to interpret the phenomena they produce, a large number of highly intelligent and learned men agree that these phenomena will gradually give humanity great and useful knowledge.

> It was in the service of this cause that our late friend gave his gift for a few years, and would no doubt have done it longer if his illness had not hindered him. His gift was outstanding and had many facets. Indridi

came to this town just as a few people had started such research. He had started as a printer's apprentice but did not complete the training. After he came here his mediumistic gift became his main preoccupation and it made him known throughout the country. If the results of psychical research in the world will become what I expect and hope, then Indridi will be remembered as one of the pioneers in this country. Without his great gift our knowledge of the remarkable phenomena would not have become what it is today, though still in its earliest stages. Nor would knowledge of it have become as widespread in our country as it is, if not for him.

I feel it my duty to mention this at the side of his coffin. It would be ungrateful of me not to do so, and I am convinced that he appreciates it, as I do who knew him so well and who was so close to him for a long time. And I believe that no one has had greater opportunity than I to observe the phenomena that occurred around him. As a token of my gratitude to him, I would like to say at the side of his coffin in this holy place where we stand, that I consider it one of the greatest fortunes in my life that I came to know and observe the phenomena that occurred in his presence....

It was not without pain, neither for him nor for some of us, to do this research, although all we sought was only the truth. I must, here at his coffin, praise him that he never lacked courage to stand by what he believed to be an important truth however much external forces were against us. In that way he was an example to many who the world held in higher esteem. Some of them lacked the courage to stand by the truth.

We who worked with Indridi in the Experimental Society have many delightful memories. I think that most of us would admit that we had never felt closer to a heavenly presence than there. We may never forget all the affection and loving care that was shown to us. If it all had its origin only in Indridi then he had far greater qualities than we have ever known before.

In his view he was only an instrument in the hands of others who had reached another world and there developed in love and kindness. He admired their loyalty and kindness to him until the end. On his death-bed he was still aware of the presence of his friends, particularly as he approached the end. During my last visit to the Vifilstadir sanatorium, he told me that he was amazed by their loyalty, for they never left him....

Indridi Indridason was buried in the Reykjavik Churchyard. No engraved stone monument was raised on his grave and the records of the graveyard burials are lost for the year 1912. No one knows where his grave is.

Brynjolfur Thorlaksson (1867-1950) immigrated to Canada in 1913 but moved back to Iceland in 1933. In his memoirs (Thordarson, 1942, p. 119), Thorlaksson wrote:

> While I stayed in Winnipeg in Canada, I once attended a kind of an experimental séance. The medium was an Icelandic woman. Besides me, there was her son who also had some mediumistic ability, an Icelandic girl, and an English actor with the Winnipeg Theatre. He possessed great spiritual energy. None of them knew anything about Indridi.[1]

> A personality spoke from the lips of this medium who said he was Indridi Indridason. His voice resembled the late Indridi´s voice. Much more convincing though was the selection of his words and how he formed sentences, it was literally exactly as Indridi used to speak when he was alive.

> Here I conclude my memoirs about Indridi Indridason the medium, who was the most amazing of all men I have come to know in my life, and has become more memorable than all other men.

—AUTHORS' TRANSLATION FROM ICELANDIC.

---

[1] This Icelandic medium in Winnipeg has not been identified. Walter Meyer zu Erpen has informed the authors that it is unlikely that she was part of a group around medical doctor Thomas Glendenning Hamilton (1873-1935) and his associates. His experimental group produced table levitations and ectoplasmic manifestations. The "English actor" was probably Canadian Pacific Railway lawyer Henry Archibald Vaughan Green (1888-1979), a long-time participant and auxiliary medium in the Hamilton experiments. He was also active in the Winnipeg theatre community, including as a playwright and director. With their shared interests in Spiritualism and theatre, Green and Kvaran – who visited Winnipeg in the 1920s – must have known one another, and Brynjolfur Thorlaksson should have been aware of Dr. Hamilton's research.

CHAPTER 34

CONCLUDING REMARKS -
THE EVIDENCE FOR SURVIVAL

Existing contemporary documents, including both published papers and the existing minute books, give detailed descriptions of incidents and phenomena that occurred in the mediumship of Indridi Indridason. They also describe the precautions that the members of the Experimental Society imposed to prevent fraud. The basic sources comprise notes made as the phenomena were happening or immediately after each séance. Most of the contemporary reports leave many questions unanswered, as they often lack sufficiently detailed descriptions of circumstances that may be crucial for a thorough and fully satisfactory assessment of the genuineness of the phenomena. However, taken as a whole, the contemporary reports that do exist offer strong support for the conclusion that the phenomena were indeed genuine. We wish to bring to attention the following arguments:

1. In his carefully controlled séances in the winter of 1908-1909, Dr. Gudmundur Hannesson did not succeed in finding any evidence of fraud, in spite of a thorough and sustained effort to do so. The phenomena were then at their height. A summary of the methods that Gudmundur used in his investigation is given in *Appendix B*. Most of Einar Kvaran's and Haraldur Nielsson's

articles were written on the basis of contemporary notes. Some were written from their memory of events, but usually they also checked the minute books. Thorbergur Thordarson also used the minute books to check Brynjolfur Thorlaksson's reports. Hence it is not perhaps surprising that our sources correspond in detail, as most of the authors consulted, and based their accounts on the minute books. However, we also have reports of witnesses describing certain events in the same manner, even though it is not mentioned that the minute books had been consulted (for example, the accounts of Gislina Kvaran, Kristjan Linnet and Thorkell Thorlaksson). Gudmundur Hannesson's reports were independently written.

2. The Experimental Society invited many outsiders to attend séances and witness Indridi's phenomena (Nielsson, 1930, p. 198). Among them were strong disbelievers and specially qualified or highly respected citizens, such as the Bishop of Iceland (Rev. Hallgrimur Sveinsson), the British Consul (probably Asgeir Sigurdsson), Dr. Gudmundur Hannesson, Bjorn Olafsson, and the magistrate who later became a Supreme Court Judge (probably Pall Einarsson (1868-1954)), to mention just a few. Those who were invited, and accepted the invitation, became convinced that the phenomena were not produced by fraud. Gudmundur Hannesson became convinced of the genuineness of the phenomena, although he is not known to have made any statement supporting or rejecting their Spiritualistic interpretation.

3. All that we know indicates that it was the sincere will of the Experimental Society to have the genuineness of the phenomena fully examined. The society's leaders were considered men of integrity and were among the most educated citizens in Iceland at that time; most of them were academics and some holding among the highest offices in the country.

4. Many of the macro-psychokinetic phenomena were "unwelcome," so to speak. For instance, the violent and destructive phenomena occurring in connection with "Jon." According to our reports, Indridi seems to have been genuinely frightened by these violent assaults.

5. Some of Indridi's phenomena occurred in full light and when he was not in trance.

It seems beyond any reasonable doubt that paranormal phenomena did take place in the mediumship of Indridi Indridason, moreover, an exceptional variety of phenomena. Forces were at work that are inexplicable by modern science and contradict some of the basic limiting principles (Broad, 1969). The inevitable question follows, what was the source of these paranormal phenomena, forces, abilities and manifestations? Did they originate solely and exclusively in the medium, or were they beyond him and working through him? This is the old question of an animistic or Spiritualistic interpretation. The Spiritualistic interpretation bears in it the consequence that life continues after death in another realm of existence.

F.W.H. Myers writes in his *Human Personality and its Survival of Bodily Death* that "the question of man's survival of death stands in a position uniquely intermediate between matters capable and matters incapable of proof" (Myers, 1903, vol. 2, p. 79). Another prominent researcher, Canadian-born American psychiatrist Ian Stevenson (1918-2007), has argued in a circumspect way that certain phenomena found in apparition, mediumship and reincarnation cases may offer evidence for survival (1982, 2001). Keeping the views of Myers as well as Stevenson in mind, let us examine with due caution, some relevant features in the mental phenomena of Indridi's mediumship, and what their meaning for the survival question might be.

Information or facts were sometimes revealed that are unknown to the medium. An example of this was the case of Sigmundur Gudmundsson who described many events in his life which were later verified by his wife. This may, and may also not, be relevant to the question of survival as it could be explained by assuming that Indridi was endowed with a great gift of telepathy.

Motivational factors. Can they be explained by psi? That seems less certain, for motivation does not provide a means of acquiring information. In the "fire in Copenhagen case" Jensen had a motivation to follow the fire in his home area in Copenhagen whereas that fire should not have interested Indridi more than fires anywhere else in the world. Hence, this case may offer some evidence for the reality and genuineness of the communicator Emil Jensen.

Personification refers to psychological and personal characteristics of the communicating entity, such as his or her manner of speech, choice of words, way of thinking, and consistency of behavior over time. There is much evidence for this in Indridi's mediumship. Rev. Steinn Steinsen and other communicators were recognized and accepted as genuine by persons who had known them when they were alive, and for the reason that they bore the personal characteristics (personality and memory) they had when they were alive. Indridi had never met them. This, more than anything else, led Haraldur Nielsson (1922a) to think that the communicating entities were real persons who had survived death.

Skills were sometimes displayed that neither the medium possessed nor anyone else present at the sittings, and not only that, no one in the whole country. The case in point is the extraordinary professional singing that took place, sometimes by a female voice and a male voice at the same time. No opera singers were living in Iceland at the time of these sittings.

Xenoglossy means speaking in languages unknown to the medium. Good evidence is found in Indridi's mediumship for speaking in languages unknown to him. Most of the singing and speaking in foreign languages was beyond Indridi's capacity. This indicates an independence of the communicating entities from the person and capabilities of Indridi and may be interpreted as evidence for their genuineness.

This brief overview shows a strong evidence for paranormal physical phenomena in the mediumship of Indridi Indridason. In addition we find an exceptional variety of phenomena that have been interpreted as pointing towards human survival of bodily death, as Myers phrased it. The manifestation of these phenomena may indicate the existence of another realm of reality of which we rarely have a glimpse. Seen that way, Indridi was a middleman (the direct translation of the term "medium" in Icelandic is "middleman"), or an interface of rare quality between these two realms.

REFERENCES

Primary sources available in English about Indridi Indridason's mediumship are marked with an asterisk.

Aksakof, A. (1894) "Ein Epochemachendes Phänomen im Gebiete der Materialisationen." *Psychische Studien*, 21, 284-299, 337-353, 385-399, 435-449, and 478-490.

Aksakof, A. (1898). *A Case of Partial Dematerialization of the Body of the Medium: Investigation and Discussion.* Boston: Banner of Light.

Alvarado, C.S. (1993). "Gifted subjects' contributions to psychical research: The case of Eusapia Palladino." *Journal of the Society for Psychical Research*, 59, 269–292.

Bennett, E.T. (1907) *The Physical Phenomena Popularly Classed under the Head of Spiritualism.* New York: Brentano.

Berger, A.S., and Berger, J. (1991) *Encyclopedia of Parapsychology and Psychical Research.* New York: Paragon House.

Bjarnason, A.H. (1906) "Ur Andaheiminum." *Reykjavik*, 7, 12 May 1906, 81-82.

Blondal, K.J. (2015) *Raddad myrkur* [Voices through Darkness. Minute Books of the Experimental Society in Reykjavik]. Reykjavik: Stafrof.

Bozzano, E. (1982). *Musica Trascendentale.* Rome: Edizione Mediterrane. (1943, first revised edition).

Broad, C.D. (1950, 1969) *Religion, Philosophy and Psychical Research: Selected Essays* New York: Humanities Press.

Bushnell, H. (1979) *Maria Malibran. A Biography of a Singer.* University Park, PA: The Pennsylvania State University Press.

Claudewitz, K. (2010) "Franek Kluski – Polens store medium." *Dansk Tidskrift for Psykisk Forskning.* 2, 19-44.

Carrington, H. (1906-1907) "An Examination and Analysis of the Evidence for 'Dematerialization' as Demonstrated in Mons. Aksakof's Book: A Case of Partial Dematerialization of the Body of a Medium." *Proceedings of the American Society for Psychical Research,* 1, 131-168.

Coleman, B. (1861) *Spiritualism in America.* London: F. Pitman.

Crookes, W. (1874) *Researches in the Phenomena of Spiritualism.* London: J. Burns.

Crookes, W. (1972) "Sittings with Daniel Dunglas Home." In R.G. Medhurst, K.M. Goldney and M.R. Barrington, *Crookes and the Spirit World.* London: Souvenir Press.

Dingwall, E.J. (1922) "Einer Nielsen. Review of experiments in Oslo." *Journal of the Society for Psychical Research,* 20 (July 1922), 327-328.

Dingwall, E.J. (1947) *Some Human Oddities: Studies in the Queer, the Uncanny and the Fanatical.* London: Home & Van Thal.

Dunraven, Earl of (1924) "Experiences in Spiritualism with D.D. Home." *Proceedings of the Society for Psychical Research,* 35, 1-284. Several reprints; most recently by White Crow Books, 2011: Viscount Adare, *Experiences in Spiritualism with D.D. Home,* with introductory remarks by the Earl of Dunraven.

Fjallkonan (1906) "Dularfull Fyrirbrigdi, Laekningatilraunir." *Fjallkonan* 13, 10 March 1906, 38.

Fodor, N. (1966) *Encyclopaedia of Psychic Science.* [New Hyde Park, NY]: University Books.

Gissurarson, L.R. (1984) "Indridi Indridason Midill. Bachelor of Arts Thesis in Psychology at the University of Iceland," no. 266.

Gissurarson, L.R., and Haraldsson, E. (1989) "The Icelandic Physical Medium Indridi Indridason." *Proceedings of the Society for Psychical Research*, 57, 53-148.

Gregory, A. (1968) "The Physical Mediumship of Rudi Schneider." Papers Presented for the Eleventh Annual Convention of the Parapsychological Association. Freiburg: Institut für Grenzgebiete der Psychologie und Psychohygiene, 1968, 76-93.

Gregory, A. (1985) *The Strange Case of Rudi Schneider*. Metuchen, NJ: Scarecrow Press.

Grunewald, F. (1922a) "Die Untersuchungen der Materialisationsphänomene des Mediums Einer Nielsen in Kopenhagen im Herbst 1921." *Psychische Studien*, 49, 409-430.

Grunewald, F. (1922b) "Undersökelsen med mediet Einer Nielsen hosten 1921 i Kjöbenhavn (forelöbig beretning)." *Norsk tidsskrift for psykisk forskning*, 1(3), 98-109.

Hannesson, G. (1908-1909) "Unpublished draft written during séances with Indridi Indridason." 12 December 1908 to 15 February 1909, 12 pages.

Hannesson, G. (1910-1911) *Nordurland*, various dates (see under Hannesson, 1951)

Hannesson, G. (1924a) "Tveir Fundir hja Tilraunafelaginu." Morgunn, 5, 217-226.

*Hannesson, G. (1924b) "Remarkable Phenomena in Iceland." *Journal of the American Society for Psychical Research*, 18, 239-272.

Hannesson, G. (1951) "I Svartaskola." *Morgunn*, 32, 20-46, 143-163. First printed in *Nordurland*, 1910, 21 December, 207-209; 1911, 21 January, 9-10, 28 January, 15-16, 31 January, 17-18, 4 February, 23-24, 11 February, 26-27; 1911, 18 March, 46-47.

Haraldsson, E. (2009) "Séra Haraldur Níelsson, sálarrannsóknir og spíritismi." *Studia Theologica Islandica Ritröd Gudfrædistofnunar [Proceedings of the Department for Theology and Religious Studies]*, 28, 9-21.

Haraldsson, E. (2010) "Seancer med Einer Nielsen i Island." *Dansk Tidsskrift for Psykisk Forskning*, 2, 46-55.

Haraldsson, E (2011) "A Perfect Case? Emil Jensen in the mediumship of Indridi Indridason. The fire in Copenhagen on November 24th 1905 and the discovery of Jensen's identity." *Proceedings of the Society for Psychical Research*, 59 (223), 195-223.

Haraldsson, E (2012a) "Further facets of Indridi Indridason's mediumship; including 'transcendental' music, direct speech, xenoglossy, light phenomena, etc." *Journal of the Society for Psychical Research*, 76(908), 129-149.

Haraldsson, E (2012b) "Cases of the Reincarnation Type and the Mind-Brain Relationship." In A. Moreira-Almeida and F.S. Santon (ed.). *Exploring the Frontiers of the Mind-Brain Relationship*, pp. 215-231. New York: Springer.

Haraldsson, E. (2012c) *The Departed Among the Living. An Investigative Study of Afterlife Encounters*. Guildford, Surrey: White Crow Books.

Haraldsson, E. (2013). *Modern Miracles. Sathya Sai Baba. The story of a modern day prophet*. Guildford, Surrey: White Crow Books.

Haraldsson, E., and Gerding, J.L.F. (2010). "Fire in Copenhagen and Stockholm. Indridason's and Swedenborg's 'Remote Viewing' Experiences." *Journal of Scientific Exploration*, 24, 425-436.

Haraldsson, E., and Stevenson, I. (1975) "A communicator of the "drop in" type in Iceland: The case of Runolfur Runolfsson." *Journal of the American Society for Psychical Research*, 69, 33-59.

Home, D.D. (1863) *Incidents in My Life (first series)*; (1872) *Incidents in My Life (second series)*; (1877) *Lights and Shadows of Spiritualism*. Republished in 2007 as *The Complete D.D. Home* (2 volumes). SDU Publications.

Hyslop, J.H. (1907) "Replies to Mr. Carrington's Criticism of M. Aksakof." *Journal of the American Society for Psychical Research*, 1, 605-611.

Hyslop, J.H. (1918) "Visions of the Dying." *Journal of the American Society for Psychical Research*, 12, 585-645.

Isafold (1906) "Krabbaveiki Madurinn.", *Isafold*, 33, 17 March 1906, 63.

Jenkins, E. (1982) *The Shadow and The Light. A Defence of Daniel Dunglas Home, the Medium*. London: Hamish Hamilton.

Jochumsson, M. (1940) "Matthias Jochumsson og Georg Brandes (1899-1915)." In *Georg og Edv. Brandes: Brevveksling med Nordiske Forfattere og Videnskabsmaend*. Kobenhavn: Morten Borup - Det danske Sprog- og Litteraturselskab. Gyldendalske Boghandel.

Jonsson, J. (1984) Personal Communication, 11 December 1984.

Kragh, J.V. (2008) "Mellem Religion og Videnskab. Spiritismen i 1800- og 1900-tallet." *Scandia*, 68(1), 53-77.

Kvaran, E.H. (1906) *Dularfull fyrirbrigði*. Reykjavik: Ísafoldarprentsmiðja.

Kvaran, E.H. (1908) "Nýjar ofsóknir." *Isafold*, 35, 14 November 1908, 278.

Kvaran, E.H. (1910) "Metapsykiske Faenomener paa Island." *Sandhedssögeren*, 6, 42-51.

Kvaran, E.H. (1924) "Tilraunirnar i S. R. F. I. [Experimenterne med Einer Nielsen hos Selskabet for Psykisk Forskning i Island]." *Morgunn*, 5, 21-76. Kvaran, E.H. (1934) "Frá landamærunum." *Morgunbladid*, 21, 6 December 1934.

Kvaran, E.H. (1959) "Indridi Indridason." In Einar H. Kvaran, *Eitt Veit Eg*. Reykjavik: Salarrannsoknarfelag Islands.

Lamont, P. (2005) *The First Psychic, The Peculiar Mystery of a Notorious Victorian Wizard*. London: Little Brown.

Logretta (1908) "Andatrubod." *Logretta*, 3, 11 November 1908, 207.

Madame Home (1888, 2009) *D.D. Home: His Life, His Mission*. Guildford, Surrey: White Crow Books (2009 reprint edition).

Madame Home (1890) *The Gift of D.D. Home*. London: Kegan Paul.

Medhurst, R.G. (1972) *Crookes and the Spirit World*. London: Souvenir Press.

Morselli, E. (1908). *Psicologia e "Spiritismo"* (vol. 1). Turin: Fratelli Bocca.

Owen, A.R.G. (1964). *Can We Explain the Poltergeist?* New York: Helix Press.

Myers, F.W.H. (1903) *Human Personality and its Survival of Bodily Death*. London: Longmans, Green and Co.

Nielsson, H. (1912) "Indridi Indridason fra Hvoli, f. 12. okt. 1883, d. 31. august 1912. Likraeda vid jardarfor hans 9. sept. 1912 [Indridi Indridason from Hvoli, born 12 Oct. 1883, died 31 August 1912. Funeral sermon at his burial, 9 September 1912]." Unpublished handwritten manuscript.

Nielsson, H. (1919a) "Um Svipi Lifandi Manna." In Haraldur Nielsson, *Kirkjan og Odaudleikasannanirnar*. Reykjavik: Isafold, 1-40. Also in Haraldur Nielsson, *Lifid og Odaudleikinn*. Reykjavik: Isafoldar-prentsmidja, 1951.

*Nielsson, H. (1919b) "Wonderful Boy Medium in Iceland." *Light*, 25 October 1919, 344; 1 November 1919, 350; and 8 November 1919, 353.

Nielsson, H. (1922a) "Egne Oplevelser paa. det Psykiske Ornraade." In Haraldur Nielsson, *Kirken og den Psykiske Forskning*. Copenhagen: Levin og Munksgaard.

*Nielsson, H. (1922b) "Some of My Experiences with a Physical Medium in Reykjavik." In C. Vett (ed.), *Le Compte Rendu Officiel du Premier Congrès International des Recherches Psychiques à Copenhague*. Copenhagen, pp. 450-465.

Nielsson, H. (1923) "Poltergeist Phenomena. (A summary of Professor H. Nielsson's paper read at the Second International Congress for Psychical Research in Warsaw in 1923)." *Light*, 29 September 1923, 615.

*Nielsson, H. (1924a) "Remarkable Phenomena in Iceland." *Journal of the American Society for Psychical Research*, 18, 233-238.

*Nielsson, H. (1924b) "Poltergeist Phenomena in Connection with a Medium Observed for a Length of Time, some of them in full Light." In *L'État Actuel des Recherches Psychiques d'après les Travaux du 2me Congrès International tenu à Varsovie en 1923 en l'Honneur du Dr. Julien Ochorowicz*. Paris: Les Presses Universitaires de France, 148-168.

*Nielsson, H. (1925) "Poltergeist Phenomena." *Psychic Science*, 4, 90-111,

Nielsson, H. (1930) "Reimleikar I Tilraunfelaginu." Morgunn, 11, 171-198. Also in Haraldur Nielsson, *Lifid og Odaudleikinn*. Reykjavik: Isafoldar-prentsmidja, 1951, 87-113,Nielsson, S.H. (1985) Personal Communication, 16 January 1985.

Norsk selskab for psykisk forskning nedsatte kontrolkomite rapport (1922). *Norsk Tidskrift for Psykisk Forskning*, 1(3), 110-133.

Politiken (1905) "Fabriksbrand i St.Kongensgade: Kjobenhavns Lampe- og Lysekronefabrik i Flammer," *Politiken*, 25 November 1905, 5.

Poynton, J. (2004) "Long Shadow over Psychical Research: An Essay Review of Johnson's Kant on Swedenborg: Dreams of a Spirit-Seer." *Journal of the Society for Psychical Research*, 68(4), 262-268.

Randall, E.C. (2010) *Frontiers of the Afterlife.* Guildford, Surrey: White Crow Books. (First published in 1922.)

Reykjavik (1906a) *"Dagbok." Reykjavik,* 7, 27 October 1906, 191.

Reykjavik (1906b) *"Andatruar-Farganid: Laekningatilraunir Ondungan-na." Reykjavik,* 7, 17 March 1906, 43-44.

Reykjavik (1908a) *"Dularfull Fyrirbrigdi."* Reykjavik, 9, 17 November 1908, 202-203.

Reykjavik (1908b) "Nyr Atvinnuvegur: Loddaraskapur, Fjardrattur." *Reykjavik,* 9, 10 November 1908, 197.

Reykjavik (1908c) "Kuklid." *Reykjavik,* 9, 24 November 1908, 205-206.

Rogo, D.S. (1970) *NAD: A Psychic Study of Some Unusual "Other-World" Experiences.* New York: University Books.

Rogo, D.S. (1972) *A Psychic Study of "The Music of the Spheres" (NAD, Volume II).* Secaucus, NJ: University Books.

Stevenson, I. (1982). "The Contribution of Apparitions to the Evidence for Survival." *Journal of the American Society for Psychical Research,* 76, 341–358.

Stevenson, I. (1984). *Unlearned Language: New Studies in Xenoglossy.* Charlottesville: University Press of Virginia.

Stevenson, I. (2001) *Children Who Remember Previous Lives: A Question of Reincarnation.* Jefferson, NC: McFarland.

Swatos, W.H., and Gissurarson, L.R. (1997) *Icelandic Spiritualism: Mediumship and Modernity in Iceland.* New Jersey: Transaction Publishers.

Tarchini, P. (1947) "La Smaterializzazione del Corpo del Medio Nelle Sedute Medianiche." *Luce e Ombra,* 47, 44-51.

Trobridge, G. (2004). *Swedenborg: Life and Teaching.* Whitefish, MT: Kessinger Publishing.

Thordarson, Th. (1942) *Indridi Midill.* Reykjavik: Vikingsutgafan.

Thurston, H. (1952) *The Physical Phenomena of Mysticism.* London: Burns Oates.

Universitetskomiteen i Kristiania (1922) *Mediet Einer Nielsen. Kontrolundersökelser av Universitetskomiteen i Kristiania.* Oslo: Gyldendal, 1922, 71 pages.

Waage, E. (1949) *Lifad og leikid*. Reykjavik: Bokfellsutgafan.

Waddington P. (2007) *Knock, Knock, Knock! Who Is There? Or how chiefly British luminaries were or were not bamboozled by the spirit 'medium' D.D. Home at London, Ealing and Florence in 1855 and what they made thereof thereafter.* Upper Hutt, New Zealand: Whirinaki Press.

Weaver, Z. (1992) "The Enigma of Franek Kluski." *Journal of the Society for Psychical Research*, 58(828), 289-301.

Wolfe, N.B. (1874) *Startling Facts in Modern Spiritualism*. Cincinnati: no publisher.

Zorab, G. (1970) "Test Sittings with D.D. Home at Amsterdam." *Journal of Parapsychology*, 34(1), 47-63.

APPENDIX A

The Sequence in which Indridi's Phenomena Occurred
This table shows the chronological sequence in which Indridi Indridason's phenomena first occurred and consequently the order in which the Experimental Society "experimented" with them.

Period	Phenomena Reported in Contemporary Sources	Comments
Beginning of 1905 until spring 1905	• Table-tilting movements in a group setting • Automatic writing • Trance • Trance speaking	Some "proofs of identity" were claimed from the very beginning.
Winter 1905-1906	• Levitations of objects (e.g., tables) • Knocks on objects and walls • Light phenomena (e.g., light-spots and large reddish light-flashes) • Clicking or cracking sounds in the air • Levitations of Indridason • Dematerializations of Indridason's arm	A short period of materialization phenomena was reported this winter when the light phenomena reached their climax.

Period	Phenomena Reported in Contemporary Sources	Comments
From February until spring 1906	• Various kinds of knocks • Olfactory (odor) phenomena • Healing experiments • "Proof of identity" claimed	Indridason became ill in February 1906. Other phenomena were obtained for the remainder of the winter.
Winter 1906-1907	• Light phenomena • Materializations of human forms • Apports	Indridason's materialization ability weakened significantly at the beginning of 1907.
Winter 1907-1908	• Levitations of objects • Violent movements of objects • Objects fly about and are thrown as if by invisible power • Levitations of Indridason • Knocks • Invisible playing of musical instruments • Invisible winding of a music box • Sitters touched and pulled by materialized limbs • Direct voice phenomena	In December 1907 a violent poltergeist outbreak took place around Indridason. A few light phenomena were reported that winter.

Period	Phenomena Reported in Contemporary Sources	Comments
Winter 1908-1909	The same phenomena as the previous winter, but also: • Breezes and gusts of wind • Singing by independent voices • Direct writing • Sitters observe materialized limbs	Dr. G. Hannesson made extensive investigations on the genuineness of the phenomena throughout that winter.

APPENDIX B

S ummary of Major Methods used by Gudmundur Hannes-
son in his Investigation. G.H. : Dr. Gudmundur Hannesson.
H.N. : Professor Haraldur Nielsson.
I.I. : The medium, Indridi Indridason.

Item	Short Description
The enclosed area of the experimental house was isolated.	The area where I.I. sat and in which various objects (trumpets, tables, etc.) were placed was isolated from the rest of the hall. G.H. nailed down a net reaching from the ceiling down to the floor, which was made of strong yarn with mesh too small for a hand to fit through. The net was fastened on all sides with wooden slats threaded through the mesh. The slats were firmly screwed into the ceiling, walls and floor.
Entrances were locked and sealed.	Doors leading to the séance hall were locked from the inside and sealed. The slit in the net, which served as the entrance into the enclosed area, was also tied together and sealed.

Item	Short Description
The hall was examined.	The whole hall was carefully searched shortly before and immediately after experimental sittings, and the ceiling, walls, floor, the panel and all crevices were carefully examined for possible clues to fraud.
Sittings were held in other houses.	The phenomena occurred at séances in other houses, for example, at the homes of the Bishop of Iceland and G.H. This supported the opinion that the experimental house was "clean." In his own home, G.H. chose the séance room shortly before the sitting.
Phosphorescent tape was put on most of the objects.	G.H. put phosphorescent tape on the objects that moved in the darkness at séances, to observe their movements. He reported that the movements were odd, and not like the movements that one would expect if I.I. (or an accomplice) had produced them by swinging the objects around with string and/or a pole.
"Multiple effects."	G.H. tried to notice whether two or more of the phenomena occurred simultaneously, in such a way that a single person could hardly have faked them. He reported several such simultaneous occurrences, for example, when he felt a strong breeze coming from a different direction than that of I.I. and the watchman. On at least two occasions he was sure he heard two different independent voices simultaneously singing the same tune.

Item	Short Description
Exclusion of accomplices.	G.H. selected disbelievers to attend some of the sittings to control for a possible deceiver among members of the Society. For the same reason, G.H. also held sittings where only a few persons he trusted were allowed to attend.
Silence.	G.H. had sittings with only a few selected people and without playing of the harmonium, to be better able to notice if someone moved around the hall. He observed many phenomena occurring during silence.
Sudden actions without time for preparation.	• Sometimes a sitter asked for a knock somewhere in the hall, and immediately the knock was heard coming from that spot. G.H. reported that the nimbleness of an impostor would have had to be amazing. • Sitters often turned on a light immediately after asking for permission. Nothing suspicious was seen at these moments. • Sometimes lights were suddenly lit without permission.
Indridi Indridason searched before sittings.	• I.I.'s clothes and hair were carefully examined. • I.I. had to change clothes before at least some of the sittings with G.H. G.H. watched him while he was doing this. • I.I.'s clothes were sewn together.

Item	Short Description
Indridi Indridason watched.	• A watchman sat by I.I. during séances holding all his limbs. • Sometimes two watchmen held I.I. • I.I. was contained in one corner of the séance room with two watchmen, one on each side, holding him. • A string was sewn around I.I. H.N. held the end of the string. That string was so short that I.I. could not reach the objects that were expected to move without H.N. noticing. • G.H. put phosphorescent tape on I.I. to see where he was. • I.I. was seated in a wicker chair, to hear if he moved in the chair or out of it.
Watchman searched.	• In our sources we are told that the watchman (H.N.) was often searched before sittings. • The watchman was held like I.I. during séances. G.H. held his hands and felt his knees while the phenomena took place. • G.H. put phosphorescent tape on the watchman to see where he was.

Item	*Short Description*
Ruling out possibilities.	• G.H. used various methods of producing light spots, to see if the lights that moved at séances were definitely the phosphorescent tape on the objects. These light spots never resembled those coming from the phosphorescent tape. • The phosphorescent tape was bought abroad. It was not possible to buy it in Iceland at the time. • Hannesson argued that nothing could explain many of the phenomena, other than if an able-bodied man was free inside the net. Three strong men had not been able to shake the pulpit which at a later séance was torn loose by the invisible power.
The objects that moved.	• G.H. examined the objects that moved during sittings, both before and after séances. He found no hidden cells in them. • Some of the objects were not owned by the Society; for example, the zither, which was often moved through the air, was borrowed from Brynjolfur Thorlaksson. • I.I. did not own any of the objects.

APPENDIX C

Comparison of Phenomena Observed in the Presence of Indridi Indridason and Daniel Dunglas Home. Home's phenomena as reported in Dunraven (1924), Crookes (1972) and Zorab (1970) were examined for the compilation of this table.

H - denotes phenomenon occurring in the presence of D.D. Home.

I - denotes phenomenon occurring in the presence of Indridi Indridason.

Trance Phenomena		
H	I	Medium falls into trance
H	I	Trance speaking
Knocks		
H		Raps, like stream of electric sparks
H	I	Clicking / cracking sound in the air
H	I	Knocks responding to sitters' questions and requests
H	I	Knocks heard on the medium himself
H	I	Loud and heavy knocks
Gusts of Wind		
H	I	Cold / hot gusts of wind
H	I	Gusts of wind strong enough to blow paper
	I	Gusts of wind as if someone was blowing air from their mouth

		Olfactory (Odor) Phenomena
H	I	Sudden fragrance in presence of medium
H	I	Other smells, e.g., smell of seaweed
H	I	Odor "clings" to sitters after touch by medium
		Phenomena in Connection with Attempted Healing
H		Strange heat radiates from medium
	I	Operation without equipment
	I	Wound heals completely in a few minutes
		Movements of Objects
H	I	Trembling of objects
H		"Earthquake effect" - séance room trembles as in an earthquake
H	I	Objects move a short distance
H	I	Light objects move a long distance
H	I	Heavy objects move a short distance
H	I	Heavy objects move a long distance
H	I	Curtains pulled to and fro by request
H	I	Light is turned off
		Levitations of Objects
H	I	Tilts
H		Objects do not fall off a table that tilts
H	I	Light object levitates high
H	I	Heavy object levitates
		Objects Moved Through the Air Without Support
H	I	Heavy and light objects move a short distance
H	I	Light object moves a long distance
	I	Heavy object moves a long distance
	I	Objects move as if they have been thrown forcefully
	I	An object moves between two places without being seen moving
		Phenomena in Connection with Musical Instruments
H	I	Musical instruments play without anyone touching them
	I	Winding of a music box by itself

H	I	Musical instruments played while being moved through the air
Movements and Levitations of People		
H		Medium walks in darkness without bumping into furniture
	I	Medium is thrown or dragged along floor
H	I	Medium levitates
H	I	People other than the medium levitate during a séance
H	I	Medium is "transported" a long distance
Fixation of Objects and/or the Medium		
H	I	Sitters cannot move medium's body or limbs
H	I	Sitters cannot move objects or stop them from moving
H		Object becomes light or heavy on request
Light Phenomena		
H	I	Fire-flashes or fire-balls
H		Small lights, stars or "phosphoric" (sic; possibly phosphorescent) balls in the air
H	I	Luminous clouds
	I	Small and large light-flashes on walls
	I	Light-spreads, as large as 10 to 12 feet
H		Luminosity of objects, clothes, letters, etc.
H		Luminosity of medium's head, hands, etc.
H	I	Luminosity of materializations
Materializations		
H	I	Only shadow/shape of materialized fingers is seen
H	I	Only a hand or foot is seen
H	I	Only shadow/shape of a human figure is seen
H	I	Complete materialized human being is seen
H	I	Sitters touch materialized fingers
	I	Sitters touch materialized limbs/trunks that do not recede
	I	Monster-like "animal" is seen*

*   Many violent phenomena were reported to have taken place in full light in Indridason's presence during poltergeist outbreaks in the winter of 1907-1908.

		Touches or Pulls by Apparently Materialized Beings
H	I	Sitters are touched
H	I	Objects are pulled
H	I	Sitters' clothes are pulled
H	I	Sitters are kissed
	I	Objects that have been firmly fastened are torn loose
	I	Sitters are violently pulled or punched
		The "Fire Test"
H		Medium handles something burning without hurting himself
		Dematerialization
	I	One of the medium's limbs becomes undetectable by touch
		Changes in the Size of the Medium
H		Elongation
H		Medium becomes shorter/smaller
		Phenomena in Connection with Essence Extraction and Production
H		Medium "withdraws" scent from a flower
H		Liquid is extracted from/out of something, e.g., spirit from brandy
H		Liquid is "moved" out of a glass/put back in a glass
	I	Medium produces unknown substance
		Sounds Heard at at Distance from the Medium
H	I	Laughter
H	I	Clatter of hoof-beats
H	I	Footsteps
H		Music or ringing of bells
H	I	Rustling noise of clothes, as if someone is moving
H		Whistle, whirr of wings, bird chirp/twitter
	I	Buzzing sound
		Direct Voice Phenomena (voices that are heard at a distance from the medium)
H	I	Whisper
H	I	A few words are spoken
	I	Voices speak through trumpets that are being moved through the air

	I	Voices speak without the help of trumpets
	I	Singing of voices
	I	Two voices sing simultaneously

Phenomena in Connection with Writing

	I	Automatic writing
H	I	Medium writes while entranced, possessed by a discarnate
H	I	Direct writing, that is, writing by a pen without human touch
H	I	Signature of a famous person is obtained through direct writing

Apports

	I	Transportation of objects through matter
	I	Transportation of medium through matter

Phenomena of the "Mental" Type

	I	Medium experiences visions
	I	Medium describes event while it is occurring
H		Medium "reads" another person's mind
H	I	Medium describes the past
H	I	Medium claims to see deceased people
	I	Medium recognizes from a photograph a deceased person whom he has not seen before
	I	Medium speaks language which he does not know
H	I	Medium provides knowledge from ostensible discarnate person

General

	I	Two or more phenomena take place simultaneously in such a way that would be impossible for one person to create through normal means.
H		Phenomena often occur in full light
	I	Phenomena seldom occur in full light
H		Small number of sitters allowed to attend sittings
	I	Large number of sitters allowed to attend sittings
H		Phenomena seldom occur spontaneously outside sittings
	I	Phenomena often occur spontaneously outside sittings

APPENDIX D

List of Séance Participants, Deceased Communicators, and Other Individuals who Witnessed or Commented upon Indridi Indridason's Mediumship.
Compiled by Walter Meyer zu Erpen and Erlendur Haraldsson.

Surname, First Names	Inclusive Years	Occupation	Relationship to Other Participants	Resident of	Other Information
Albertsson, Kristjan	1897-1989			Reykjavik, Iceland	did not know Indridi Indridason personally as Sigurdur Haralz did, but remembered clearly Indridi Indridason's involvement in a public political meeting in Reykjavik
Auduns, Dagny	1908-1991		wife of Reverend Jon Auduns	Reykjavik, Iceland	two minute books of the Experimental Society were discovered among Dagny Auduns' archives
Auduns, Jon, Reverend	1905-1981	clergyman; Dean of Reykjavik Cathedral	husband of Dagny Auduns	Reykjavik, Iceland	a prominent Spiritualist who had studied theology under Professor Haraldur Nielsson
Bjarnadottir, Ragnheidur					attended a healing "operation" by Indridi Indridason in early March 1906
Bjarnason, Agust H.	1875-1952	later Professor of Philosophy and Psychology at the University of Iceland		Reykjavik, Iceland	superficial critic of the Experimental Society and Indridi Indridason's mediumship after attending a single lecture by Einar Kvaran
Bjarnason, Thorsteinn		a farm worker		Grimsstadir, Iceland	witness to direct voice phenomena while Indridi Indridason was outside, in broad daylight
Bjornsson, Sigridur, Miss			cousin of Haraldur Nielsson	Reykjavik, Iceland	attended at least one séance with Indridi Indridason, on 4 February 1907
Brandsdottir, Ingveldur	1892-1941		wife of Indridi Indridason (married 1911)	Reykjavik, Iceland	
Brynjolfsson, Groa			wife of Skafti Brynjolfsson	Reykjavik, Iceland	attended séances with Indridi Indridason during June 1909; observed a dark spot in the middle of the phosphorescent tape as though it was being held by two fingers as it moved about in the air; attested with her husband Skafti Brynjolfsson to Gudmundur Hannesson's report of the 11 June 1909 séance
Brynjolfsson, Skafti			husband of Groa Brynjolfsson	Reykjavik, Iceland	attended séances with Indridi Indridason during June 1909; attested to two voices singing at the same time and reported on physical phenomena that occurred while assigned with Haraldur Nielsson to control the medium inside the area enclosed by the net; attested with his wife Groa Brynjolfsson to Gudmundur Hannesson's report of the 11 June 1909 séance
Danielssen, Daniel Cornelius	1815-1894	Norwegian doctor	none known	Norway	a frequent spirit communicator/control in the Indridi Indridason séances
Einarsdottir, Soffia Emilia (Mrs. S. Gunnarsson)	1841-1902		wife of Sigurdur Gunnarsson	Stykkisholmi	a spirit communicator at an Indridi Indridason séance (date not clear); she provided proof of her identity by materializing her hand for her husband
Einarsson, Indridi	1851-1939	economist and prominent playwright	a relative of Indridi Indridason; Indridi was living at his home in 1905 when his psychic abilities were discovered	Reykjavik, Iceland	attended early séances with Indridi Indridason

254

Surname, First Names	Inclusive Years	Occupation	Relationship to Other Participants	Resident of	Other Information
Einarsson, Jon	ca. 1856-1906		none known	Westman Islands, Iceland	a disruptive spirit communicator in the Indridi Indridason séances who was eventually pacified by another spirit communicator, Reverend Hallgrimur Petursson
Einarsson, Pall	1868-1954	magistrate who later became a Supreme Court judge		Reykjavik, Iceland	believed to have been the magistrate who was invited to witness Indridi Indridason's phenomena
Erlendsson, Hinrik	1879-1930	medical student in 1905; received medical licence in 1912		Reykjavik, Iceland	witness to disappearance of Indridi Indridason's arm during séance held on 20 December 1905
Fjeldsted, Jon	1878-1932			Reykjavik, Iceland	witness to the disappearance of Indridi Indridason from the courtyard of the Hotel Island following the séance held on 4 January 1908
Gislason, Engilbert	1877-1971		paternal grandfather of Indridi Indridason	Reykjavik, Iceland	witness to destructive phenomena in the presence of Indridi Indridason in December 1907
Gislason, Indridi	1822-1898		and younger brother of Konrad Gislason	Hvoli, Saurbae, Iceland	one of Indridi Indridason's main spirit controls
Gislason, Konrad	1808-1891	Professor of Icelandic and Nordic Studies and a prominent scholar in Copenhagen	older brother of Indridi Indridason's paternal grandfather	Copenhagen, Denmark	one of Indridi Indridason's main spirit controls; thanks to Hallgrimur Scheving, for whom he worked as a farm hand, Konrad Gislason received an education and was able to study at the University of Copenhagen; Konrad did not return to Iceland; though Indridi did not meet him, he would have heard about Konrad as a child
Grieg, Edvard	1843-1907	Norwegian composer	none known	Norway	one of the spirit communicators at Indridi Indridason's séances, who first appeared on 14 September 1907, only ten days after his death
Gudmundsen, Thorgrimur					participated at the Indridi Indridason séance, on 3 February 1908, and questioned the spirit communicator Thordur from Leira
Gudmundsson, Gudny			widow of Sigmundur Gudmundsson	Gufudal, Iceland	
Gudmundsson, Sigmundur	1838-1897			Gufudal, Iceland	frequent spirit communicator at Indridi Indridason séances during 1907-1908
Gudmundsson, Thorarinn Th. (also referred to as Thor Gudmundsson)				Reykjavik, Iceland	present at the Hotel Island after the séance with Indridi Indridason on 25 September 1907; as a French-speaking participant, he felt that the French singer understood him
Gudnadottir, Jona	1892-1909		fiancée of Indridi Indridason, daughter of Gudni Jonsson and Gudny Nielsdottir	Reykjavik, Iceland	

Surname, First Names	Inclusive Years	Occupation	Relationship to Other Participants	Resident of	Other Information
Gunnarsson, Sigurdur, Reverend	1848-1936	clergyman	husband of Soffia Emilia Einarsdottir	Stykkisholmi, Iceland	attended at least one séance with Indridi Indridason (date not clear), at which his deceased wife's hand materialized
Hannesson, Gudmundur, Dr.	1866-1946	professor of medecine at the University of Iceland	husband of Karolina Isleifsdottir	Reykjavik, Iceland	an avowed skeptic; he conducted the best controlled experiments with Indridi Indridason throughout the winter of 1908-1909
Haralz, Jonas	1919-2012	bank director	brother of Sigurdur Haralz & son of Haraldur Nielsson	Reykjavik, Iceland	did not know Indridi Indridason personally, but attested to his older brother Sigurdur Haralz' good memory
Haralz, Sigurdur	1901-1990	seaman	brother of Jonas Haralz & son of Haraldur Nielsson	Reykjavik, Iceland	witness to direct voice phenomena while Indridi Indridason was outside, in broad daylight
Isleifsdottir, Karolina (Mrs. G. Hannesson)	1871-1927		wife of Gudmundur Hannesson	Reykjavik, Iceland	had stated her disbelief in the séance phenomena, but then attended a séance with Indridi Indridason held in her home, on 12 December 1908
Jakobsson, Gudmundur	1860-1933			Reykjavik, Iceland	attended at least one séance with Indridi Indridason, on 17 September 1907, at which his hat was thrown into the air and disappeared temporarily
Jensen, Lovisa, Mrs.					attended at least one séance with Indridi Indridason, on 21 October 1907
Jensen, Thomas Emil (known as Emil Jensen in the séances)	ca. 1848-1898	Copenhagen manufacturer and coffee merchant	none known	Copenhagen, Denmark	Emil Jensen was the new spirit communicator who reported the fire in Copenhagen during the 24 November 1905 séance; in 2009, Erlendur Haraldsson was able to identify him as Thomas Emil Jensen
Jochumsson, Matthias	1835-1920	Icelandic poet and clergyman		Akureyri, Northern Iceland	attended some seances with Indridi Indridason during 1906
Jonsson, Ari					attended a séance with Indridi Indridason on 11 June 1909
Jonsson, Bjorn	1846-1912	editor; minister of Iceland		Reykjavik, Iceland	one of the founders of the Experimental Society; frequent participant in séances with Indridi Indridason
Jonsson, Gudmundur	1888-1945	later became a well-known writer in Denmark and Iceland and changed his name to Gudmundur Kamban	husband of Gudny Nielsdottir, father of Jona Gudnadottir, and brother-in-law of Haraldur Nielsson	Reykjavik, Iceland	attended séances and observed physical phenomena with Indridi Indridason
Jonsson, Gudni	1843-????	farmer		Grimsstadir, Iceland	witness to direct voice phenomena while Indridi Indridason was outside, in broad daylight

Surname, First Names	Inclusive Years	Occupation	Relationship to Other Participants	Resident of	Other Information
Jonsson, Jakob, Reverend	1904-1989	clergyman		Reykjavik, Iceland	corresponded with Erlendur Haraldsson; recalled that Professor Haraldur Nielsson had mentioned Indridi Indridason's mediumship in a lecture to students at the theological faculty at the University of Iceland
Jonsson, Jon	dd. 16 March 1906	patient who received healing		Reykjavik, Iceland	attended healing sessions with Indridi Indridason and several members of the group for three to four weeks during February and March 1906
Jorgenson, Jorgen	1780-1841	Danish-born adventurer and commander of a British warship	none known		occasional spirit communicator; as commander of a British warship, he had captured Iceland and declared it independent during the Napoleonic wars; the British Navy captured and sentenced him to transportation for life to Australia
King, John			none known		spirit communicator at Indridi Indridason séance on 23 January 1908
Kristjansson, Bjorn	1858-1939	merchant; member of Icelandic parliament		Reykjavik, Iceland	attended a séance with Indridi Indridason on 11 June 1909
Kvaran, Einar Hjorleifsson	1859-1938	writer and editor		Reykjavik, Iceland	established the first Icelandic circle (October 1904) to investigate mediumship; one of the founders of the Experimental Society; Einar Kvaran's name at birth was Hjorleifsson and he adopted the surname "Kvaran"
Kvaran, Gislina, Mrs.	1866-1945		wife of Einar Kvaran	Reykjavik, Iceland	sometime referred to as Mrs. G.H. (possibly Gislina Hjorleifsson, using her husband's name before he adopted "Kvaran")
Linnet, Kristjan	1881-1958	senior government servant (syslumadur)		Reykjavik, Iceland	attended séances with Indridi Indridason; when interviewed by Thorbergur Thordason, he recalled several distinct phenomena, including direct voice singing and Indridi's reaction to the "beast"
Malibran, Francois Eugene	1781-1836	a wealthy French plantation owner in the United States	husband of Maria Felicia Malibran	New York	a one-time spirit communicator (date not clear; possibly 1907), in search of his also deceased wife "Madame Malibran"
Malibran, Maria Felicia, Madame	1808-1836	French mezzo-soprano opera singer	wife of Francois Eugene Malibran	born in Paris, France	a frequent spirit communicator at Indridi Indridason séances during 1907-1908
Nielsdottir, Gudny	1856-1947		wife of Gudni Jonsson, mother of Jona Gudnadottir, and sister of Haraldur Nielsson	Grimsstadir, Iceland	possible witness to direct voice phenomena while Indridi Indridason was outside, in broad daylight
Nielsson, Haraldur	1868-1928	clergyman; professor of theology at the University of Iceland	father of Jonas Haralz and Sigurdur Haralz, who adopted Haralz as their surname	Reykjavik, Iceland	one of the founders of the Experimental Society; one of the main investigators and proponents of the authenticity of Indridi Indridason's mediumship
Oddgeirsson, Pall	1888-1971	merchant	brother of Thordur Oddgeirsson	Reykjavik, Iceland	witness to destructive and violent phenomena in presence of Indridi Indridason, probably on 17 December 1907

Surname, First Names	Inclusive Years	Occupation	Relationship to Other Participants	Resident of	Other Information
Oddgeirsson, Thordur	1883-1966	clergyman	brother of Pall Oddgeirsson	Reykjavik, Iceland	shared rooms with Indridi Indridason at the Experimental House; witness to destructive and violent phenomena in his presence, during December 1907
Ol. Dav.					reported by Gudmundur Hannesson as having spoken at the séance with Indridi Indridason on 1 February 1909; assumed by the authors to have been one of Indridi's control personalities or spirit communicators
Olafsson, Bjorn	1862-1909	ophthalmic surgeon		Reykjavik, Iceland	Gudmundur Hannesson chose Bjorn Olafsson to assist him in his experiments with Indridi Indridason
Olafsson, Julius					attended at least one Indridi Indridason séance, on 7 December 1907
Olafsson, Kjartan	thirteenth-century historical person				with Gudrun Osvifursdottir, a leading figure in a famous Icelandic saga; infrequent spirit communicators
Olafsson, Magnus	1862-1937	photographer		Reykjavik, Iceland	assisted with attempt during December 1907 to photograph one of the spirit controls at a séance with Indridi Indridason
Osvifursdottir, Gudrun	thirteenth-century historical person				with Kjartan Olafsson, a leading figure in a famous Icelandic saga; infrequent spirit communicators
Palmadottir, Ingibjorg S.				Reykjavik, Iceland	attended a healing "operation" by Indridi Indridason in early March 1906
Petursson, Gisli					attended séances with Indridi Indridason in June 1909
Petursson, Hallgrimur, Reverend	1614-1674	famous Icelandic religious poet		Saurbae, Iceland	spirit control who helped pacify the very disruptive spirit, Jon Einarsson, in the Indridi Indridason séances
Rosinkrans, Olafur	1852-1929	gymnastics education instructor		Reykjavik, Iceland	around Christmas 1905, was unable to repeat the remarkable gymnastic feats that Indridi Indridason had performed while in a trance state
Scheving, Hallgrimur	1781-1861	teacher at Bessastada gymnasium		Bessastadir, Iceland	Rector who helped Konrad Gislason with his education
Sigurdsson, Asgeir	1877-1936	British Consul		Reykjavik, Iceland	believed to have been the British Consul who was invited to witness Indridi Indridason's phenomena
Simonarson, Kristin, Mrs.					attended at least one séance with Indridi Indridason, on 21 October 1907
Sk.Th.					all that is known is that Sk.Th. was a young man; he attended the séance with Indridi Indridason on 20 December 1905 at which Indridi's arm disappeared

Surname, First Names	Inclusive Years	Occupation	Relationship to Other Participants	Resident of	Other Information
Smith, Oddny, Mrs.					spirit communicator at séance with Indridi Indridason on 11 September 1907
Stefansson, Stefan		school director		Reykjavik, Iceland	school director who claimed in or before 1908 to have been refused admission to Indridi Indridason's séances
Steinsen, Steinn, Reverend	1838-1883	clergyman		Hvammi, Iceland	one of Indridi Indridason's main spirit controls; he sometimes communicated through direct voice; his voice was recognized by Sveinbjorn Sveinbjornsson
Sveinbjornsson, Sveinbjorn	1847-1927	Icelandic composer		Edinburgh, Scotland	attended 14 September 1907 séance with Indridi Indridason and recognized the voice of his deceased friend Reverend Steinn Steinsen
Sveinsson, Hallgrimur, Reverend	1841-1909	clergyman; Bishop of Iceland	uncle of Haraldur Nielsson	Reykjavik, Iceland	attended a 1907 séance with Indridi Indridason and later asked for a séance to be held in his own home
Sveinsson, Sveinn		carpenter		Reykjavik, Iceland	carpenter who was asked to repair the steps of the pulpit in the Experimental House, to ensure that they were firmly attached
Thordarson, Thorbergur	1888-1974	published author		Reykjavik, Iceland	writer who recorded Brynjolfur Thorlaksson's memories of Indridi Indridason and edited and published them as the book *Indridi, the Medium* (1942)
Thordur				Leira, Iceland	a spirit communicator at the 3 February 1908 séance with Indridi Indridason who was questioned by Thorgrimur Gudmundsen
Thorlaksson, Brynjolfur	1867-1950	organist at Reykjavik Cathedral	brother of Thorkell Thorlaksson	Reykjavik, Iceland	played the harmonium at Indridi Indridason's séances; became a close personal friend; observed spontaneous phenomena in Indridi's presence
Thorlaksson, Thorkell	1869-1946	ministry secretary	brother of Brynjolfur Thorlaksson	Reykjavik, Iceland	attended Indridi Indridason séances and also observed spontaneous phenomena in his presence
Waage, Eufemia	1881-1960		daughter of Indridi Einarsson	Reykjavik, Iceland	attended a sitting in the early period of Indridi Indridason's mediumship which she wrote about in her autobiography (1949)
Zoega, Geir T.	1857-1928	first master at the Grammar School of Reykjavik		Reykjavik, Iceland	attended a séance with Indridi Indridason on 17 September 1907; as an Icelandic linguist who spoke French at a time when few Icelanders did, he spoke to Madame Malibran, the French singer, in French and believed that she understood him

ACKNOWLEDGEMENTS

A grant from the Tate Fund of the Society for Psychical Research is gratefully acknowledged. Thanks go to Bjorg Jakobsdottir for various assistance, and my grandson Logi Haraldsson for solving many formatting and computer problems. Kaare Claudewitz, President of Selskabet for Psykisk Forskning in Copenhagen, Professor Adrian Parker at the University of Gothenburg, Jon Mannsåker President of Norsk Parapsykologisk Selskab in Oslo, Guy Playfair and Gudjon Albertsson were helpful in searching for various items of information. Last but not least, thanks go to archivist / historian Walter Meyer zu Erpen for a thorough reading and editing of the manuscript, many valuable suggestions for improvement, and for asking on many occasions for additional information which has greatly improved the value of this work.

THE WRITING OF THIS BOOK

T he authors' preoccupation with Indridi Indridason spans several decades. The primary author first read about Indridi in the
1960s, perhaps earlier. After joining the Psychology Department at the University of Iceland in 1973 he would discuss Indridi in his
course on paranormal phenomena. Loftur Reimar Gissurarson, one of
his students, became interested and undertook to write a Bachelor of
Arts thesis about Indridi and searched for whatever sources were available. He completed an excellent 205-page thesis (Gissurarson, 1984).

Based on that work, we jointly wrote the monograph *The Icelandic
Physical Medium Indridi Indridason* that was published as a *Proceed-
ing of the Society for Psychical Research* (Gissurarson and Haraldsson,
1989). The monograph was subsequently reprinted in part or in whole
in *Renaitre 2000* in France, *Luce e Ombra* in Italy, and *Parapsykolo-
giske Notiser* in Norway.

Loftur continued the work and wrote jointly with William Swatos
Icelandic Spiritualism: Mediumship and Modernity in Iceland (Swatos
and Gissurarson, 1997), much of it dealing with Indridi, and the history of mediums and Spiritualism in Iceland.

Shortly after the year 2000, two minute books of the Experimental
Society were unexpectedly found and contained much new information
(Haraldsson, 2009). As soon as time allowed, the first author became
deeply involved in this material and this resulted in three major articles being published in the *Proceedings and the Journal of the Society*

for Psychical Research (Haraldsson, 2011, 2012a) and also in the *Journal of Scientific Exploration* (Haraldsson and Gerding, 2010). It soon became obvious that only a book would do justice, as the story of the mediumship of Indridi Indridason deserved to be known to a wider international audience.

INDEX

A

Adare, Lord (later 4th Earl of Dunraven), 138-142, 230

air movement, *see* gusts of wind (paranormal)

Aksakof, Alexander, xv, 51, 229-230, 232

Albertsson, Kristjan, 212

Alvarado, Carlos S., xiii-xvii, 212, 261

Amsterdam (The Netherlands), 59, 138, 236

apports, xiv, 1, 17, 71, 75-77, 146, 238, 251

auditory phenomena, xiv, 109-124 *see also* direct voice phenomena

Auduns, Dagny, 3

Auduns, Jon, 3

automatic writing, 12, 15, 82

B

Bennett, Edward T., 119, 229

Bentzen, Fire Chief, 32-33

Berger, Arthur S., 130, 229

Berger, Joyce, 130

Bishop of Iceland, 30, 73

Bjarnadottir, Ragnheidur, 54

Bjarnason, Agust H., 156

Bjarnason, Thorsteinn, 111, 213

Bjornsson, Hafsteinn, 229

Bjornsson, Sigridur, 74

Blondal, Karlotta J., 3, 229

Bozzano, Ernesto, 119, 230

Brandes, Georg, 135, 232

Brandsdottir, Ingveldur, 9

breezes – *see* gusts of wind (paranormal)

Broad, Charlie D., 39, 41, 227, 230

Brynjolfsson, Groa, 182, 184, 187

Brynjolfsson, Skafti, 114, 181-184

Brynjolfur, *see* Thorlaksson

Bushnell, Howard, 117, 130, 208, 230

C

Carrington, Hereward, 52, 59, 230, 232

Castel, William, 39

clairvoyance, 36, 42

Claudewitz, Kaare, 79, 230, 261

Coleman, Benjamin, 117-118, 230
communicators, deceased, xv, 10, 12, 13, 16, 19, 41, 56, 67, 71, 74, 96, 100, 105-107, 120, 121, 125, 127, 130, 145, 159, 162, 187, 188, 201, 208, 215, 228, 232, 253-259
conferences, psychical research, 4, 58-59 (photos), 203, 234
conjurors, 157, 158, 195
control personalities, 13, 71, 74, 96, 101, 145, 149, 176, 201
controls, experimental, 5, 20, 21, 24, 105, 164, 169, 166
Cook, Florence, xiv
Copenhagen (Denmark), 128, 130, 135, 162, 188, 203, 215
Copenhagen fire, 29-36, 41, 60 & 66 (photos), 227, 231, 234, 261
Cox, Serjeant, 142, 144
criticism, 151-162
Crookes, Carrie, 142
Crookes, Nellie, 142
Crookes, Walter, 142
Crookes, William, Sir, 5, 100, 106, 135, 142, 143, 146-148, 150, 187, 198, 230, 233, 247
Crookes, William, Mrs., 144

D

Danielssen, Daniel Cornelius, 55, 84, 106, 126, 188 (photo)
Danish Metapsychic Society, 30
Dansk Tidsskrift for Psykisk Forskning, 231
deceased communicators – see communicators
dematerializations, 47-52
d'Espérance, Elizabeth, xv, 51, 52
Dingwall, Eric J., 152, 174, 230

direct voice phenomena, 11, 21, 22, 28, 75, 82, 94, 97, 101, 109-119, 127, 134, 135, 145, 147, 153, 159, 163, 166, 176, 210-213, 238, 250
direct writing, 11, 105, 129, 163, 201, 207, 208, 239, 251
disruptive spirits, 81-94
Dunraven, 3rd Earl of, 117, 138-139, 142, 146-147, 150, 187, 230, 247

E

Einar, see Kvaran
Einarsdottir, Soffia Emilia (Mrs. S. Gunnarsson), 9, 75
Einarsson, Indridi, 7, 25,
Einarsson, Jon, 82, 83, 85, 86, 90-92, 94, 96, 97, 99, 101-103, 107, 110, 133, 161, 176, 210, 211, 226
Einarsson, Pall, 226
Erlendsson, Hinrik, 50
Eva C. (Marthe Béraud), xiv
Everitt, Mrs., 118
Experimental House, 3, 9, 12, 14, 22, 61 (photo), 75, 89-92, 94, 114, 125, 161, 164, 166, 172, 175, 187, 191-192 (photos), 206, 208-210, 241-242
Experimental Society, 2-3, 15, 17, 19, 105, 157, 226

F

fixation, 11, 93, 170, 249
Fjallkonan, 54
Fjeldsted, Jon, 99
Fodor, Nandor, 52, 230
fraud, xvi, 61 & 63 (photos), 153, 160, 225
French, Emily S., 117

G

Galton, Francis, 142
Geley, Gustav, 59, 79
Gerding, Hans, 39, 232, 264
Gislason, Engilbert, 97
Gislason, Indridi, 16, 215
Gislason, Konrad, 9, 16, 20, 25, 27-28, 51, 55-56, 67-68, 99, 106, 113, 125, 127, 176, 188 (photo), 216
Gissurarson, Loftur Reimar, iii-iv, xi, xiv-xvii, 230-231, 235, 263
Goligher, Kathleen, xiv
Gothenburg (Sweden), 39, 41, 52
Green, Henry A.V., 224
Gregory, Anita, 150, 231
Grieg, Edvard, vi, 113, 121 (photo), 125, 127-131, 162, 194, 208
Grunewald, Fritz, 59, 151, 231
Gudmundsen, Thorgr., 68
Gudmundsson, Gudny (Mrs. S. Gudmundsson), 68
Gudmundsson, Sigmundur, 68, 227
Gudmundsson, Thor, 115
Gudmundur, see Hannesson
Gudnadottir, Jona, 9, 111, 212
Gunnarsson, Sigurdur, 69, 75
gusts of wind (paranormal), 10, 24, 36, 178, 202, 239, 242, 247
Guzyk, Janek, xiv, 79

H

Hamilton, Thomas Glendenning, 224
Hannesson, Gudmundur, 109, 114, 148, 159, 160, 163-187, 194 (photo), 195-203, 205, 207-208, 216, 225- 226, 241
Haraldsson, Erlendur, xi, xiv-xvi, 29, 39, 54, 102, 107, 108, 152, 231-232, 253, 261, 263-264

Haraldur, see Nielsson
Haralz, Jonas, 212
Haralz, Sigurdur, 109, 111, 157, 212, 213
healing, v, xiv, 19, 53, 55
Helsinki (Finland), 51
Hjern, Olle, 41
Hollis, Mary J., 118
Home, Daniel Dunglas, xiv, 5, 117, 124 (photo), 137-139, 141-142, 146-147, 174, 230, 232, 233, 236, 247
Home, Julie (Madame Home), 138
Human Personality and Its Survival of Bodily Death, 2, 107, 227, 233
Humphrey, Mrs., 142
Hyslop, James H., 52, 119, 232

I

Ibsen, Henrik, 127
Iceland, mediums in, 2, 8, 107, 224
Icelandic Scientific Society, 5, 163
Icelandic Society for Psychical Research, 2, 152
Indridason, Indridi
   attitudes toward, 155-162
   death, 9, 219
   disappearance of his arm, 47-52
   early mediumship, 15-18
   general phenomena, 9-12
   life of, 7-9, 219-224
   photographs of, ix, 63-65
   spontaneous phenomena, 17, 77-78, 145, 174, 251
   state of health, 9, 55, 67, 75
   visions of, 8, 251
International Congress for Psychical Research, 4, 58-59 (photos), 203, 234
Isafold, 55, 155, 232-233

Isleifsdottir, Karolina (Mrs. G. Hannesson), 175

J

Jakobsson, Gudmundur, 91, 207
James, William, 42
Jenkins, Elizabeth, 139, 232
Jensen, Anna Sofie, 45
Jensen, Edvard Julius, 45
Jensen, Julie Caroline, 45
Jensen, Lorenz Ferdinand, 45-46, 61 (photo)
Jensen, Louise Emilie, 45
Jensen, Lovisa, Miss (Copenhagen), 45
Jensen, Lovisa, Mrs. (Reykjavik), 83
Jensen, Thomas Emil (Emil), 25, 26, 29-34, 66, 72, 73, 75
Jochumsson, Matthias, 135, 232
Jon, *see* Einarsson
Jonsson, Ari, 185
Jonsson, Bjorn, 3, 49, 50, 54, 91, 96, 98, 216, 155, 158
Jonsson, Gudmundur, 91, 96, 98, 99
Jonsson, Gudni, 213
Jonsson, Inge, 41
Jonsson, Jakob, 77
Jonsson, Jon, 55, 156
Jorgenson, Jorgen, 162
Joseph of Copertino, Saint, 174
Journal of the American Society for Psychical Research, 231-232, 234-235
Journal of the Society for Psychical Research, xi, 229-230, 232, 234, 236

K

Kamban, Gudmundur, *see* Jonsson, Gudmundur

Kant, Immanuel, 39, 41, 234
King, John, 118, 130, 131
Kluski, Franek, xiv, 79, 230, 236
Koons, Jonathan, 117, 130
Krabbe, Knud H., 151
Kragh, Jesper Vaczy, 46, 233
Kristiania (Oslo, Norway), 59, 151
Kristjansson, Bjorn, 181-182, 184-185
Kvaran, Einar Hjorleifsson, xiv, 2-4, 7-9, 14-17, 19-20, 22-28, 30-31, 33-34, 37, 43, 46-47, 49-51, 53-56, 57 (photo), 67, 71-73, 75, 81, 84-85, 89-90, 94, 96-100, 102, 105-106, 109-110, 115, 122 (photo), 125, 130, 135, 152, 155-158, 161, 170, 175, 179, 182, 185, 209-210, 219, 224-226, 233
Kvaran, Gislina (Mrs. E.H. Kvaran), 31, 50, 226

L

Lamont, Peter, 138, 233
Leonard, Gladys Osborne, 131
levitation of objects, xii, xiv, 1, 10, 19, 26, 94, 150, 160, 163, 206, 209, 224, 237-238, 248
levitation of medium, 10, 17, 26-28, 83, 134, 147, 160-161, 174, 205, 209, 237, 238, 249
life after death (survival), vii, 2, 67, 107, 225, 227-228, 233, 235
light conditions, 12, 14, 16, 19, 21, 48, 49, 50, 52, 55, 75, 81-84, 90, 92, 96, 97, 109-111, 118, 128, 152, 160, 161, 163, 178, 196, 197, 199, 208, 210, 212, 226, 237, 238, 243
light phenomena, xiv, xvi, 1, 51, 10, 11, 14, 19, 20, 22-26, 37, 38, 43,

44, 67, 71, 72, 74, 98, 125, 134, 137, 139, 145, 147, 153, 202, 232

Linnet, Kristjan, 78, 110, 209-210, 226

Logretta, 155-156, 233

London (England), xi, 59, 107, 116, 118, 138, 149

M

Malibran, Maria Felicia, Madame, 106, 120 (photo), 130, 208, 230

Malibran, Francois Eugene, 116, 117

Mannsåker, Jon, 127, 261

materializations, 17, 25, 71

Medhurst, Richard G., 106, 142, 230, 233

Meyer zu Erpen, Walter, 224, 253, 261

minute books, xii, 2-4, 43, 62 (photo), 68, 86, 89, 99, 102, 105, 106, 109, 123 (photo), 126, 127, 130, 133, 134, 139, 146, 150, 187, 193 (photo), 215, 225, 226, 229, 263

Morgunn, 231, 233-234

Morselli, Enrico, xiv, 233

movement of objects, 10, 19, 21, 134, 150, 182
    see also apports; levitation of objects

Mulacz, Peter, 119

Musica trascendentale, 113-119

Myers, Frederic W.H., 2, 107, 148, 161-162, 227-228, 233

N

New York (United States), xvii, 59, 116

Nielsdottir, Gudny, 111, 212-213

Nielsen, Einer, xvi, 46, 123 (photo), 148-153, 174, 189 (photo), 230-231, 233, 235

Nielsson, Haraldur, xiv, 2-4, 7-9, 11, 13-14, 16-17, 19-28, 30, 33, 37, 43, 49, 51, 56, 58-59, 60 (photo), 71-77, 81-86, 89-93, 95-99, 105, 109-111, 122 & 123 (photos), 126, 130, 135, 157, 159, 163-164, 167-168, 170, 172-173, 175-177, 181-182, 184, 186-187, 192, 202-203, 205, 207-209

Nordraak, Rikard, 127-129

Nordurland, 231

Norsk Selskab for Psykisk Forskning, 151

Norsk Tidskrift for Psykisk Forskning, 234

O

Oddgeirsson, Pall, 97

Oddgeirsson, Thordur, 82, 89, 90, 92, 93, 96, 97, 156

odor sancti, 54

odors, 10, 54, 147, 151, 153, 202, 248

Ol. Dav., 201

Olafsson, Bjorn, 126, 164, 175,

Olafsson, Julius, 85

Olafsson, Kjartan, 162

Olafsson, Magnus, 84

olfactory phenomena, see odors

Osty, Eugene, 149

Osvifursdottir, Gudrun, 162

out-of-the-body experiences, 36

Owen, A.R.G. (George), xvi, 233

P

Palladino, Eusapia, xiv-xv, 14, 18, 130, 229

Palmadottir, Ingibjorg S., 55

Paris (France), 59, 116-117, 138, 149

Parker, Adrian, 41, 52, 261

Partridge, Charles, 117

Petursson, Gisli, 101-102, 162, 181,
    183, 185-186

Petursson, Hallgrimur, 101, 102, 162

phosphorescent tape, xiii, 160, 171,
    176, 178, 181, 182, 185, 186, 195,
    197, 198, 205, 242, 244, 245

photographic experiment, 81, 84-86,
    208

photographs, 91, 102, 120-124, 126,
    151

Piper, Leonora, 107

Politiken, 30-34, 36, 40, 234

poltergeist phenomena, xvi, 10, 14,
    95, 133, 146, 161, 234, 238, 249
    see also violent disturbances

Poynton, John C., 41, 234

Price, Harry, 149

primary control personality – *see*
    control personalities

Proceedings of the Society for
    Psychical Research, 41, 139, 142,
    230-232, 263

proof of identity, xv, 16, 19, 67-70

psychical research in Iceland, 235,
    263

R

Randall, Edward C., 117, 235

Reykjavik, xi, xv, 1, 41, 59, 73, 82,
    156-157

Rogo, D. Scott, 119, 235

Rosinkrans, Olafur, 28

Runolfsson, Runolfur (Runki), 102,
    232

S

Saemundsson, Thorsteinn, 33

Sai Baba, Sathya, xi, 54, 232

Scheving, Hallgrimur, 9

Schneider, Rudi, xiv, xvi, 18, 121
    (photo), 148-151, 153, 231

Schneider, Willi, 149

Sigurdsson, Asgeir, 226

Simonarson, Kristin, 83

sitters, numbers of, 13, 14, 19, 28,
    31

Sk.Th., 50

Smith, Oddny, 216

Society for Psychical Research, xi,
    107

Sörensson, Stefan, 119

spirit communicators – see
    communicators

spirit controls – see control
    personalities

Spiritualism in Iceland, 263

Stefansson, Stefan, 158

Steinsen, Steinn, 22, 70, 106, 113,
    128, 135, 228

Stevenson, Ian, 29, 102, 108, 115,
    227, 232, 235

Stockholm fire, 39-42, 232

Stockholm (Sweden), v, 39-41

surgical-like operations, xi, 53-56

survival – *see* life after death

Sveinbjornsson, Sveinbjorn, 69, 113,
    121, 127, 162, 194 (photo)

Sveinsson, Hallgrimur, 30, 73, 226

Sveinsson, Sveinn, 95

Svendsen, Johan, 127

Swatos, William H., Jr., 235, 263

Swedenborg, Emanuel, v, 39-42, 120
    (photo), 232, 234-235

T

table-tilting phenomena, 7, 14, 15, 237

Tarchini, Pietro, 77, 235

Thjodolfur, 155

Thordarson, Thorbergur, 4, 11, 14, 17, 27, 37, 78, 99, 109-110, 190 (photo), 210, 226, 235

Thordur, 82, 89, 90, 92, 93, 96, 97, 156

Thorlaksson, Brynjolfur, 4, 77-78, 92-93, 114-117, 127-130, 190 (photo), 193 (photo), 206-212, 224, 245

Thorlaksson, Thorkell, 73, 78, 96, 114, 210, 226

Thurston, Herbert, 54, 174, 235

trance, 17, 145, 164, 166, 182, 202, 209, 211, 212, 226, 237, 247, 251

trance controls – *see* control personalities

trance speech, 1, 9, 15, 145 *see also* direct voice

Trobridge, George, 40, 235

U

Universitetskomiteen i Kristiania (Oslo), 151, 235

University of Iceland, xiii, 2, 156, 230

V

violent disturbances, 8-10, 14, 81-95, 115, 133, 141, 146, 161, 172, 184, 201, 226, 238, 249-250

von Knobloch, Charlotte, 39

von Schrenck-Notzing, Albert, 59, 149

W

Waage, Eufemia, 25, 134, 236

Waddington, Patrick, 138, 236

Weaver, Zofia, 79, 236

wind – *see* gusts of wind (paranormal)

Winnipeg (Canada), 224

Winther, Christian, 151

Wiseman, Richard, xi-xii

Wolfe, N.B. (Napoleon Bonaparte), 118, 236

Wriedt, Etta, 131

Wydenbruck, Nora, 119

Wynne, John, 140

Wynne, Mrs., 139-141

X

Xenoglossy, 232

Z

Zoega, Geir T., 115

Zorab, Georg, 138, 236, 247

Paperbacks also available from
White Crow Books

Elsa Barker—*Letters from
a Living Dead Man*
ISBN 978-1-907355-83-7

Elsa Barker—*War Letters from
the Living Dead Man*
ISBN 978-1-907355-85-1

Elsa Barker—*Last Letters from
the Living Dead Man*
ISBN 978-1-907355-87-5

Richard Maurice Bucke—
Cosmic Consciousness
ISBN 978-1-907355-10-3

Arthur Conan Doyle—
The Edge of the Unknown
ISBN 978-1-907355-14-1

Arthur Conan Doyle—
The New Revelation
ISBN 978-1-907355-12-7

Arthur Conan Doyle—
The Vital Message
ISBN 978-1-907355-13-4

Arthur Conan Doyle with
Simon Parke—*Conversations
with Arthur Conan Doyle*
ISBN 978-1-907355-80-6

Meister Eckhart with Simon Parke—
Conversations with Meister Eckhart
ISBN 978-1-907355-18-9

D. D. Home—*Incidents in my Life Part 1*
ISBN 978-1-907355-15-8

Mme. Dunglas Home; edited,
with an Introduction, by Sir
Arthur Conan Doyle—*D. D.
Home: His Life and Mission*
ISBN 978-1-907355-16-5

Edward C. Randall—
Frontiers of the Afterlife
ISBN 978-1-907355-30-1

Rebecca Ruter Springer—
Intra Muros: My Dream of Heaven
ISBN 978-1-907355-11-0

Leo Tolstoy, edited by Simon
Parke—*Forbidden Words*
ISBN 978-1-907355-00-4

Leo Tolstoy—*A Confession*
ISBN 978-1-907355-24-0

Leo Tolstoy—*The Gospel in Brief*
ISBN 978-1-907355-22-6

Leo Tolstoy—*The Kingdom
of God is Within You*
ISBN 978-1-907355-27-1

Leo Tolstoy—*My Religion:
What I Believe*
ISBN 978-1-907355-23-3

Leo Tolstoy—*On Life*
ISBN 978-1-907355-91-2

Leo Tolstoy—*Twenty-three Tales*
ISBN 978-1-907355-29-5

Leo Tolstoy—*What is Religion
and other writings*
ISBN 978-1-907355-28-8

Leo Tolstoy—*Work While
Ye Have the Light*
ISBN 978-1-907355-26-4

Leo Tolstoy—*The Death of Ivan Ilyich*
ISBN 978-1-907661-10-5

Leo Tolstoy—*Resurrection*
ISBN 978-1-907661-09-9

Leo Tolstoy with Simon Parke—
Conversations with Tolstoy
ISBN 978-1-907355-25-7

Howard Williams with an Introduction
by Leo Tolstoy—*The Ethics of Diet:
An Anthology of Vegetarian Thought*
ISBN 978-1-907355-21-9

Vincent Van Gogh with Simon Parke—
Conversations with Van Gogh
ISBN 978-1-907355-95-0

Wolfgang Amadeus Mozart with Simon
Parke—*Conversations with Mozart*
ISBN 978-1-907661-38-9

Jesus of Nazareth with Simon Parke—
Conversations with Jesus of Nazareth
ISBN 978-1-907661-41-9

Thomas à Kempis with Simon
Parke—*The Imitation of Christ*
ISBN 978-1-907661-58-7

Julian of Norwich with Simon
Parke—*Revelations of Divine Love*
ISBN 978-1-907661-88-4

Allan Kardec—*The Spirits Book*
ISBN 978-1-907355-98-1

Allan Kardec—*The Book on Mediums*
ISBN 978-1-907661-75-4

Emanuel Swedenborg—*Heaven and Hell*
ISBN 978-1-907661-55-6

P.D. Ouspensky—*Tertium Organum:
The Third Canon of Thought*
ISBN 978-1-907661-47-1

Dwight Goddard—*A Buddhist Bible*
ISBN 978-1-907661-44-0

Michael Tymn—*The Afterlife Revealed*
ISBN 978-1-970661-90-7

Michael Tymn—*Transcending the
Titanic: Beyond Death's Door*
ISBN 978-1-908733-02-3

Guy L. Playfair—*If This Be Magic*
ISBN 978-1-907661-84-6

Guy L. Playfair—*The Flying Cow*
ISBN 978-1-907661-94-5

Guy L. Playfair —*This House is Haunted*
ISBN 978-1-907661-78-5

Carl Wickland, M.D.—
Thirty Years Among the Dead
ISBN 978-1-907661-72-3

John E. Mack—*Passport to the Cosmos*
ISBN 978-1-907661-81-5

Peter & Elizabeth Fenwick—
The Truth in the Light
ISBN 978-1-908733-08-5

Erlendur Haraldsson—
Modern Miracles
ISBN 978-1-908733-25-2

Erlendur Haraldsson—
At the Hour of Death
ISBN 978-1-908733-27-6

Erlendur Haraldsson—
The Departed Among the Living
ISBN 978-1-908733-29-0

Brian Inglis—*Science and Parascience*
ISBN 978-1-908733-18-4

Brian Inglis—*Natural and Supernatural:
A History of the Paranormal*
ISBN 978-1-908733-20-7

Ernest Holmes—*The Science of Mind*
ISBN 978-1-908733-10-8

Victor & Wendy Zammit —*A Lawyer
Presents the Evidence For the Afterlife*
ISBN 978-1-908733-22-1

Casper S. Yost—*Patience
Worth: A Psychic Mystery*
ISBN 978-1-908733-06-1

William Usborne Moore—
Glimpses of the Next State
ISBN 978-1-907661-01-3

William Usborne Moore—
The Voices
ISBN 978-1-908733-04-7

John W. White—
The Highest State of Consciousness
ISBN 978-1-908733-31-3

Stafford Betty—
The Imprisoned Splendor
ISBN 978-1-907661-98-3

Paul Pearsall, Ph.D. —
Super Joy
ISBN 978-1-908733-16-0

**All titles available as eBooks, and selected titles available in Hardback and
Audiobook formats from www.whitecrowbooks.com**

Lightning Source UK Ltd.
Milton Keynes UK
UKOW04f2228150216

268418UK00002B/38/P